THE HOME DEPOT

DECK
PLANS & IDEAS

DREAM IT · BUILD IT

TURN YOUR DREAMS INTO REALITY

The world's largest and first in home improvement retailer—The Home Depot®—together with HomeStyles, the leader of the home- and project-plan industry, provide the inspiration, the plans, the tools and the materials to fulfill your home-building dreams. Select your deck, backyard project or dream home from our inventory of more than 10,000 plans. When you're ready to build, visit **www.homedepot.com** to locate The Home Depot store nearest you.

For more information on the projects in this book and many others, as well as on thousands of home plans, visit **www.DreamIt-BuildIt.com** or call **1-888-314-1303**.

For additional help with your building or decorating needs, look for these other Home Depot titles:
- *Home Improvement 1-2-3*
- *Outdoor Projects 1-2-3*
- *Decorating 1-2-3*
- *Kitchens & Baths 1-2-3*
- *Wiring 1-2-3*
- *Decks 1-2-3*
- *Landscaping 1-2-3*

More titles are coming soon.

Other titles available in the **Dream-It, Build-It** series:
- *Classic American Home Styles*
- *Shed and Garage Plans & Ideas*
- *Backyard Project Plans & Ideas*

HomeStyles
Founders: Jeff Heegaard and Roger Heegaard
Operations and Project Management: Kyle J. Coolbroth
Sales and Marketing: Jim Plucker

Staff for *Deck Plans & Ideas*
Production Director: Bruce Krause
Managing Editor: Pamela Robertson
Designer: Scott Woodbury
Content: Steve Gramins
Project Plans: Brian Binstock, Mark Englund, Jason Lucas, Roger Wittrock
Editors: Kirk Baruth, Sara Freund, Josh Kimball
Production Artist: Lynn Colbjornsen

The Home Depot
Marketing Manager: Nathan Ehrlich
Global Product Merchant: Brian Haubenschild
Merchant Assistant: Debbie Cooke
Internet Editor: Anna J. Siefken
Designer: Phil King

St. Remy Media Inc.
President: Pierre Léveillé
Vice President, Finance and Operations: Natalie Watanabe
Managing Editor: Carolyn Jackson
Managing Art Director: Diane Denoncourt
Systems Director: Edward Renaud
Director, Business Development: Christopher Jackson

Staff for *Deck Plans & Ideas*
Senior Editors: Marc Cassini, Pierre Home-Douglas
Senior Editor, Production: Brian Parsons
Art Directors: Philippe Arnoldi, Francine Lemieux, Robert Paquet
Editor: Rob Lutes
Writer: Robert Labelle
Illustrators: Gilles Beauchemin, Vincent Gagnon, Jacques Perrault
Researcher: Lance Blomgren
Photographer: Robert Chartier
Photo Researcher: Linda Bryant
Production Coordinator: Dominique Gagné
Prepress Technician: Jean Angrignon Sirois
Scanner Operator: Martin Francoeur

The following persons also assisted in the preparation of this book:
Danny-Pierre Auger; Ken Balcer, Sandi Construction; Lorraine Doré; Joey Fraser; Pascale Hueber; Patrick Jougla; Solange Laberge; Odette Sévigny; Roxanne Tremblay.

Picture Credits
4 Ernest Braun/California Redwood Association
5 George Lyons/California Redwood Association
8 Dan Sellers/California Redwood Association
9 Tom Jacques/Hickory Dickory Decks
10 (upper) Wolmanized® Wood, (lower) Tom Rider/California Redwood Association
11 Tom Jacques/Hickory Dickory Decks
12 (upper) Tom Jacques/Hickory Dickory Decks, (lower) Marvin Sloben/California Redwood Association
13 Wolmanized® Wood
14 Ernest Braun/California Redwood Association
15 (upper) Wolmanized® Wood, (lower) Sico Inc.
16 (upper) Tom Jacques/Hickory Dickory Decks, (lower) Marvin Sloben/California Redwood Association
17 Ernest Braun/California Redwood Association
24 (upper left) Dan Sellers/California Redwood Association, (lower left) Southern Forest Products Association, (lower center) Tom Jacques/Hickory Dickory Decks, (right) Ernest Braun/California Redwood Association
25 DekBrands
27 (upper) Tom Jacques/Hickory Dickory Decks, (lower) Wolmanized® Wood
29 Ernest Braun/California Redwood Association
30 Wolmanized® Wood
32 Robert Chartier
33 Sico Inc.
35 Robert Chartier
36 (upper) Robert Chartier, (lower) Tom Jacques/Hickory Dickory Decks
37 (upper) Robert Chartier, (lower) Southern Forest Products Association
38 Wolmanized® Wood
39 (upper) Tom Jacques/Hickory Dickory Decks, (lower) Wolmanized® Wood
40 Tom Jacques/Hickory Dickory Decks
41 (left) Wolmanized® Wood, (right) Elizabeth Benham/Suntuf
42 Balthazar Korab/California Redwood Association

Front cover: Ernest Braun/California Redwood Association

The Home Depot® is a registered trademark of Homer TLC, Inc.
The Home Depot® is not affiliated with HomeStyles®.

© Copyright 2001, HomeStyles®. All rights reserved. Printed in U.S.A. The trademark HomeStyles is registered in the U.S. Patent and Trademark Office by Gruner and Jahr, Inc., and is used under license therefrom.

ISBN 1-56547-120-2

HomeStyles
Saint Paul, Minnesota

St. Remy Media Inc.
Montreal, Quebec

A curved railing skirts two sides of this scallop-shaped, low-level deck. Pots of flowering plants help the deck blend in with the outdoors.
(Photo: courtesy California Redwood Association; Designer: Bonnie Brocker-Beaudry)

FOREWORD

It starts with a dream. A dream of a place between sky and earth, between the indoors and the outdoors. A meeting place for family and friends; a place to dine, converse, play and just relax.

Today's home owners envision the backyard deck as an extension of the home, an outdoor space with the style and amenities once reserved for the inside of our homes. The deck plans and ideas in this book will help you transform your dreams into reality.

Who better to bring you this book than the world's largest home-improvement retailer—The Home Depot—in conjunction with the leader of the home- and project-plan industry, HomeStyles?

Working together we have developed a truly unique and valuable book that addresses your needs as a do-it-yourselfer. This book includes 16 of the most popular deck plans in full detail from HomeStyles, coupled with suggested materials lists from The Home Depot so that you may visit your local Home Depot store and purchase the materials to complete your project. In addition, you'll find lots of ideas that will inspire you to create the perfect outdoor destination.

"To accomplish great things, we must not only act, but also dream; not only plan, but also believe."
Anatole France, writer and Nobel laureate
(Photo: courtesy California Redwood Association; Designer/builder: Decks by Kiefer)

Contents: THE IDEAS

	Dream Your Deck	**9**
1	**Plan Your Deck**	**18**
	Legal Considerations	20
	Traffic Control	21
	Location, Location, Location	22
	The Road to Building a Deck	24
2	**Get the Look You Want**	**26**
	Decking Patterns	26
	Railing Designs	28
	Stair Styles	30
	Wheelchair Access	31
3	**Deck Materials**	**32**
	Deck Underpinnings	34
	Deck Hardware	35
4	**Fancy Add-ons**	**36**
	Let There Be Light	36
	A World of Water	37
	Benches, Tables, Planters and Storage	38
	Arbors, Screens and Overheads	40

Contents: The Plans

5 Our Most Popular Deck Plans — 42

- The Derrick — 43
- The Drake — 50
- The Scout — 57
- The Durvin — 64
- The Dorchester — 71
- The Portside — 78
- The Ridgeview — 84
- The Tackleberry — 93
- The Irondale — 102
- The Plymouth — 111
- The Highbridge — 120
- The Longview — 129
- The Royale — 137
- The Clifton — 147
- The Gatsby — 155
- The Newcastle — 165

Glossary — 176

INTRODUCTION

A well-considered design gives this intimate sitting area its distinctive character. The bull's-eye pattern of the decking echoes the octagonal shape of the built-in table and of the deck itself.
(Photo: courtesy Tom Jacques, Hickory Dickory Decks)

DREAM YOUR DECK

Building a deck to your specifications has a multitude of payoffs. You will not only enlarge your living space, but also improve your home aesthetically and increase its value. But where can you get the information and inspiration you need to build the deck of your dreams? The deck plans, ideas and photos in this book are a great starting point. The plans and ideas will fulfill the information side of the equation, while the photos will supply plenty of inspiration. The photos aren't necessarily tied to the plans; rather, they are intended to inspire you by providing vivid examples of creative deck design. Whether it's an interesting decking pattern, a distinctive stair and railing design or planters and overheads that blur the boundary between garden and living room, the following pages—along with the helpful employees at The Home Depot—will help you put a personal stamp on your chosen deck plan. At the end of the process, you may find yourself sitting under your new deck's leafy arbor, a gentle breeze in the air—just the right setting to lie back and…dream!

Basking in the shade of leafy trees and a broad overhead, this deck derives its natural appeal from the distinctive color and grain pattern of redwood. A strong relationship with nature is reflected in the massive post-and-beam construction of the overhead and by the living tree accommodated in an opening in the decking. Matching curves that define the edges of the overhead and the deck's upper level are a design touch that ties the overhead to the structure.
(Photo: courtesy California Redwood Association; Designer/builder: Jamie Turrentine)

INTRODUCTION

Pools of light give this multilevel deck an inviting evening atmosphere and serve to blur the boundaries between interior and exterior living spaces.
(Photo: courtesy Wolmanized® Wood)

INTRODUCTION

A deck design doesn't have to be simple or humdrum. The Oriental style of this detached combination gazebo and deck creates a fanciful backyard retreat. Railings and an upper border made from curved balusters add the finishing touch to the structure's exotic design.
(Photo: courtesy Tom Jacques, Hickory Dickory Decks)

This detached, low-level deck makes use of built-in planters and benches to define the deck area and direct traffic, while a series of lattice panels creates an attractive privacy screen for bathers in the spa.
(Photo: courtesy California Redwood Association; Designer: John Hemingway)

INTRODUCTION

OPPOSITE PAGE:
Because of their load, deck spas need a great deal of structural support. Here, a deck-level spa rests on the ground, requiring the deck surface to be built up to the spa. This challenge is met to great effect here with a two-tiered deck platform, which creates a well-defined and sheltered spa area.
(Photo: courtesy Wolmanized® Wood)

Privacy doesn't necessarily mean shutting out the outside world. The widely spaced lattice in the panels skirting this low-level deck lets in sun and breezes on a private eating area. Imaginative "portholes" for planters enhance the open effect.
(Photo: courtesy Tom Jacques, Hickory Dickory Decks)

This beautiful high-level deck may require a lot of space and a hefty budget, but the ideas it inspires can be adapted to any plan. Dramatic curves create an interesting contrast to the straight decking. Curved horizontal rails lining both the bench area and deck accentuate its wide expanse.
(Photo: courtesy California Redwood Association; Designer/builder: Scott Padgett Construction)

INTRODUCTION

With the right stain, pressure-treated wood can look natural. This island deck, with its railing-free lower level, makes an inviting meeting place that complements the surrounding terrain. Built-in benches accent the deck's irregular shape. Your local Home Depot store can help you choose the best finish product for your deck.
(Photo: courtesy Wolmanized® Wood)

Cedar is attractive to start with, and the finish on this deck brings out the wood's grain and character while serving as a protective topcoat. The deck's rich quality is enhanced by a series of contrasting lines created by the diagonal decking, the parallel benches, an octagonal table and patterned railing panels.
(Photo: courtesy Sico Inc.)

OPPOSITE PAGE:
The narrow, tapered shape of this poolside deck is made to appear wider with parallel decking laid perpendicular to the deck's length. The elegant curved railing is code-compliant by maintaining a 4-inch spacing between the balusters.
(Photo: courtesy California Redwood Association; Land architect: Scott Smith)

INTRODUCTION

OPPOSITE PAGE:
Design means working with what you have. Rather than extending directly out over a steeply inclined lot, this multitiered deck follows the terrain, creating a variety of individual activity areas. Built-in planters and benches complete the design and mark the deck's perimeter.
(Photo: courtesy California Redwood Association; Designer: Gary Cushenberry)

ABOVE:
This simple deck and suburban bungalow harmonize well. A high, wooden privacy fence along one side creates a feeling of intimacy, while low-level benches bordering the other sides open the space up to the patio and garden.
(Photo: courtesy Tom Jacques, Hickory Dickory Decks)

A unique railing design gives this redwood deck an elegant touch. The wood overhead lets in air and light while serving as a trellis for climbing plants.
(Photo: courtesy California Redwood Association; Designer/builder: Joseph D. Wood, Wood's Shop)

CHAPTER 1

PLAN YOUR DECK

How can you be sure your new deck will fulfill your needs and suit your lifestyle? Start by thinking about the backyard activities you and your family enjoy. Will the kids need a play area on the deck? Do you intend to cook, dine and entertain on the deck? Will the deck enclose a pool? Perhaps your dream deck is a quiet space for lounging in the sun.

Beginning on page 43, you'll find a series of deck plans to help your dreams take form. Decks come in many shapes and sizes, but most belong to one of the categories shown on the page opposite. And virtually all share the basic parts shown below. Whether you tackle the project yourself or plan to hire out the work, becoming familiar with deck anatomy will help you fine-tune your design. Either way, your design should harmonize with the style of your home and garden. Choosing a deck of the appropriate size can be difficult; it's not easy to visualize from a plan how much space you'll need. Before making a final decision, use a garden hose to mark off the area where your deck will be built. Then, lay out the space as you plan to use it. Position the grill and a table and chairs. Reserve an area for benches or lounge chairs. Feeling a little crowded? Move the hose further out. Keep in mind, however, that there are limits on the size of a deck. Local bylaws in many areas have strict rules on how much of your property can be occupied by a deck (*page 20*).

The next few pages will explore the many issues you need to consider as you plan and design a new deck. These include everything from getting building permits and knowing how to read and understand plans to considering traffic patterns on your deck and placing the deck in the best possible location in your yard. Don't hesitate to consult the employees at your local Home Depot. Their expertise will help you make purchasing decisions you'll be happy with. The result will be a deck that looks like it has always been there, one that provides years of pleasure and convenience.

THE PARTS OF A DECK:
Building Blocks of Design

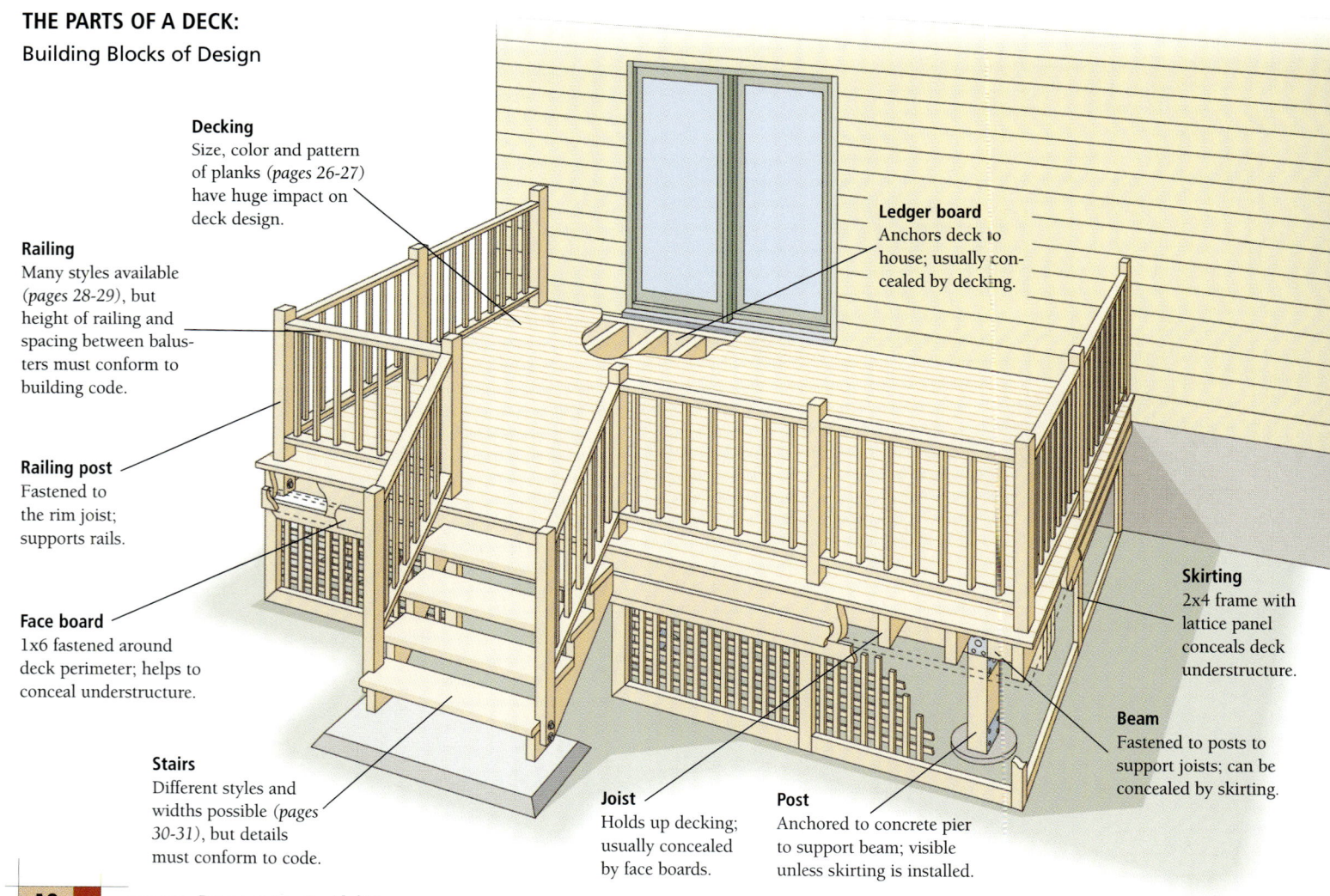

Decking
Size, color and pattern of planks (*pages 26-27*) have huge impact on deck design.

Railing
Many styles available (*pages 28-29*), but height of railing and spacing between balusters must conform to building code.

Railing post
Fastened to the rim joist; supports rails.

Face board
1x6 fastened around deck perimeter; helps to conceal understructure.

Stairs
Different styles and widths possible (*pages 30-31*), but details must conform to code.

Ledger board
Anchors deck to house; usually concealed by decking.

Skirting
2x4 frame with lattice panel conceals deck understructure.

Beam
Fastened to posts to support joists; can be concealed by skirting.

Joist
Holds up decking; usually concealed by face boards.

Post
Anchored to concrete pier to support beam; visible unless skirting is installed.

CHAPTER 1

A GALLERY OF DECK TYPES

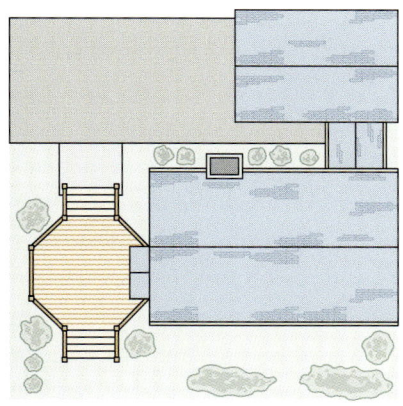

Octagonal
A good choice with a rectangular home since this deck's offbeat shape breaks up the home's straight lines and creates a visually wider living area.

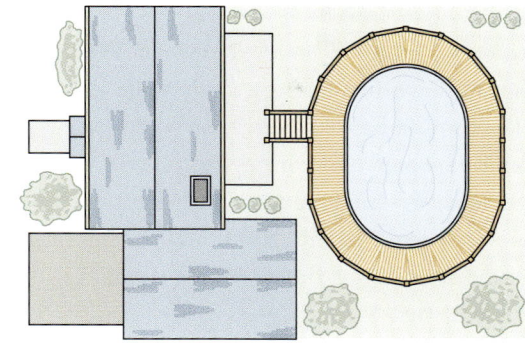

Circular with pool
This raised deck creates an easy-access area for an above-ground pool.

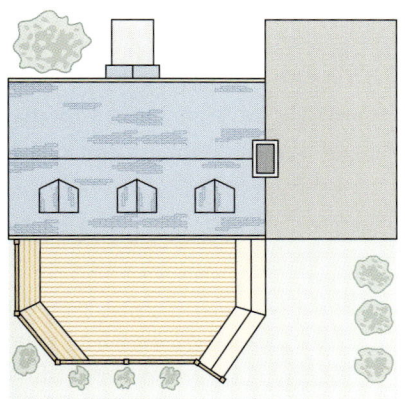

Low level
Ideal for homes with low foundations, low-level decks turn yard space into living space. Wide steps can double as benches and provide greater access to the deck.

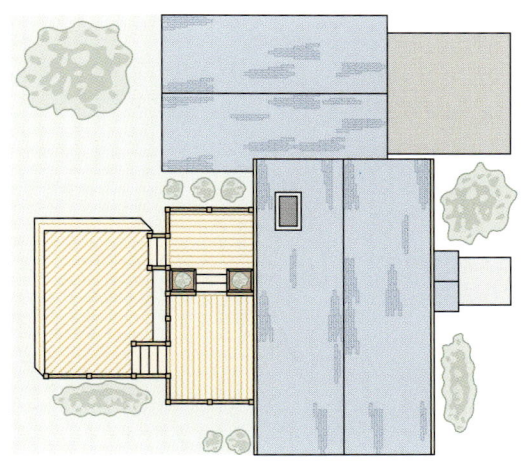

Multilevel
This type of deck works well on a lot with changes in elevation. You can achieve a multilevel effect by linking two or more decks of varying heights. The final result is visually interesting and creates a multi-purpose deck.

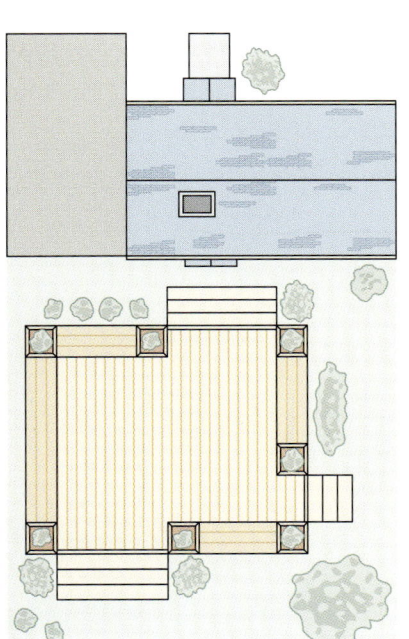

Detached
A detached deck can be situated anywhere in the yard. A quiet retreat, it can be linked to the home with an attractive walkway.

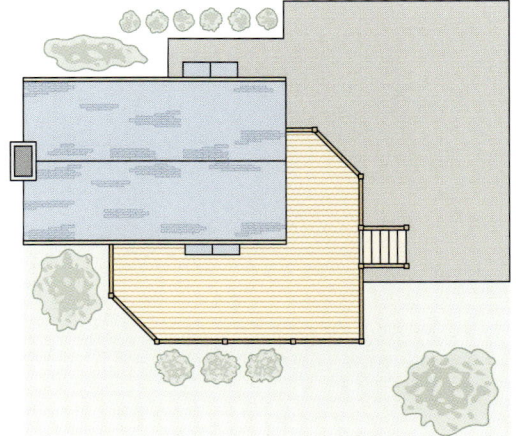

Wraparound
The shape of this deck forms two activity areas and because the deck faces two sides of the home, it can usually also provide a sunny area and a shaded area at the same time.

www.homedepot.com

CHAPTER 1

Legal Considerations

Once you've chosen a deck plan, one of the first things you have to take care of is making it legal. In most areas, any deck more than 30 inches high requires a building permit. Visit your local building-permit department to see what applies to you. Expect to have to submit a copy of your plan to ensure it conforms to local building codes and zoning restrictions. If your project requires extensive wiring, such as new electrical circuits or plumbing for a spa or hot tub, additional permits may be needed. Fees for building permits are often determined by the cost per square foot of the project, so try to supply a well-thought-out estimate with your plan.

Building codes and zoning restrictions serve to protect home owners and the community from substandard building practices. The building codes governing decks cover everything from the depth of footings and the height of railings to the sizes and capacities of building materials. Although the deck plans in this book conform to building codes in most areas and include lists of building materials, you'll need to make sure that the sizes and strengths of the lumber and fasteners you use meet local standards. Although standards are fairly uniform throughout the U.S., there are exceptions. In earthquake-prone zones such as California, for example, special joist hangers and anchors must be used. Meanwhile, footings in northern climates must usually be dug below the frost line.

Zoning restrictions also have an aesthetic side, ensuring that building projects do not disfigure the neighborhood. Some common restrictions are illustrated below. **Setback** restrictions determine how close you can build to a neighbor's property line. **Lot-coverage limits** require that a deck does not cover a larger portion of your lot than is allowed. **Height limits** put a cap on how high you can build. But unless you have plans for a backyard tower, this is seldom an issue for decks. **Easements** are corridors across your property that you can't build on because they provide access to your lot, usually for utility workers. Check your property deed for easements and any additional stipulations that govern the design or location of new structures on your property.

If your building department rejects your plan, don't despair. Appeals are common and you can obtain a variance or exception to an ordinance if you can show good reason for your design choice and are willing to make some alterations. Apply early for such appeals. There is often a long waiting list, a factor that can throw you off schedule.

IN THE ZONE: Restrictions You Should Know About

Height limit

Easement

Lot-coverage limits

Setback

CHAPTER 1

Traffic Control

A large part of choosing a deck of the right style, shape and size is making sure people using the deck do not collide or crowd each other. To prevent problems, sketch the different activity areas you anticipate and draw traffic patterns in and out of the areas. Do the lines intersect or are they well spaced? Grilling and eating on the deck, for example, will inevitably result in frequent trips to and from the kitchen. Don't design the deck so these trips cut across a lounging or play area. If the existing kitchen entrance is a single door, you may want to expand it to accommodate a set of double sliding doors to improve access to the deck. For a multipurpose deck, consider adding a second door onto the deck. As shown at right, two doors split traffic to and from the deck, helping to prevent disruptions. You can cut down on the cost of framing a new door by converting a window opening into a door.

The design and location of deck stairs can have a significant impact on deck traffic. On the deck at right, a set of wide stairs centered between the two doors prevents traffic from converging on the deck. Wide stairs also facilitate moving unwieldy items such as a table or grill on and off the deck. They can also double as a seating area when you are entertaining. The second set of stairs at the side of the deck enables visitors to access the driveway without detouring across the deck and the yard.

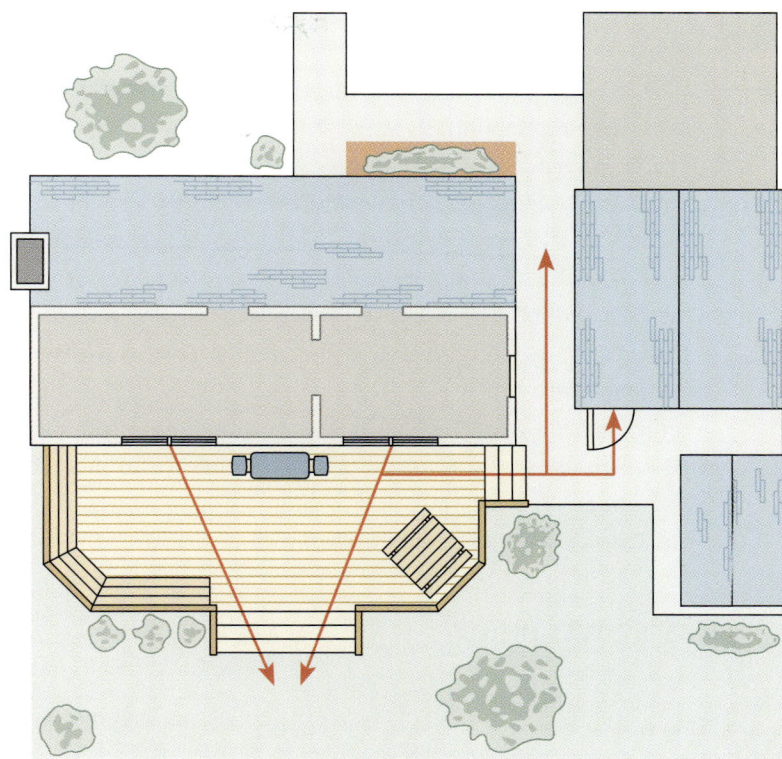

READING THE DECK PLANS

Knowing how to interpret the plans in this book will help you choose the deck that's best for you. The plans are all produced to professional standards, clearly indicating the layout, size and position of all the elements making up each deck. They are all drawn to scale, which varies from plan to plan. Most of them include the following elements:

- The **RENDERING** is an artist's representation of the deck.

- The **PLAN VIEW** shows an overhead view of the deck. It includes exterior dimensions, the location of the house and some details such as the suggested sizes of decking, railing posts and stairs.

- Next, the **PIER LAYOUT** indicates the positions and distances between the concrete piers that support the structure. Also shown is the process by which these measurements are found—with mason's lines elevated on batterboards. The location of any concrete pad for the stairs is also shown. **PER SITE CONDITIONS** indicates the positions and dimensions of any items that depend on the final height of the deck.

- The **FRAMING PLAN** repeats the plan view with the decking stripped away. Here, the dimensions and types of materials for the understructure are shown. The abbreviation **O.C.** refers to "on center," meaning that all measurements shown are taken from the center of each structural element to the center of the next one.

- **ELEVATIONS**, also referred to as side views, indicate vertical dimensions as well as types and sizes of materials.

- **DETAILS** reveal the understructure of the deck shown from the side. A below-ground cutaway of the concrete pier is also shown. This view, combined with the other details of the structure, includes all the necessary materials and dimensions for the deck.

Although you will very likely find a deck plan in this book that suits your needs and design sense, none of the plans are cast in stone. It's possible to make adjustments to the size or shape of a deck. A rule of thumb for adjusting a plan is to work from the top down, beginning with the railing and decking, then making the necessary changes to the understructure. Work through all adjustments with a professional deck designer or builder who will be able to recommend appropriate structural changes.

CHAPTER 1

Location, Location, Location

How would you describe the climate of your own backyard? Does the sun beat down on it all day long or is it a shady oasis? Perhaps it is a little of both, with some areas of the yard more inviting than others. Even though you may be inclined to attach a new deck to your home, you may discover that the underused back corner of the yard is really the most climate-friendly area on your property.

One of the most important factors in locating your deck is the orientation of your house. Depending on the location of shade trees, the south-facing wall typically receives the most sun, the north much less. The east face usually captures the cooler morning rays, while the west receives the warm afternoon sun. As most decks are of necessity placed in the back and sometimes side yards, this is a good opportunity to get out the compass and establish your home's bearings. Given the choice, you may find yourself rethinking a basic backyard deck in favor of a wraparound model that offers a combination of both sunny and shady areas.

You should also consider the region where you live. If your home is in an arid desert zone, you won't want the same amount of sun as someone living near the Canadian border. A seaside deck might receive sun all afternoon, but it will also benefit from the cooling ocean breezes. Region also affects the amount of daylight hours your deck will receive. Northern homes enjoy long hours of summer daylight, while days and nights in the southern states are more or less equal.

BACKYARD MICROCLIMATES

You should also consider your yard's individual climate factors. Large deciduous trees provide shade during the hot sum-

HERE COMES THE SUN

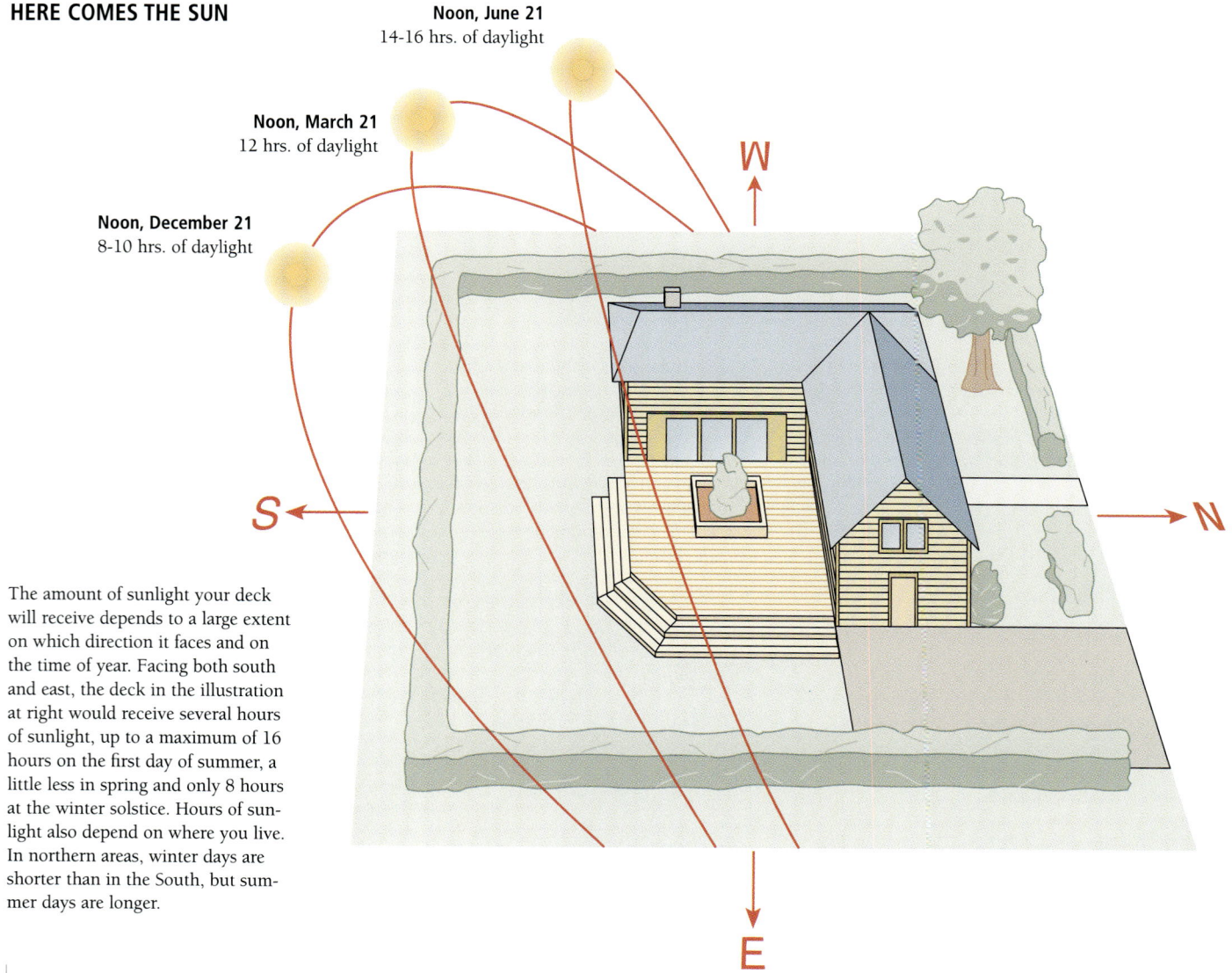

Noon, June 21
14-16 hrs. of daylight

Noon, March 21
12 hrs. of daylight

Noon, December 21
8-10 hrs. of daylight

The amount of sunlight your deck will receive depends to a large extent on which direction it faces and on the time of year. Facing both south and east, the deck in the illustration at right would receive several hours of sunlight, up to a maximum of 16 hours on the first day of summer, a little less in spring and only 8 hours at the winter solstice. Hours of sunlight also depend on where you live. In northern areas, winter days are shorter than in the South, but summer days are longer.

mer days but allow the sun's rays in when they lose their leaves in winter. The walls of your home, particularly where they meet at inside corners, can create sheltered areas that are dramatically different from unprotected spaces. Light-colored siding or masonry will reflect light and heat all day long, while brick will absorb heat during the day and radiate it in the evenings.

If your situation dictates that you must put your deck in a somewhat unfavorable climate zone, all is not lost. Short of moving the sun in the sky, there are a number of adjustments you can make to enhance or improve climate conditions. Arbors and vines can produce the same effect as tree shade, while screens and overheads (*page 40*), can provide warming shelter.

WIND AND WEATHER

The difference between an afternoon breeze and a strong, blustery wind can make life on your new deck either pleasant or unbearable. Winds can be categorized as annual prevailing winds, localized breezes or high-velocity storm winds. Annual prevailing winds can be the most troublesome since you may find your chosen deck location to be uncomfortably windy. Test the area by posting flags or ribbons at various spots on the site. Take note of the wind's direction and use this information to help determine where to construct screens or baffles to deflect its force. Before deciding to include this additional construction, however, consider how to better take advantage of the walls of your home—they will make the best windbreak of all.

If your area experiences strong seasonal storms and winter snow, you may have to take some precautions to protect your deck. Again, locating your deck near the protective walls of your home will deflect some of the effects of driving rains, but make sure a proper runoff system of gutters and downspouts is installed above the deck to prevent water from pouring off your roof onto the deck surface. As for snow, the main danger is weight. An accumulated snow pile can put an incredible amount of weight on your deck. Clearing it regularly will help, but sudden heavy falls may cause the deck to collapse. If your area is prone to heavy snowfalls, check the structural requirements with a professional. You may need to increase the size of your deck's framing members or increase the number of supports. No matter how strong your deck, weather will eventually take its toll. Regular maintenance (*page 25*) is the best way to keep your deck in peak form.

WIND BREAKERS

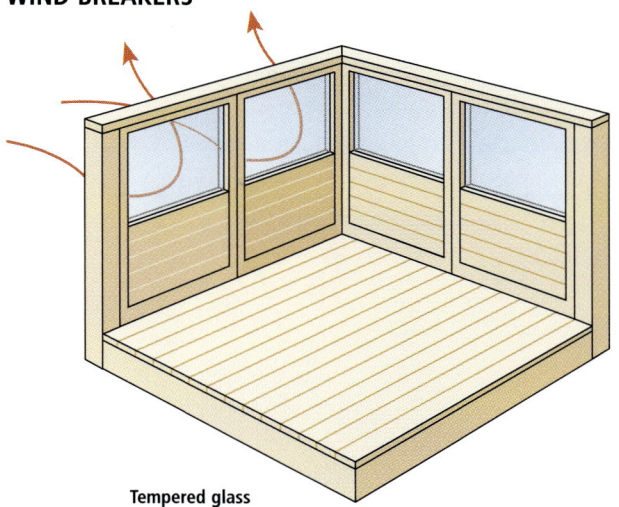

Tempered glass
Ideal for chilly, windy areas, a tempered glass shelter will allow the sun to warm the deck while blocking wind and harmful ultraviolet (UV) rays.

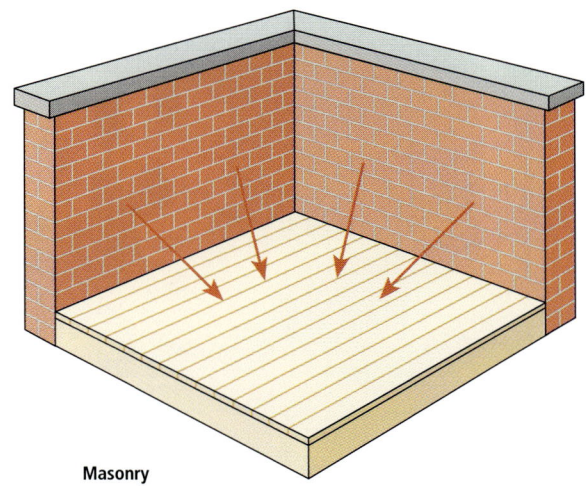

Masonry
An inside corner of brick or stone will shelter your deck during the day and add warmth to the space after sundown when the bricks radiate stored heat.

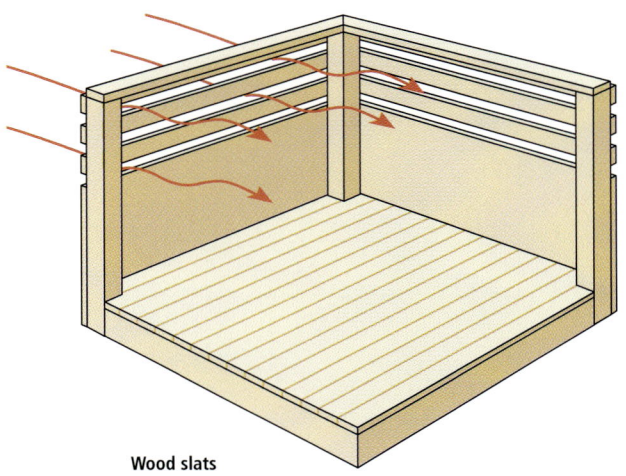

Wood slats
Slats or lattice will allow air to circulate while effectively reducing the wind's full force.

CHAPTER 1

The Road to Building a Deck

In addition to choosing a deck plan, you have to decide whether you will tackle the project yourself or hire a contractor. These two pages are not intended to provide an in-depth, step-by-step how-to guide to constructing a deck. Rather, the idea is to give you an appreciation of the process and of the basic steps involved so that you can choose to execute certain parts of the construction yourself and contract others out. Although this book focuses on deck design and style, the often-overlooked issue of attending to construction details has a huge impact on the appearance of a deck.

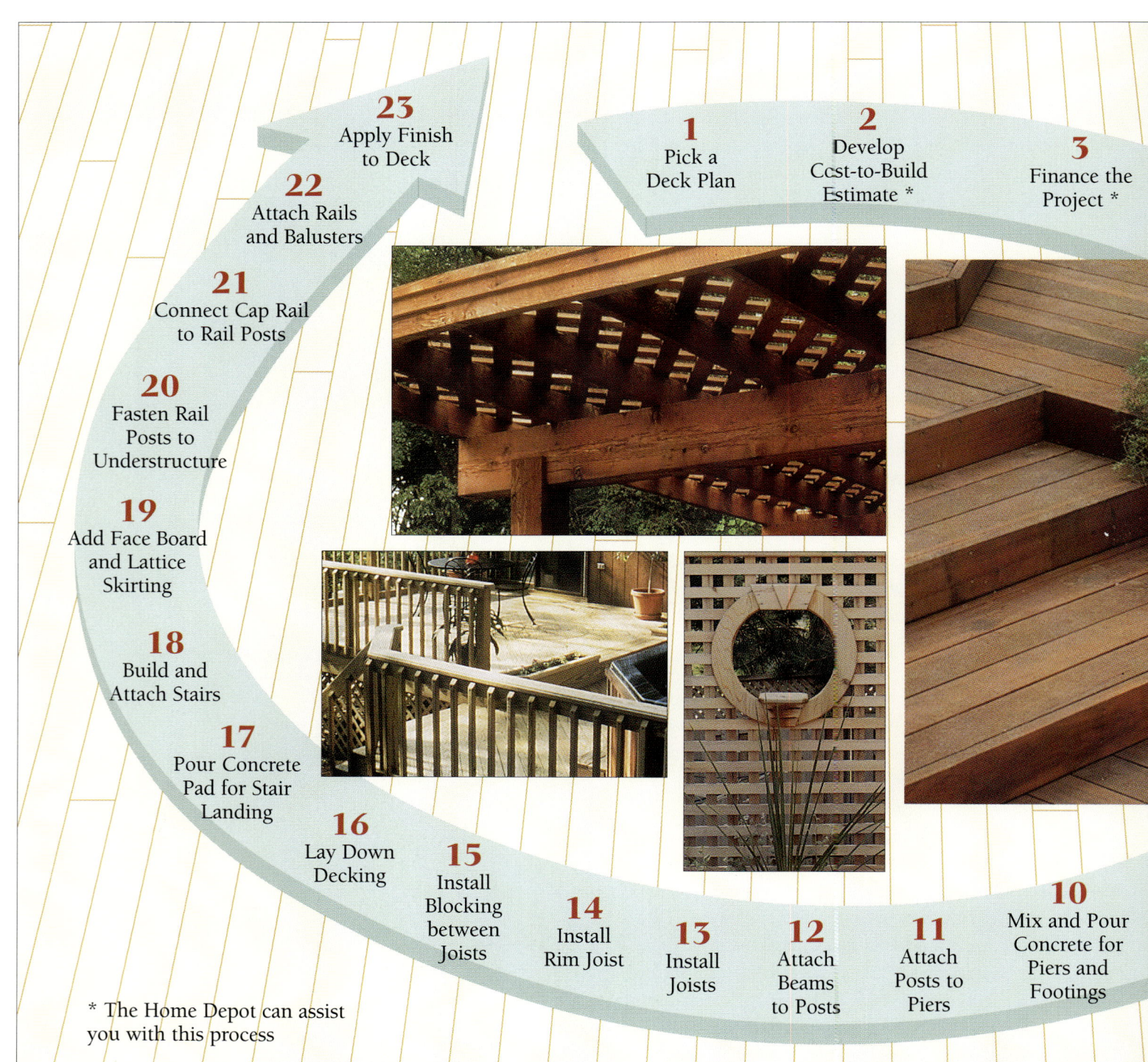

1. Pick a Deck Plan
2. Develop Cost-to-Build Estimate *
3. Finance the Project *
10. Mix and Pour Concrete for Piers and Footings
11. Attach Posts to Piers
12. Attach Beams to Posts
13. Install Joists
14. Install Rim Joist
15. Install Blocking between Joists
16. Lay Down Decking
17. Pour Concrete Pad for Stair Landing
18. Build and Attach Stairs
19. Add Face Board and Lattice Skirting
20. Fasten Rail Posts to Understructure
21. Connect Cap Rail to Rail Posts
22. Attach Rails and Balusters
23. Apply Finish to Deck

* The Home Depot can assist you with this process

CHAPTER 1

Floating Foundation Deck System

Over the life of a deck, the frost heave that occurs in winter can lift posts from their original positions, causing significant damage to the structural integrity of the deck. The standard method for preventing this damage is to anchor the posts to concrete piers dug and poured down to the frost line, with deeper and wider concrete footings at the bottom.

With no holes to dig and no concrete to mix, **DekBrands** floating foundation deck system offers an easier and less expensive solution to frost-heave damage. As shown in the illustration, the system uses precast piers that sit on top of the ground, moving up and down to accommodate frost movement. The **DekBrands** floating foundation deck system is strong, durable and safe. Designed in accordance with all national building codes, it far exceeds minimum structural construction requirements when built according to plan. For more information on deck foundations, see page 34.

4 Take Your Plan to Building-Permit Department

5 Hire a Contractor (if necessary)

6 Buy Materials *

7 Mark Post Locations

8 Dig Holes for Piers and Footings

9 Fasten Ledger Board to House

BUY NOW, PAY LATER!

The Home Depot Consumer Credit Account offers a financing solution to your home improvement needs. To make purchases more affordable, take advantage of our special offers and attractive deferred billing programs available only to Home Depot Consumer Account Holders.* Apply for a Consumer Credit Account at any store or online at homedepot.com to buy the merchandise that you need today!

*Interest may accrue

PRESSURE-TREATED LUMBER
Safety Alert!

Always wear eye protection, a dust mask and long clothes when cutting and handling pressure-treated lumber. Be sure you are working safely by checking out the important handling tips at www.epa.gov/opp00001/citizens/1file.htm.

AN OUNCE OF PREVENTION . . .

The work doesn't end when your new deck is finally built. Daily wear and tear and exposure to the elements will inevitably make their mark on the deck. Sunlight breaks down wood fibers. Dirt and moisture encourage rot and the growth of mildew. The good news is that there is a lot you can do to protect and restore your deck. The secret is to keep an eye out for problems and make regular cleaning a part of your routine. Here are some additional tips and pointers on how to keep your deck in top shape:

- For maximum protection from moisture and the sun's ultraviolet (UV) rays, refinish your deck at the intervals suggested by the finish manufacturer, typically every year or two.
- Reposition deck furnishings such as benches and planters regularly to prevent moisture damage under them.
- Clean dirt between deck boards with a putty knife or the spray from a garden hose. This will maintain air circulation between the boards, preventing moisture and mildew buildup.
- Clean the deck with a solution of water and detergent, applying it with a stiff brush and working with the wood grain, then rinse with a hose. If you have a large deck, consider renting a power washer. Water at high pressure will help dislodge ground-in surface dirt and clear away debris trapped in gaps. Make sure the washer isn't too powerful. Otherwise, you risk peeling the grain up.
- Remove mildew stains with a solution of household liquid bleach and water.
- Because stairs are subjected to heavy traffic, they may need more frequent cleaning; and stair treads may need replacement sooner than other deck components.
- Inspect the decking for nail stains, splintering, splits, and popped nails. You can reset popped nails with a nail set and a hammer or reinforce them with galvanized deck screws. Remove rust and chemical stains with sodium percarbonate; if that fails, try an acid-based oxalic cleanser.
- To test for rot, insert an awl into any wood surface near the ground. If the wood crumbles instead of splintering, chances are it is rotting and needs to be replaced.
- Warped boards can be flattened by replacing the nails with galvanized deck screws.

CHAPTER 2

GET THE LOOK YOU WANT

This chapter will help you put a personal stamp on your new deck. The most visible parts of a deck—the decking, the railing and the stairs—allow plenty of room for experimentation. With decking, for example, the standard arrangement involves laying the boards parallel to the longest side of the deck. Although this pattern has the advantage of coaxing the eye forward and making the surface seem larger, there are other possibilities. A sampling is shown below.

Railings can be designed in several ways (*pages 28-29*) as long as you respect building codes. Motifs range from ranch-style railings to a traditional Swiss chalet look. The associates at your local Home Depot can guide you with design decisions.

Decking Patterns

Any of the decking patterns shown below will make your deck a focal point by drawing attention to the deck's surface and accentuating its shape. An intricate pattern can help transform a nondescript backyard into a showpiece. Just be sure the decking won't clash with what you already have. For guidance in choosing the right pattern, look to the design features of your home. The basketweave design, for instance, is a large-scale version of wood parquet flooring. So it may be a good choice if a room adjoining the deck has parquet flooring. Laying the decking in a basketweave pattern would integrate the interior and exterior spaces of the home.

As shown in the illustrations below, you may need to reinforce the understructure to properly support the deck boards. Depending on the pattern, you may have to double some

DESIGN-SAVVY DECKING PATTERNS

Bull's-eye
Joists must be doubled under the end joints of deck boards.

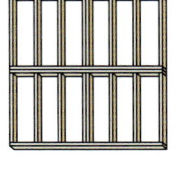
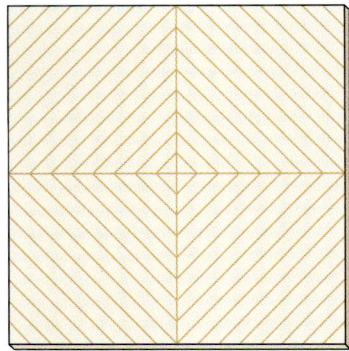

Diagonal
Joists can be arranged in a parallel pattern, but must be placed closer together than with straight decking.

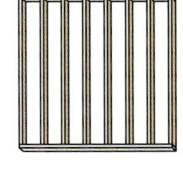

Picture frame
Blocking around perimeter supports outside boards.

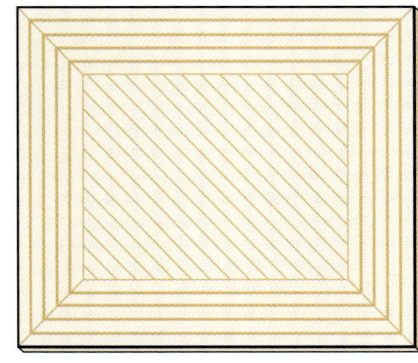

Basketweave
Blocking between joists bolsters decking.

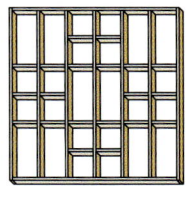

ENDS IN SIGHT

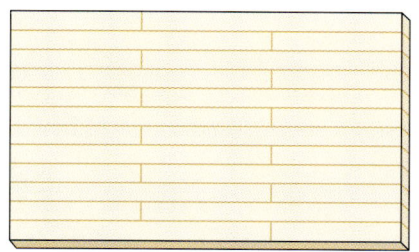
Alternating
End joints in every second row line up.

Random
No effort is made to align end joints.

Grouped
End joints in three consecutive rows line up.

joists, add blocking between joists or place the joists closer together than you otherwise would. The basic principle is that the deck boards must be supported by joists at specified intervals (typically every 16 inches) and at each end of every board.

NAILING DOWN YOUR DESIGN

Although you can get deck boards up to 20 feet long, lengths of 8, 10, 12 and 16 feet are more common. As a result, most decks have boards butting end to end. With careful planning, you can turn end joints into design features. Three different designs are shown above. To ensure the strength of the deck, there are a couple of limits on your creativity. Every end joint must be centered over a joist and all the boards should be long enough to span across at least three joists. Some builders prefer not to align end joints in consecutive rows. The grouped pattern flouts this rule, so it is not as strong as the others.

A bull's-eye pattern transforms this deck area into the focal point of the backyard. The pattern complements hexagonal- or octagonal-shaped decks well. Built-in benches and angled stairs echo the design.
(Photo: courtesy Tom Jacques, Hickory Dickory Decks)

A basketweave pattern visually divides this deck area into square segments. In this example, the design contributes to the symmetrical placement of deck furniture and decor.
(Photo: courtesy Wolmanized® Wood)

DIMENSION AND DESIGN

The most common lumber for decking is 1x6 or 2x6. However, for a different design, you can use 2x2s or 2x4s or combine different board widths, alternating 2x6s and 2x2s, for example. Deck boards are typically laid flat, but for an interesting appearance you can install 2x4s on edge. This method will increase materials costs—you end up needing twice as much lumber as you would with the boards laid face down—but there is a savings in building the understructure: 2x4s on edge can be installed directly on beams. Joists aren't required.

CHAPTER 2

Railing Designs

The style of your deck's railing is limited only by your own creativity. Codes vary somewhat between jurisdictions, but many regulations are standard across North America. If your deck will be 30 inches off the ground or higher, it must have a railing. In general, the railing must be at least 36 inches high, although many deck railings, including some of those featured in the plans in this book, rise to 42 inches. As an additional safety feature—even if you do not have small children—gaps between railings or balusters should not be any wider than 4 inches. A deck railing has to be sturdy. If you are engineering your own, bear in mind that it must be strong enough to resist a lateral force of 20 pounds per square foot.

In choosing a railing design, think about how your railing posts will be fastened to your deck's understructure. Heavier railings may demand a more substantial post structure. Different options are shown in the illustrations below. The deck's supporting posts can be used as railing posts, giving the railing the full support of the deck foundation. In a standard deck railing design, railings are supported by posts bolted to the rim joists.

Once the supporting posts have been installed, there are several ways to attach the railings. Typically, a cap rail links the tops of the posts and upper and lower rails span the posts. The lower rail must be no more than 4 inches above the deck surface. In the simplest, sturdiest design, these rails are fastened to the faces of the posts, but a more streamlined look can be created by locating the rails between the posts. On standard deck railings, vertical balusters made from 2x2 stock are then attached to the rails at no more than 4-inch intervals. But you shouldn't necessarily limit yourself to these tried-and-true methods. Nowadays, builders have an enormous variety of design options. By putting some of them to work, you can add visual appeal and character to your deck.

A WORLD OF STYLES

As with your choice in decking patterns, choose railing details to match and enhance the style of your home. These design choices may include creating spacing patterns with vertical balusters, replacing vertical rails with horizontal ones or investing in turned posts and balusters and decorative post caps—the perfect touch for a deck attached to a Victorian home. Alternative materials to standard 2x2 balusters include prefabricated lattice panels, metal rods or rails, tempered glass and even stretched awning cloth. Each of these materials and designs will impart its own distinctive appearance and, in some cases, provide effective privacy or screen the deck from the wind. Other railing possibilities include cutout motifs from wider sections of board.

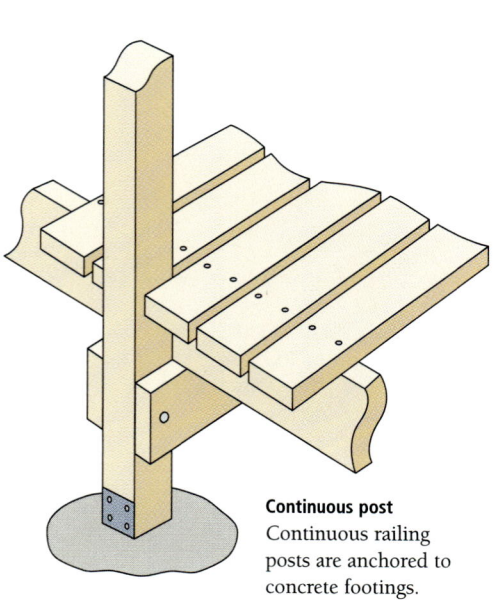

Continuous post
Continuous railing posts are anchored to concrete footings.

Sandwich post
Pairs of 2x4 railing posts sandwich the joists.

Post mounted to rim joist
Railing posts are attached to the outside of rim joist.

CHAPTER 2

Lattice screens attached to the top and bottom of the rails lend a country charm to this expansive deck, adding a measure of privacy and providing a buffer from the breeze.
(Photo: courtesy California Redwood Association; Designer: Rex Higbee)

These simple repeated patterns can give your deck its own signature design. Consult the helpful employees at your local Home Depot for guidance.

Railings need not be straight lines connecting posts. One popular trend is the use of curved railings. Although they require more work to construct and may increase your costs, the smooth flowing lines of curved rails make a pleasing contrast to parallel decking patterns and are a fitting alternative to standard straight rails.

A GATED DECK

If you have small children and want your deck to double as a safe play area, you may want to close off the stairs with a gate. Gates keep children out as well as in, adding an extra element of safety to a deck surrounding a pool or spa. A gate is essentially a section of railing attached with hinges to the posts bordering the stairs. Gates are made in many different ways. Commonly, a diagonal brace is usually fastened to the structure, running from the bottom of the hinge side to the top of the latch side. For added security, code dictates that gates must be designed to open away from the stairs.

Decorative balusters
Profiled balusters fastened between 2x4 rails provide a distinctive look.

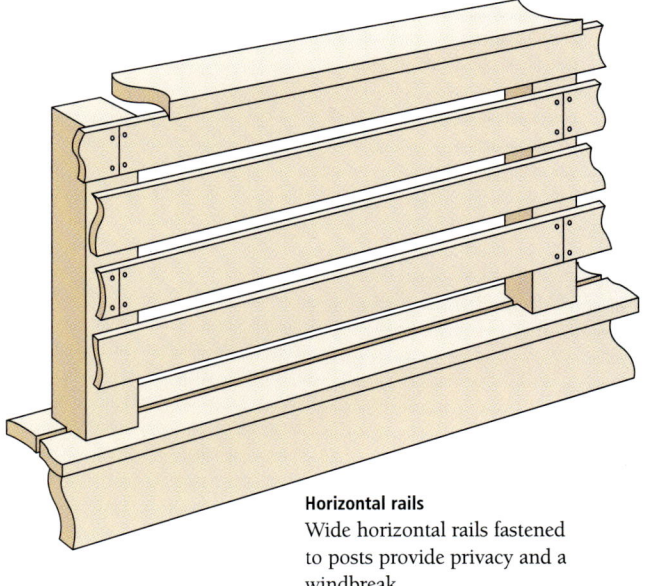

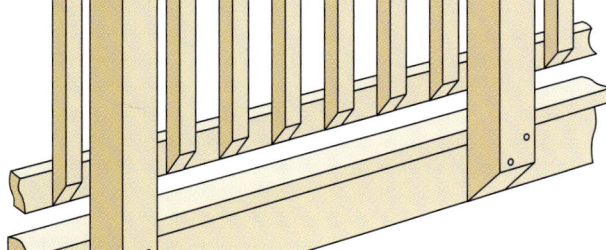

Standard railing
Vertical balusters are fastened to 2x4 horizontal rails at top and bottom.

Horizontal rails
Wide horizontal rails fastened to posts provide privacy and a windbreak.

CHAPTER 2

Stair Styles

Deck stairs do more than simply provide access on and off a deck. They guide traffic, hide the deck's understructure and, especially on low-level decks, provide extra space for seating and planters. Although most of the deck plans in this book feature stairs that are 4 feet in width—ample room for one person to access at a time—you may want to plan for wider stairs if you're likely to have a lot of deck traffic. Adding an extra 2 feet of stair width will permit simultaneous up and down traffic without crowding. Wider stairs also make it easy to move furniture on and off the deck.

For decks more than 8 feet high, the stair design usually includes a landing to change the direction of the stairs and conserve space. Landings make stairways less imposing and easier to climb. They also create mini activity areas—ideal spots for built-in benches or planters. You can also include a change in direction in your stair design if you are building a low-level deck. Winders—angled stairs that gradually change stair direction—add visual appeal and are often used to direct traffic away from the yard to a path or drive at the side of the deck.

As you design your deck, make sure that stair components—the treads, risers and handrails—match the style and pattern of the deck railing and decking. Stair handrails should link with the deck railing without a break and stair treads ought to harmonize with the decking. But this does not mean that there are no attractive alternatives for stair styles. If you are using 2x6 boards for the decking, for example, you can consider framing doubled 2x6 stair treads with mitered 2x2s. This will blend with the look of your decking, widen the stair treads and impart a refined, finished appearance to the entire deck.

The stringers that support stairs may be either notched or left unnotched, in which case the treads are fastened with cleats. Unnotched stringers, which close the sides of the steps, add a feeling of strength. One pair of stringers is adequate for 4-foot-wide stairs. Wider stairs require additional stringers.

An elegant staircase links the two levels of this expansive deck. With ample width and a large landing, the stairs are designed to avoid congestion as traffic moves between levels.
(Photo: courtesy Wolmanized® Wood)

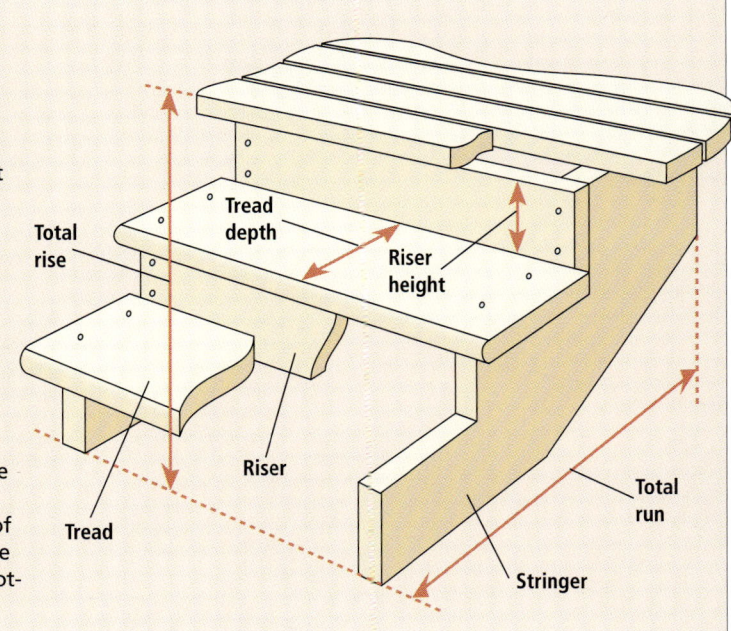

RISE AND RUN TO STAIR DESIGN

The deck plans in this book specify the height and placement of stairs as being determined "per site conditions." That's because stairs must follow guidelines that can't be worked out until the exact distance between the top of the decking and the ground—the total rise—can be measured. To determine how many steps you'll have, divide the total rise by 7 inches, the ideal height of a riser (the vertical distance between steps). A deck 35 inches high, for example, would have five steps. If the result is a fraction, round the number of steps up or down to a whole number. Make the tread depth between 10 and 11 inches, then multiply this figure by the number of steps to determine the horizontal distance between the edge of the deck and the bottom of the stairs, known as the total run.

CHAPTER 2

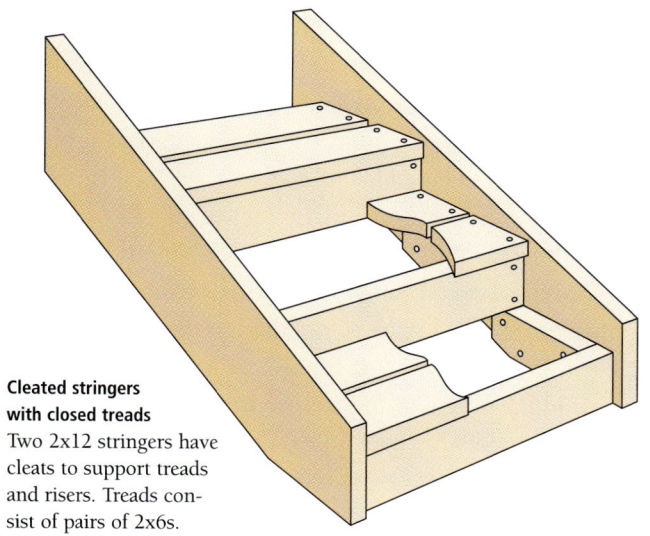

Cleated stringers with closed treads
Two 2x12 stringers have cleats to support treads and risers. Treads consist of pairs of 2x6s.

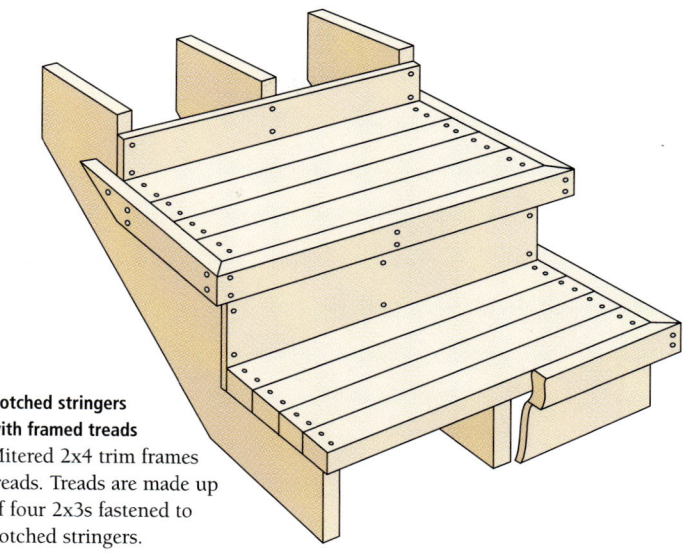

Notched stringers with framed treads
Mitered 2x4 trim frames treads. Treads are made up of four 2x3s fastened to notched stringers.

Wheelchair Access

Outfitting your deck with a ramp makes it accessible to guests and family members with reduced mobility. It also enables you to easily maneuver such wheeled items as strollers and wheelbarrows on and off the deck. An attractive ramp will also add to the resale value of your home.

The Americans with Disabilities Act sets strict standards for ramps. A minimum width of 42 inches is required and the rise should be no more than 1 inch for every 12 inches of run. This means that a deck with an elevation of 2 feet will need a ramp that is 24 feet long; however, this rule is relaxed for decks less than a foot high as the danger of rolling or tipping out of control is much less on a short rise. Ramps also require a 5- by 5-foot level landing to accommodate turning on and off the deck and a level resting place every 30 feet.

To conserve space, many ramps are built in two sections, zigzagging back and forth or wrapping around two sides of the deck. At the bottom, many ramp designs include a sloped concrete pad to allow for a smooth transition onto a walkway, driveway or other flat surface.

The support structure for a ramp is not significantly different from that for a deck. Posts on concrete piers or footings are positioned on each side every 5 feet. Beams fastened to each set of posts support the joists on which the ramp decking is fastened. For ramps leading off a deck 30 inches high or higher, a continuous railing 32 to 36 inches high is required. This railing can be built in the same style and with the same materials as the rest of the deck railing.

When it comes to designing a ramp for your deck, consider whether you want to integrate the structure into the backyard or make it a focal point. You can soften the appearance of a ramp with shrubs and other plantings. A curving, serpentine design, on the other hand, will grab attention and add visual interest. The employees at your local Home Depot can assist you with your design questions.

Wheelchair lifts or elevators are another choice for bringing a deck up-to-date with the current trend toward making decks wheelchair-accessible. An elevator requires much less space than a long ramp and can be useful for transporting heavy loads on and off a deck and into the home. If you consider investing in such a unit, make sure the model you choose is built to withstand the elements in your region.

Concrete Mixing System

Mixing the concrete for piers or a stair pad can be the most back-breaking and time-consuming part of building a deck. But with **Scepter**'s mixing system, you can prepare a batch of concrete quickly and easily. First, pour a measured volume of water into the drum with the calibrated lid. Then, add premixed concrete and screw the lid shut. After rolling the drum on its side for only 30 seconds, you're ready to open the lid and pour the concrete.

CHAPTER 3

DECK MATERIALS: WHAT YOU GET IS WHAT YOU SEE

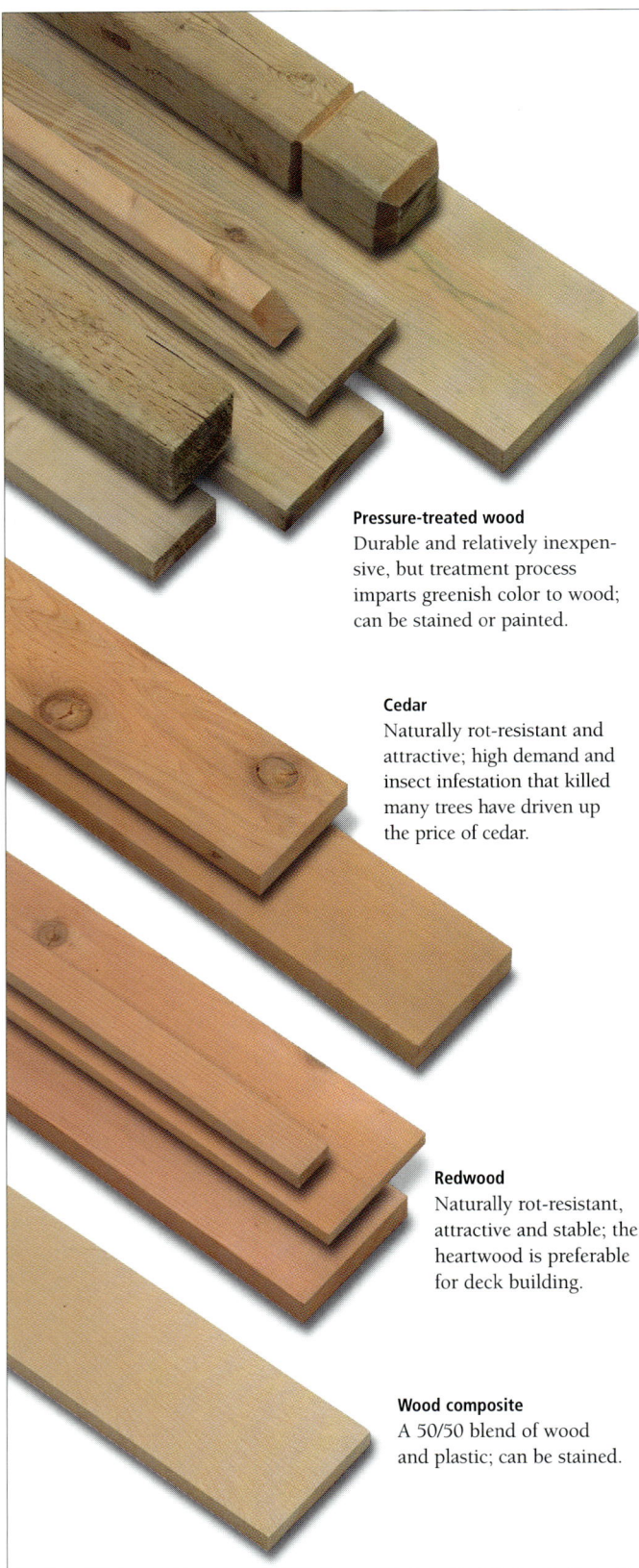

Pressure-treated wood
Durable and relatively inexpensive, but treatment process imparts greenish color to wood; can be stained or painted.

Cedar
Naturally rot-resistant and attractive; high demand and insect infestation that killed many trees have driven up the price of cedar.

Redwood
Naturally rot-resistant, attractive and stable; the heartwood is preferable for deck building.

Wood composite
A 50/50 blend of wood and plastic; can be stained.

Along with labor costs, materials are where the money goes in deck construction. Wood is the traditional material for building decks, but as discussed below and on page 33, a variety of synthetic and composite materials is available for decking, railings and stairs. Whichever material you choose, you will need to balance several, often competing factors: durability, cost, appearance and design. And although they aren't always as visible as the wood surfaces, the concrete piers that hold up the deck and the fasteners and connectors that hold it together are a big part of this equation *(pages 34-35)*. Apart from having to withstand the elements year after year, hardware can have a huge impact on design. Fasteners that rust, for example, will stain and decay the surrounding wood. They will also eventually loosen, threatening the deck's structural integrity. A wide range of deck materials as well as design services are available at your local Home Depot store.

A WORLD OF WOOD

There are two basic types of lumber for you to consider: naturally decay-resistant woods, such as redwood and cedar, and pressure-treated wood. The chart opposite compares them.

Whatever your preference in wood, a good rule of thumb when choosing lumber is to stay away from lower grades. Warped and knotty lumber is hard to work with and will not be worth the savings. As a compromise, purchase a quantity of higher-grade boards for deck surfaces and save money with mid-grade lumber for the understructure.

SYNTHETICS AND COMPOSITES

Synthetic and composite materials are gaining popularity with an increasing number of deck designers and builders. Produced mainly of recycled plastics, they are environmentally sound choices, helping to conserve forest timber. Since the plastics contained in these materials do not absorb moisture, they are completely decay-resistant and maintenance-free.

Many of these materials are usually more expensive than wood, but long-term savings in maintenance will eventually offset initial costs. A common complaint about synthetic materials is that although they can be painted, they cannot be stained in the same way as wood. To answer this charge, wood composite decking was developed. A 50/50 blend of wood by-products and recycled plastic, this material effectively simulates the look and feel of wood and it can be stained like wood. Both recycled plastic and composite

DECK WOODS	COLOR	CHARACTERISTICS	COST	USES
Redwood	Heartwood is tawny, reddish; sapwood is lighter-colored	Resistant to rot and attractive; very stable, making warping less likely; can be sanded to produce an extremely smooth surface; heartwood is knot-free; sapwood is not as dense, stable or decay-resistant as heartwood	Relatively expensive	Visible parts of deck—decking, railings and stairs; lower grades of sapwood not recommended for decking, but suitable for deck furniture, trellises or planters
Western red cedar	Reddish brown	Resistant to rot and attractive; brittle and not as strong as redwood	Relatively expensive	Visible parts of deck—decking, railings and stairs
Pressure-treated spruce, pine or fir	Preservatives turn wood greenish or brownish; color weathers to a light gray	Widely available in most regions; very durable; typically guaranteed for up to 40 years, provided ends cut during installation are coated with preservative; high resistance to moisture; the most widely used of all decking materials	A bargain compared to redwood and cedar	Any part of deck, but especially less visible understructure—joists, beams and posts

wood materials are as yet only available in limited dimensions and colors. A composite or recycled plastic deck must still rely on wood for the deck understructure. And since these materials are heavier than wood, the understructure needs to be bolstered.

A FINISH FOR YOUR DECK

It's advisable to finish any wood deck. A good finish will seal out moisture, block harmful ultraviolet (UV) radiation and prevent breakdown of wood fibers. The amount of finishing work you need to do depends mainly on the deck material you have chosen. Composite wood products do not require any finishing at all for maintenance purposes, although they can be stained or painted. Woods such as cedar or redwood are resistant to decay; however, no wood is completely indestructible and the effects of sun and water will show after time. Even pressure-treated lumber will last longer if it is treated and its color can be preserved with most finishes.

A sealing finish should be applied to a new deck as soon as the lumber has completely dried. Many manufacturers recommend treating decking before building since board ends—which may be difficult to get at after assembly—are in greatest need of protection. Follow the manufacturer's instructions as to the type of applicator and the sealant's drying time.

Today, the wide variety of deck finishes available allows deck builders to choose from a full spectrum of color and tone. These range from semi-transparent stains to solid-color stains, which can either combine with the wood's existing tone or completely mask its original color. In addition to giving your deck a unique design element, pigmented sealants are often more effective for longer periods than clear sealants, providing your colorful new deck with greater protection against the elements.

A deck finish isn't just for appearances' sake. Although the finish on this deck imparts an arresting burgundy hue to the wood, its more important function is to serve as a moisture barrier between the elements and the deck. You know a finish is doing its job when water beads on the surface rather than sinking in.
(Photo: courtesy Sico Inc.)

WOOD PURCHASING POLICY

The Home Depot is committed to building a better world through sustainable business practices. Responsible wood purchasing is one step toward sustainability and presents a tremendous opportunity to meet our customers' demand for wood products while sustaining the forests for generations to come.

To learn more about The Home Depot's wood purchasing policies, please visit our web site at www.homedepot.com.

CHAPTER 3

Deck Underpinnings

Although they will be partially or completely hidden when your deck is finished, the foundation and understructure are prime design considerations. After all, they are what will hold up your deck.

FOUNDATIONS

The illustrations below feature three common options for deck foundations. Represented in the deck plans in this book, the concrete pier is the traditional means of supporting decks. A hole is dug below the frost line—up to 48 inches deep depending on where you live—a base of crushed stone is shoveled into the hole and concrete fills a fiber tube form, which gives the pier its cylindrical shape. Meanwhile, concrete that overflows at the bottom of the form creates a wide footing. A metal post anchor *(page 35)* is embedded in the wet concrete and a post is fastened to the anchor once the concrete dries.

Precast pier blocks with built-in post anchors also sit atop a hole dug to the frost line. In this case, however, no tube form is used. Instead, concrete poured into the hole forms a footing and the pier block is set in the wet concrete. As with concrete piers, a post is fastened to the preattached anchor.

Concrete piers that sit directly on the ground offer a work-saving alternative to concrete piers and precast pier blocks. With this type of foundation, known as a floating foundation system, there are no holes to dig or concrete to prepare and pour. For more information on concrete piers, see page 25.

POSTS, BEAMS AND JOISTS

Because the lumber that supports the deck is close to the ground and its moisture most builders use pressure-treated wood for these components—the posts, beams, joists and ledger board. Even for decks with railings and decking made from a naturally rot-resistant wood such as cedar or redwood, it makes sense to build most of the understructure from pressure-treated wood since it is seldom visible. However, if you won't be putting up skirting around the understructure, you may want to use cedar or redwood for the posts since they will be visible. Other options include natural poles, which make attractive posts for decks attached to log cabins or beach houses. Usually treated with preservatives, poles are available with the bark left on. Steel posts and beams, another option, offer exceptional strength. Because of high cost, however, structural steel members are usually only used for extreme loads or unusually long spans.

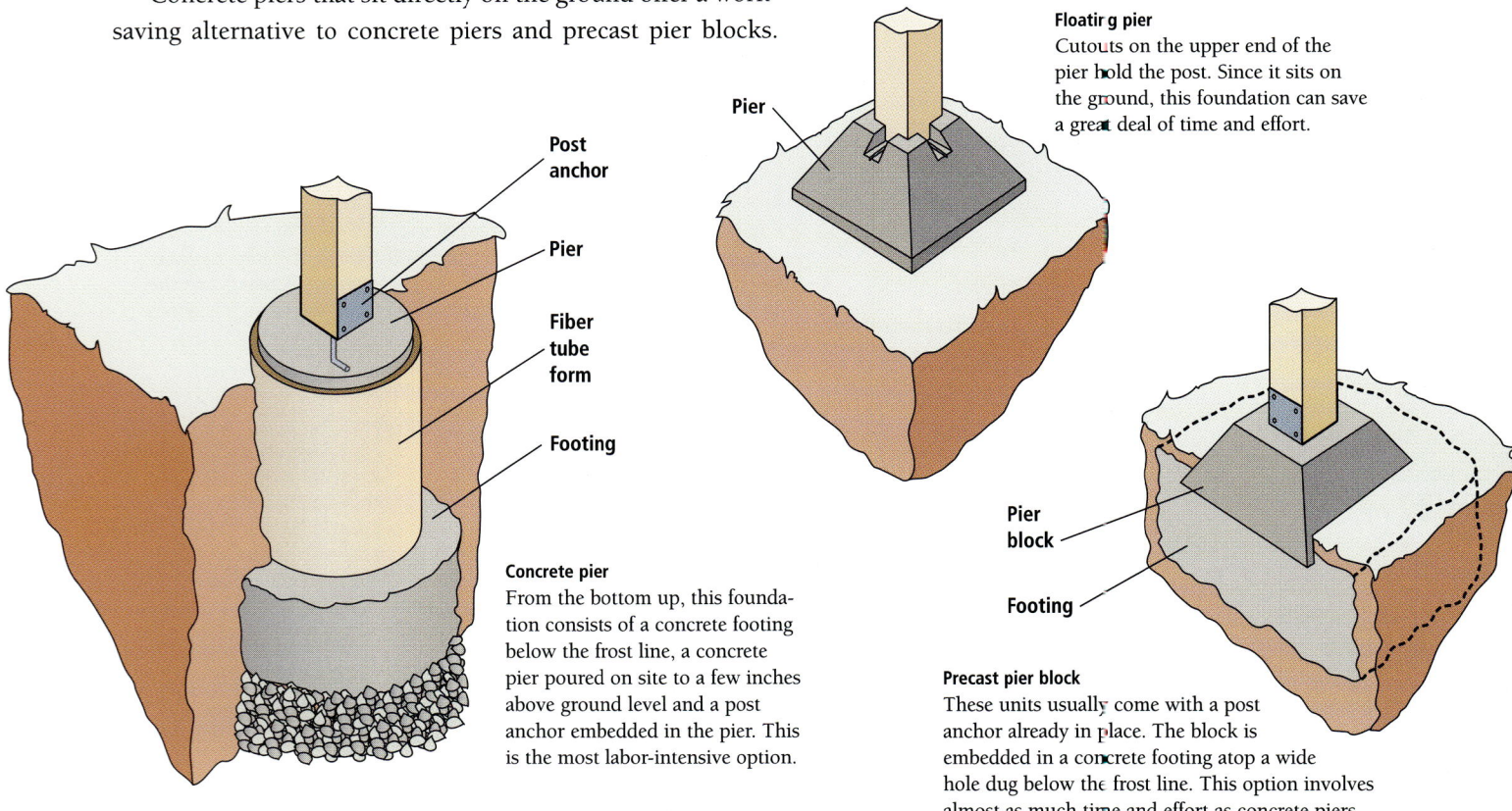

Concrete pier
From the bottom up, this foundation consists of a concrete footing below the frost line, a concrete pier poured on site to a few inches above ground level and a post anchor embedded in the pier. This is the most labor-intensive option.

Floating pier
Cutouts on the upper end of the pier hold the post. Since it sits on the ground, this foundation can save a great deal of time and effort.

Precast pier block
These units usually come with a post anchor already in place. The block is embedded in a concrete footing atop a wide hole dug below the frost line. This option involves almost as much time and effort as concrete piers.

CHAPTER 3

Deck Hardware

Most of the fasteners and connectors shown in the photos at right—from joist hangers to post anchors—will never see the light of day once your deck is up and running. Others, like the deck screws or nails that anchor the decking to the joists, are front and center. (Then again, if you don't want nails or screws to show on your decking, you can use deck clips to fasten the deck boards to the joists.) If you think all these pieces of deck hardware don't play an important role in deck design, think again. These fasteners and connectors must be able to hold the deck together without staining the wood around them or working loose.

Galvanized nails and decking screws, hot-dipped in rust-resistant zinc, are a good example. Their bumpy, silver-gray coating seals out the moisture that promotes corrosion. The coating makes them more difficult to drive into wood, but it also makes them impervious to loosening.

The workhorses of deck framing (anchors, connectors and hangers) provide strength at key points in the construction process and make life easier for deck builders. For example, a joist cut too short to fit snugly between the ledger board and the rim joist will not present any problem when it is secured in a joist hanger.

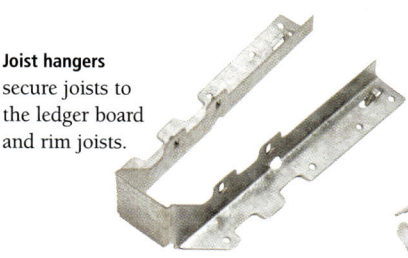

Post anchors secure the posts to the piers. The J-bolt is embedded in wet concrete and threaded to the anchor.

Post/beam connectors join beams to the top of posts.

Joist hangers secure joists to the ledger board and rim joists.

Deck clips are an alternative to nails or screws for laying decking. Fastened to the sides of the boards, they are invisible once all the decking is in place.

Universal or seismic anchors connect joists to beams. Recommended in areas prone to earthquakes.

Angle irons anchor the base of stair stringers to the concrete pad.

Lag screws, with their thick shanks and hex heads, are used to fasten the ledger board to the wall of the house.

Hex-head bolts are used where the bolt extends all the way through the members, creating a stronger connection than screws.

Carriage bolts attach railing posts to joists.

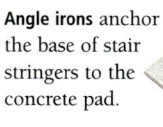

Decking screws have greater holding power than nails and are easier to remove for maintenance and repair.

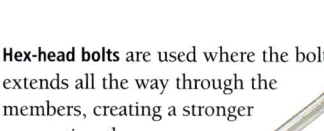

Stainless-steel screws cost twice as much as hot-dipped galvanized fasteners, but are corrosion-proof.

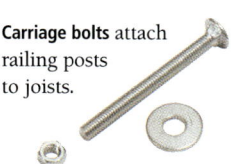

Hot-dipped galvanized nails have a thick anti-rust coating that is less likely to flake off than the coating of electroplated nails.

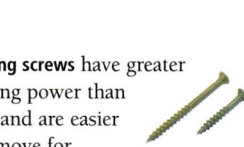
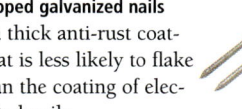

A Well-Connected Deck

A deck is subjected to a great deal of physical stress. The weather beats on it year after year. The ground under it constantly shifts. And if you live in hurricane country, annual storms put every structural joint to the test. And years from now, a deck is supposed to look as good as the day it was built.

Simpson Strong-Tie makes steel connectors designed to connect, support and strengthen joints in wood decks. From joist hangers that fasten joists to ledger boards to angle irons that secure treads to stringers, **Simpson Strong-Tie** connectors make deck building easier. In addition to adding strength and safety, connectors cut down on the number of nails required for installation and eliminate the need for complicated construction techniques such as toenailing—driving a nail into one piece at a 45-degree angle so the nail tip penetrates an adjoining piece. Although connectors were once optional parts of construction projects, they are now required by building codes in some areas.

www.homedepot.com   35

CHAPTER 4

Fancy Add-ons

The next few pages explore features you can add to a deck to enhance its appearance and functionality. Additions include lighting and plumbing fixtures *(below and opposite)*; benches, tables and planters *(pages 38-39)*; and screens, arbors and overheads *(pages 40-41)*. Your local Home Depot can help you with both design and purchasing advice.

Let There Be Light

If you think you have to stop using a deck at sundown, think again. Proper lighting adds magical appeal to nighttime, transforming a deck into a fully functioning outdoor room. You can illuminate a large area with overhead floodlights or create focused lighting with low-voltage lights, highlighting small, often used areas. Although a single 300-watt overhead floodlight may be economical, its starkness makes many deck designers seek the more sophisticated effects of low-voltage lights. Of the lights shown at right above, all are low-voltage except the rope light and motion-sensor floodlight.

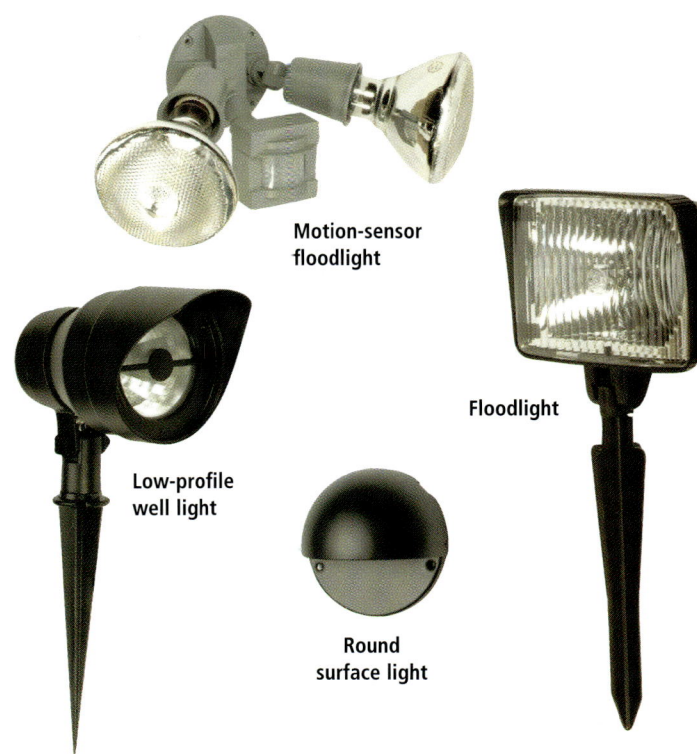

Motion-sensor floodlight

Floodlight

Low-profile well light

Round surface light

Round surface lights installed in the stair risers of this deck add atmosphere and enhance safety by making the stairs easier to negotiate when natural light is low.
(Photo: courtesy Tom Jacques, Hickory Dickory Decks)

The choice depends largely on how you plan to use your deck. A grilling area must be well lit, preferably by overheads. Mount floodlights 15 feet overhead, angling them downward at a 45-degree angle. Bouncing the light off a white wall or lightly colored surface will temper its stark effects. Light can also be softened by concealing fixtures behind a translucent wall or divider.

Low-voltage lighting is available in 12-volt system kits that include a transformer and in most cases do not require a permit for installation. There are as many styles of low-voltage lighting as there are uses. Lights for stairs and pathways are set low to the ground; they are available in styles as varied as freestanding poles and insulated boxes inset in or bracket-mounted beside stair risers. Here's a simple test for placing these lights: Light a few candles and place them in areas you think need the most light. Move them around. Add more if necessary. This will give you an idea of how much light these fixtures supply and where they'll work best.

Purely decorative low-voltage lighting systems are designed more for mood than practicality, although if they are placed in the right areas these lights can enhance safety, defining steps or the deck perimeter. Decorative ideas include rope lights installed along railings or small fixtures placed amid deck plants or shrubs.

THE SIMPLICITY OF LOW-VOLTAGE OUTDOOR LIGHTING SYSTEMS

The "low voltage" in a low-voltage lighting system is provided by a transformer that steps down 120-volt household current to 12 volts. Many low-voltage lighting kits are simply plugged into a standard outlet. Because of moisture, code requires all outdoor outlets to be protected by a ground-fault circuit interrupter (GFCI). GFCIs shut off power to a circuit virtually the instant a ground leak is detected, preventing you from receiving a potentially fatal shock. As for connecting the lights, low-voltage systems are simple to install. They generally have a two-wire cable that connects to the fixtures without any stripping or splicing of cable. The transformer should be installed in a sheltered area at least 1 foot above ground.

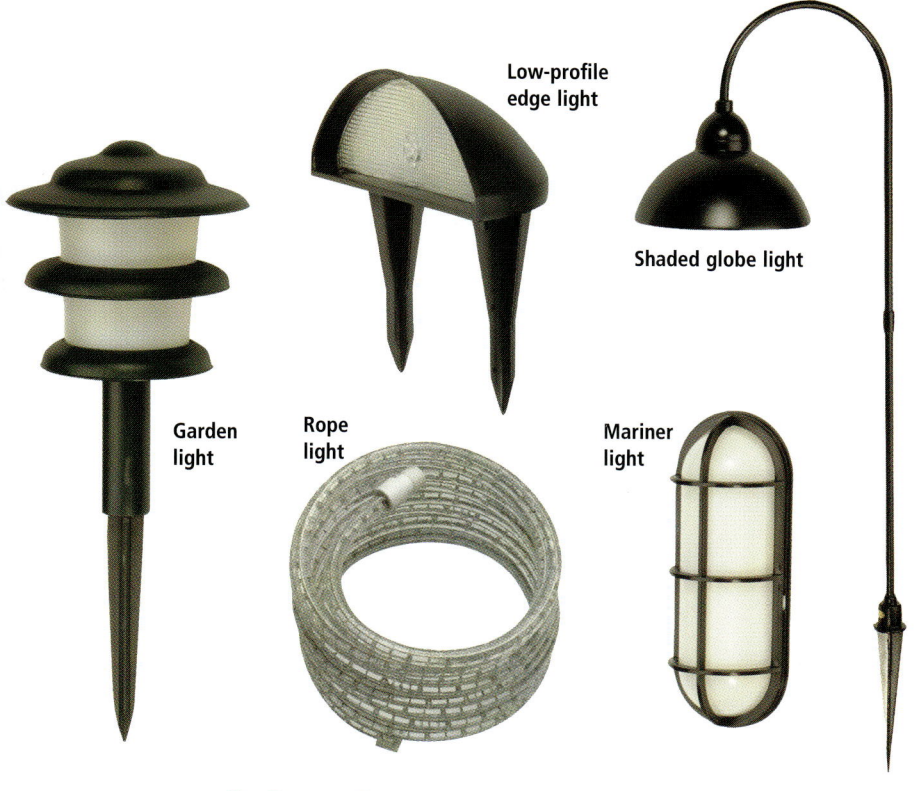

A selection of outdoor lighting fixtures
Standard 120-volt outdoor floodlights often include motion detectors or photocells that automatically turn the light on at dusk or when movement is detected. Rope lights, sold in 12- to 16-foot lengths, are most effective when installed along railings or benches. Low-voltage lights frequently come pole-mounted. They can be stuck in the ground to light paths or to create effects with plants or screens. Other low-voltage lights are mounted on brackets or recessed in components to illuminate deck edges, railings, stairways or the different levels of a multilevel deck.

A World of Water

Whether it's for gardening or the installation of a lavish spa, an outdoor water connection will provide your deck with increased comfort and convenience. A simple hose connection or hose bibb can easily be installed after your deck is completed, especially if the structure is attached to your house wall. You can tap into your home's water supply line, extending it from the interior to the outdoors. Hose bibbs should be located several feet above the deck surface and can be concealed effectively along with a garden hose in a storage box or hinged bench (*page 39*).

Supplying water to a hot tub or spa takes a little more planning. In addition to adding the necessary supply pipes and electricity to power heaters and pumps, freestanding spas—units that rest on top of the deck—require a reinforced deck understructure. Although they appear to be supported by the deck that surrounds them, built-in spas actually sit on a concrete pad set in the ground. The deck frame is then built around the spa at a level that allows the decking boards to fit under the lip of the spa. Because decking generally conceals plumbing and electricity for heaters and pumps in both types of spas, an access trapdoor is commonly included on the deck surface for maintenance and repair.

Another consideration for outdoor water is winter temperatures. In northern areas, chances are pipes will freeze and burst if they are not drained before the winter. Freeze-proof hose bibbs are equipped with an extra long stem valve that extends inside the house, effectively shutting off the water before it reaches the cold outside air. You may need to install special insulation for water pipes that supply spas or hot tubs that operate outdoors in winter weather. Before installing your spa, check to be sure your design will be able to meet the demands of your region and satisfy local building codes.

The framing under the spa area of this deck requires special reinforcement to support the additional weight of a spa filled with water. Built-in spas generally sit on a concrete pad set at ground level.
(Photo: courtesy Southern Forest Products Association)

DECKS 1-2-3

The Home Depot's *Decks 1-2-3* shows how to install low-voltage lighting and provides other step-by-step instructions, tips from the pros, material and tool information, and design inspiration to help you design, build and maintain your deck.

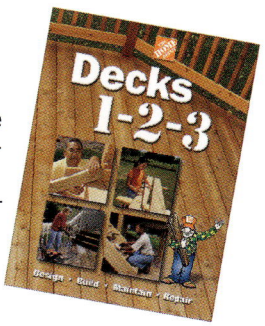

CHAPTER 4

Benches, Tables, Planters and Storage

You can incorporate built-in amenities in your deck design at the planning stage or add them after you've lived with your deck for a while. Of course, benches, tables, planters and storage spaces can all be installed separately, but building these items at the same time as your deck will generally yield better results. Your materials will match and you'll be better able to harmonize the deck design.

More than any other built-in accessory, benches can accent deck design by reinforcing perimeter lines, defining activity areas and visually breaking up long lines of railing. Benches can use deck and railing posts as supports, but they also can be simply fastened to the deck understructure without being attached to railings, which enables you to place them in virtually any location on the deck. In these cases, they are usually installed after the framing is complete but before the decking is laid.

As you consider bench design, consider comfort, height and size. A bench with a backrest will be more comfortable. If the seat is 15 inches high, the bench can double as a low table. As for size, you can design a bench to extend along the entire length of a railing or limit it to a small nook on an irregularly shaped deck.

Today's deck designers use tables as important design tools for defining activity areas on a deck. Although movable patio-style tables may be preferable for a multipurpose deck area, round or octagonal tables built into a corner with benches around them can create an inviting area for small gatherings or informal meals.

This inviting seating area is located "off the beaten track," transforming an otherwise underused deck area into a gathering place. The large deck posts are structural elements that serve as supports for the benches, the railing and the overhead.
(Photo: courtesy Wolmanized® Wood)

Basic planter
In this design, the outer sides are made from tongue-and-groove siding framed by solid wood trim. The interior is exterior-grade 3/4-inch plywood. Set on 2x4 cleats, the bottom consists of a plywood panel with drain holes.

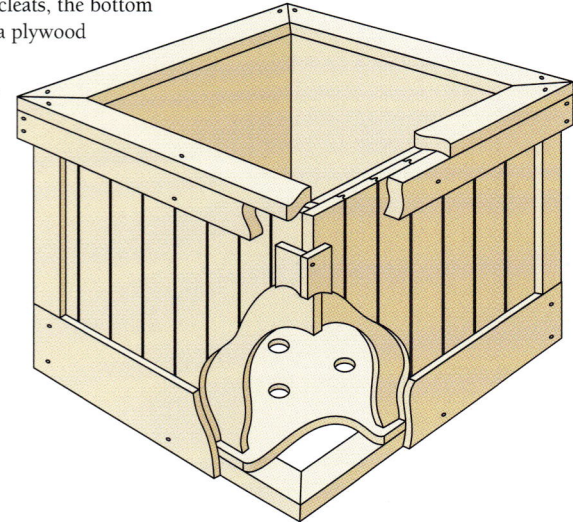

Basic bench
Made of 2x4s, the seat and back slats of this bench are fastened to seat and back supports that can be attached to railing posts.

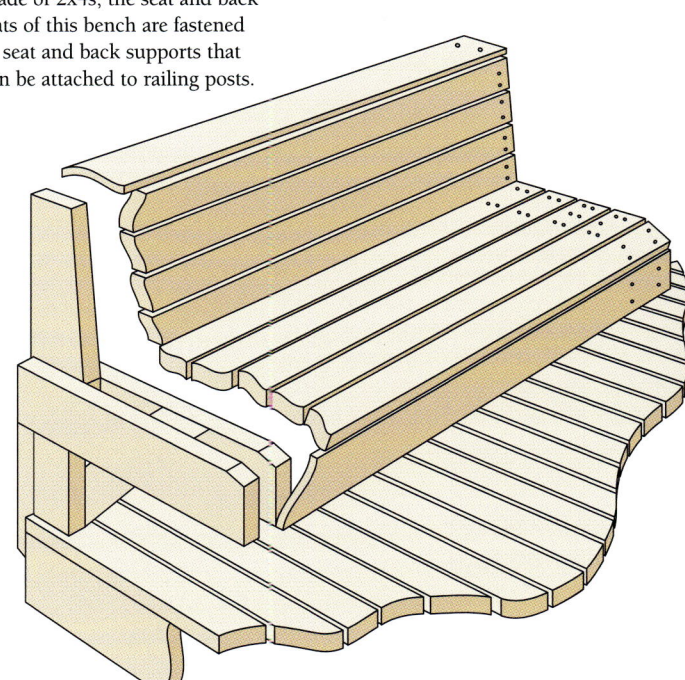

Planters add color and greenery to your deck area, highlighting to great effect the outdoor aspect of deck living. They also can serve to define or accentuate the shape of the deck. On multilevel decks, attractive planter borders built into the short walls between the levels can serve to enclose stair areas and direct traffic.

Although freestanding furniture can be placed and moved wherever you like, it must be moved regularly to prevent moisture buildup because it stands directly on decking. This is especially true for planters, which can cause decking decay as a result of the additional moisture from watered soil. Planter boxes should be lined with a waterproof barrier such as heavy-duty plastic or sheet metal. They should also be constructed with an air space between the base and the decking. Don't forget, full planters can be quite heavy. Adding casters will make them easier to shift across the decking surface.

One of the often overlooked advantages of a backyard deck is the storage space it can provide. By building a trapdoor into your decking surface, as shown below, or a door in the skirting, the space under the deck can be accessed easily and turned into storage for garden tools, hoses or even toys. The only additional materials you'll need are supports for the trapdoor and the lumber to build a hidden storage box. Handy storage areas can also be created under benches. By sealing off the front and sides of a bench with additional boards and incorporating a hinged section in the bench seat, you can easily create another deck hiding place.

One of the secrets to a successful storage area is keeping it inconspicuous. In a way, the same is true of all deck furnishings. Unless you are using an addition as a contrasting element or an accent, your deck additions should generally fit in with your deck's original design. If you follow the lines of your deck and maintain a consistency of materials, your deck additions will blend in seamlessly, making your deck a winner for style as well as function.

A curved planter does double duty as a colorful low wall, dividing activity areas of the deck, and as an attractive visual focal point.
(Photo: courtesy Tom Jacques, Hickory Dickory Decks)

The benches on this freestanding deck transform the structure into an inviting sitting area and create a visual and physical corridor to the water's edge.
(Photo: courtesy Wolmanized® Wood)

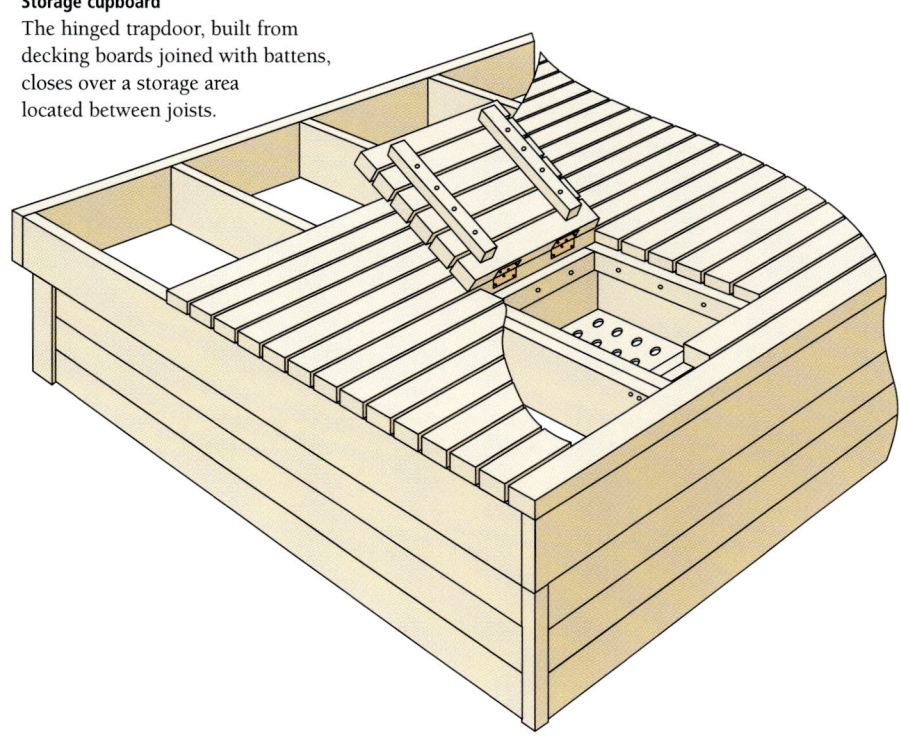

Storage cupboard
The hinged trapdoor, built from decking boards joined with battens, closes over a storage area located between joists.

CHAPTER 4

Arbors, Screens and Overheads

The concept of the deck as an extension of your home's interior comes to life with the addition of arbors, screens and overheads. With these structures, you can tame the elements to your liking, creating shade without shutting out the sun, deflecting the wind while letting in a refreshing breeze and ensuring privacy without enclosing the space.

Since most decks are raised above ground and are located in backyards that adjoin those of their neighbors, privacy screens are a common addition. Framed lattice is a traditional screen material and is still an economical and lightweight favorite. Extending the railing posts upward will provide adequate support for a series of lattice panels. Lattice is available in cedar, redwood, pressure-treated wood and plastic and comes in varying "grid densities," depending on how much of the outside world you want to close off. Other screen materials include translucent plastic panels, shade cloth and, for a more natural look, woven reed or bamboo. Woven materials have the advantage of being raised or lowered like a blind, but

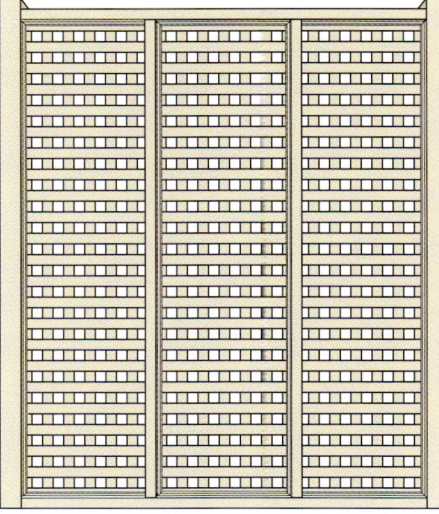

Framed lattice
Lattice panels come in 4x6-, 1x8-, 2x8- and 4x8-foot sizes, and a variety of thicknesses and spacing arrangements. The most common patterns are diagonal and, as shown here, checkerboard.

they are likely to prove less hardy in facing the elements than lattice or plastic panels.

Covering an area of your deck with an overhead or arbor should be planned out in much the same way as your initial deck plan. Perhaps it is an eating area that would most benefit from shade and shelter or maybe you'd like to create a relaxation zone away from the main traffic areas. Familiarize yourself with the sun's path over your home and deck (*page 23*) and consider the effects of increased shade on your home. Placing your overhead too close to your house wall may cut off light to the interior of your home. Take into account as well the notion of architectural harmony when choosing your arbor design. A traditional gazebo design goes well with a Victorian-style home, while a simpler design of parallel laths or boards makes a good match with a more modern ranch- or bungalow-style home.

Overhead design usually consists of basic post-and-beam construction, with roofing made up of either rafters to sup-

This fencelike privacy screen blocks neighbors' views into the deck area and cuts down on the wind, creating a private, sheltered dining area.
(Photo: courtesy Tom Jacques, Hickory Dickory Decks)

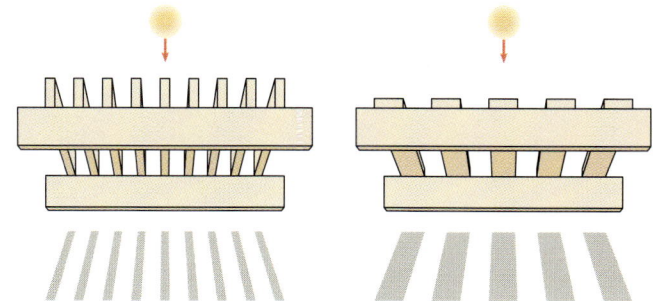

Shade from an overhead
The dimension and orientation of overhead boards determine the amount of shade they provide. When the sun is straight overhead, as shown, boards laid flat will provide more shade; however, boards set on edge will create more shade later or earlier in the day when the sun is angled.

port a finished roof or lighter weight boards that let in light and air. Posts can be fastened to the deck understructure; however, if you build your overhead at the same time as the rest of your deck, posts supporting the deck can be extended above the deck surface to support overhead beams.

The roofing for your overhead will determine the amount of shade you get. Lattice panels, translucent plastic or woven materials will create a more complete shelter, while boards or narrow laths will allow variations of light and shade. As shown in the diagram on page 40, the dimension of the lumber making up your overhead and how it is positioned will influence how much sunlight it blocks. Before fastening the boards in place, try different spacing patterns and compare laying them on edge with laying them flat. Testing your roofing when the sun is at its highest (around noon) will best demonstrate the full impact of your new deck addition. Once you've decided on just the right configuration, fasten your roofing with deck screws. This will give you the option of easily repositioning or removing roofing if your needs change.

Arbors, screens and overheads are traditional supports for climbing plants. Picture sunlight filtering through a covering of green leaves and you'll have some idea of the effect of sitting beneath a vine-covered arbor or overhead. Hanging planters can be suspended from overhead rafters or an arbor structure can be used to support built-in plant boxes. Either of these ideas will add greenery to your deck and impart an attractive finishing touch to your new outdoor living space.

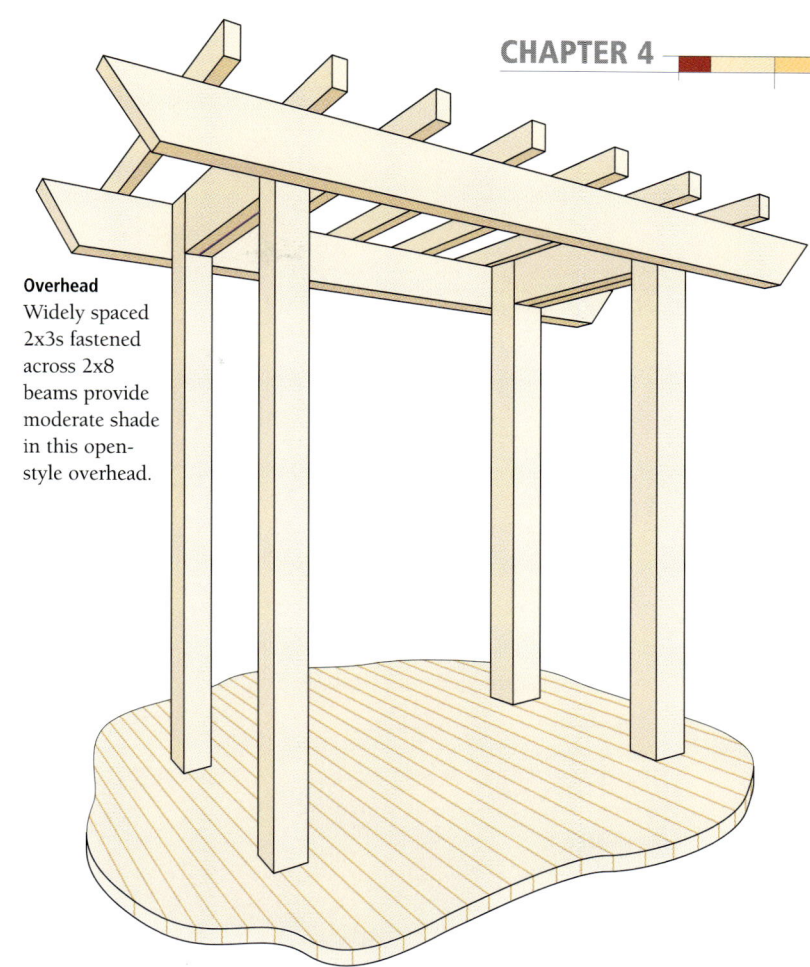

Overhead
Widely spaced 2x3s fastened across 2x8 beams provide moderate shade in this open-style overhead.

A "Tuff" Alternative for Overheads

A deck overhead doesn't have to be made exclusively of wood. Corrugated polycarbonate sheets manufactured by **Suntuf** offer many of wood's advantages and possess several benefits that wood cannot match. Combining light weight with strength, **Suntuf** sheets resist wind and hail as well as physical abuse and they won't distort in hot weather or become brittle in winter. They are available in a wide variety of transparent, translucent and opaque colors to suit most designs. And while transparent and translucent sheets transmit light with the clarity of glass, all three types provide protection from harmful ultraviolet rays. This makes **Suntuf** sheets a good choice for an overhead above a deck with a pool or spa or a deck that will be exposed to direct sunlight.

Perhaps best of all, **Suntuf** sheets don't require professional installation. If you can build a deck yourself, then you can install these sheets. They are easy to handle and can be cut and drilled with standard tools.

(Photo: courtesy Elizabeth Benham, Suntuf)

The 2x2s comprising the roofing of this overhead shield the deck area from the full force of the sun while letting in enough light to allow plants beneath it to flourish.
(Photo: courtesy Wolmanized® Wood)

CHAPTER 5

OUR MOST POPULAR DECK PLANS

On the pages that follow we present our most popular deck plans. To both inspire you and fulfill your deck building needs, we have included a complete plan and material list for each project. Depending on the complexity of the deck, the following drawings may be included:

- Plan Rendering
- Plan View
- Pier Layout
- Framing Plan
- Elevations
- Details

Find the plan you like, add the features that suit your particular lifestyle or landscape and bring the result to your local Home Depot store to purchase everything you'll need to begin construction.

For more information on these plans or to see our other project plans, visit us at **www.DreamIt-BuildIt.com**, where you'll find these additional building aids:

- A comprehensive list of recommended materials
- A tools list
- "Build-It Guide" with illustrations
- Tips on how to build your project smarter and safer
- A glossary of project-related building terms

To see the quality of our complete project plans, download our FREE doghouse project. Our site also offers the largest online inventory of home plans. **Call 1-888-314-1303 for more information.**

"He who plans and follows out that plan, carries a thread that will guide him through the maze of the most busy life. But where no plan is laid, chaos will soon reign."
Victor Hugo
(Photo: courtesy California Redwood Association; Designer: Richard O'Grady)

DISCLAIMER

Building Codes: Variations in building codes, specific local development covenants or site conditions may require modification to the design of the project plans and other information contained in this publication. You are ultimately responsible for complying with all applicable permit, building codes and other regulatory requirements. Be sure to review the plans with your local building inspector and acquire all appropriate building permits before starting your project. The project plans have been designed in accordance with the Uniform Building Code (UBC 1997).

Accuracy: There always exists a possibility for errors or omissions in the project plans and other information contained in this publication. Therefore, you and/or your building contractor(s) shall assume the responsibility of verifying all conditions and dimensions contained within a project plan prior to the start of construction. Please report any discrepancies to HomeStyles, Inc. at 1-888-314-1303 for verification and/or correction before proceeding with construction. You and/or your building contractor(s) shall assume responsibility for errors that are not reported. HomeStyles' warranty for errors and omissions is limited to, and may not exceed, the amount of fees collected for the design services related to the purchase of these plans. The Home Depot, Inc. and its directors, officers, employees, affiliates and subsidiaries specifically disclaim all warranties and conditions of any kind.

Liability: Neither The Home Depot, Inc. and its directors, officers, employees, affiliates and subsidiaries nor HomeStyles shall have any liability or responsibility for your action or inaction in connection with any project plan or any other information contained in this publication or for any damage or liability that arises during the construction and/or use of any project or project plan. Always read and observe all of the safety precautions provided by any tool or equipment manufacturer and follow all accepted safety procedures.

Materials Lists: Materials Lists are based upon the drawings contained in this plan set. Actual quantities may vary based upon actual site conditions.

CHAPTER 5

THE DERRICK

HPM-1100

This spacious deck has plenty of room for outdoor living and incorporates an effective entrance and exit plan removed from the center of activity. Set off from the main area of the deck, two staircases conveniently direct traffic to opposite sides of the yard, while sturdy rails provide sunbathers and young ones with a feeling of security.

Dimensions for this deck are 16' X 14'.

Derrick

Plan View

Scale: 1/4" = 1'-0"

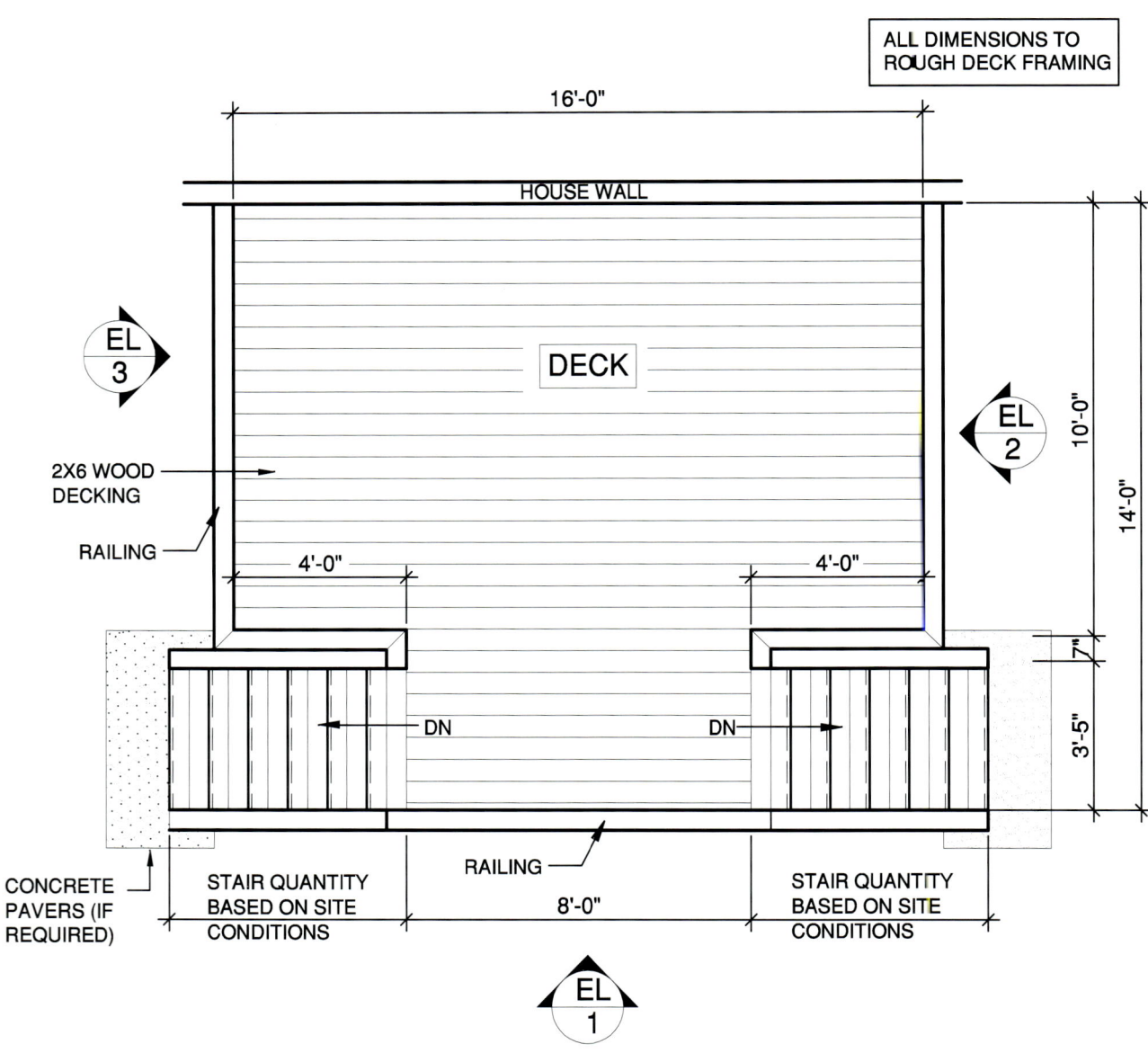

DERRICK — Pier Layout

Scale: 1/4" = 1'-0"

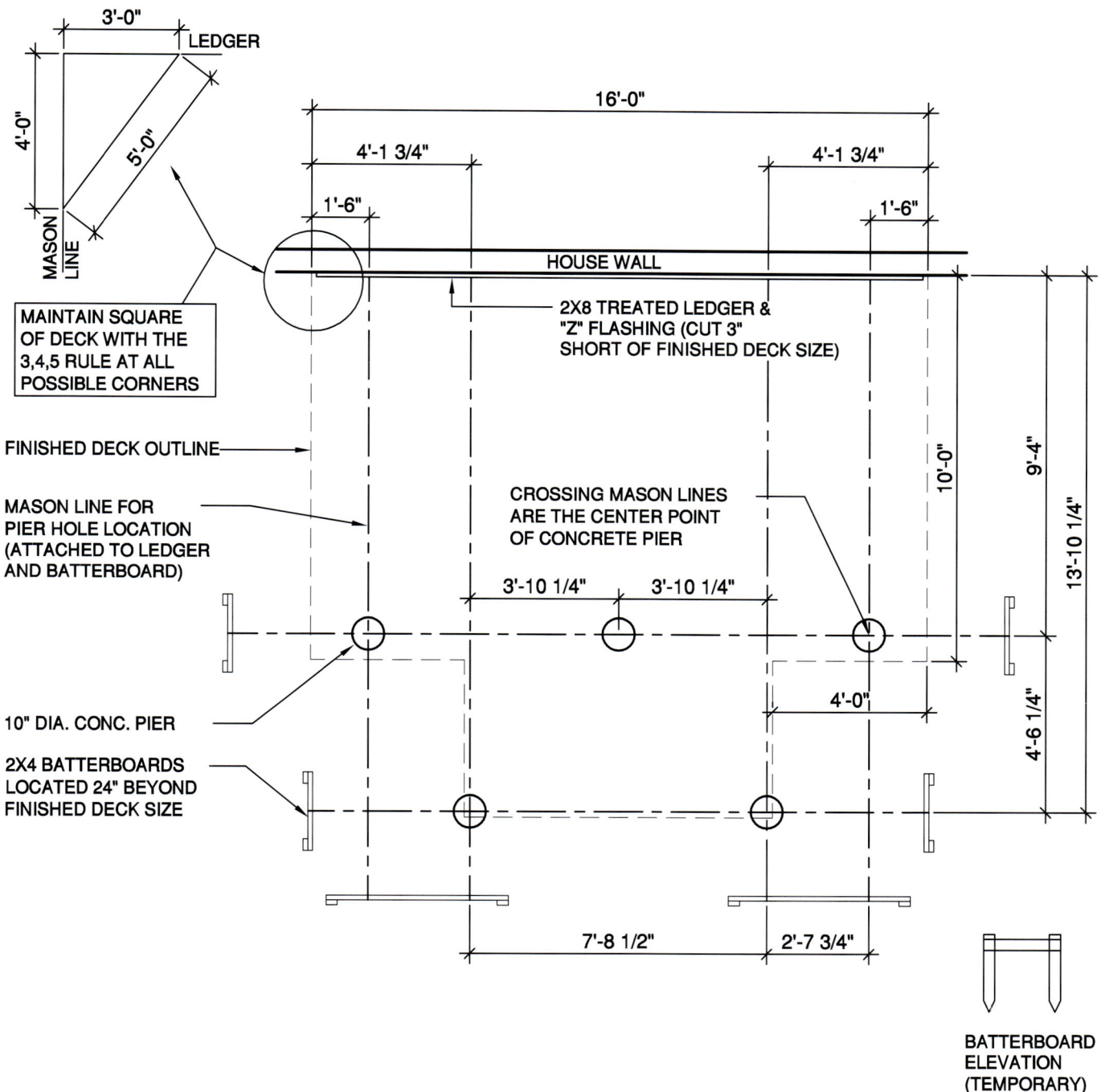

BATTERBOARD ELEVATION (TEMPORARY)

www.homedepot.com 45

DERRICK — Framing Plan

Scale: 1/4" = 1'-0"

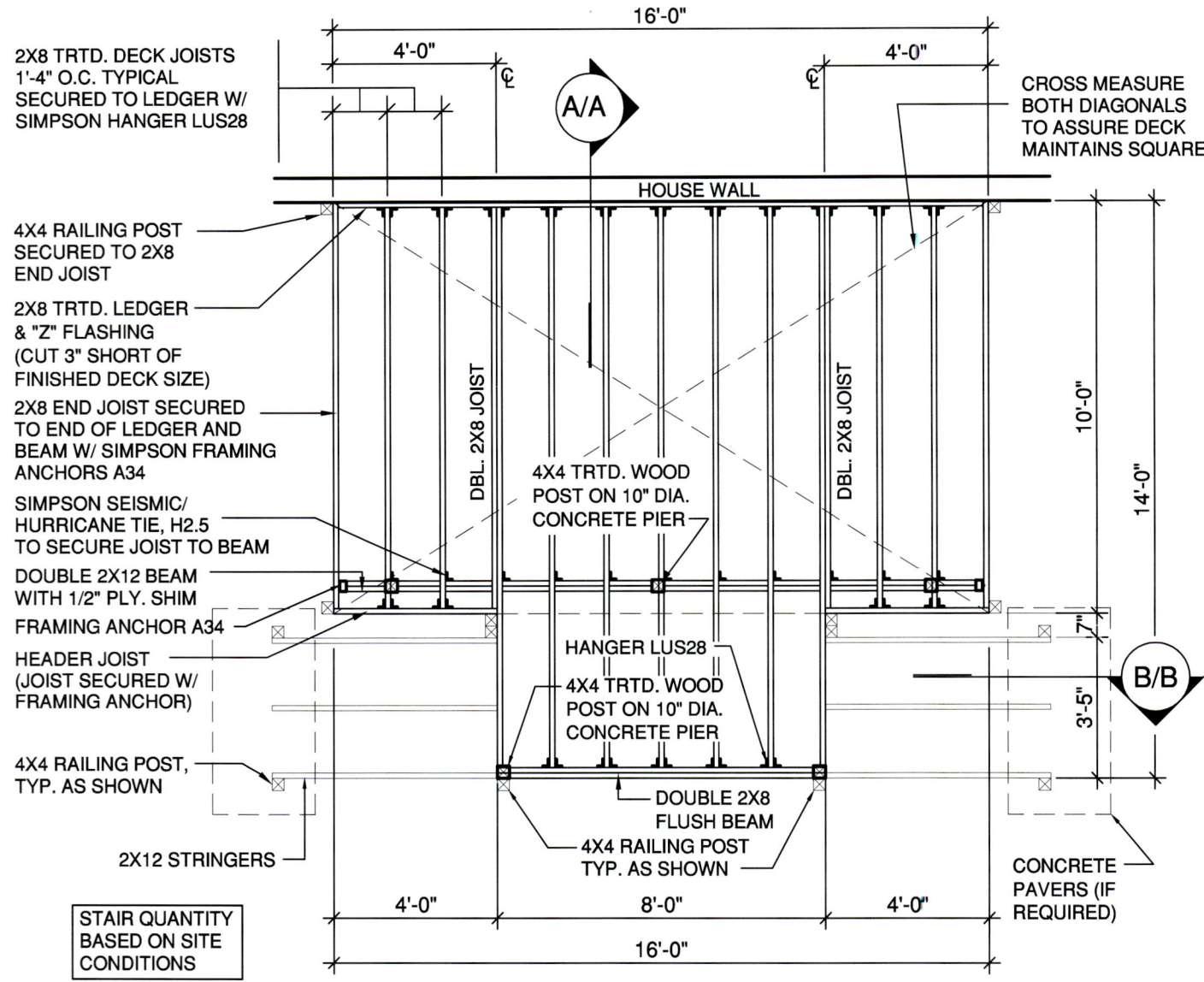

DERRICK — Elevations

Scale: 1/4" = 1'-0"

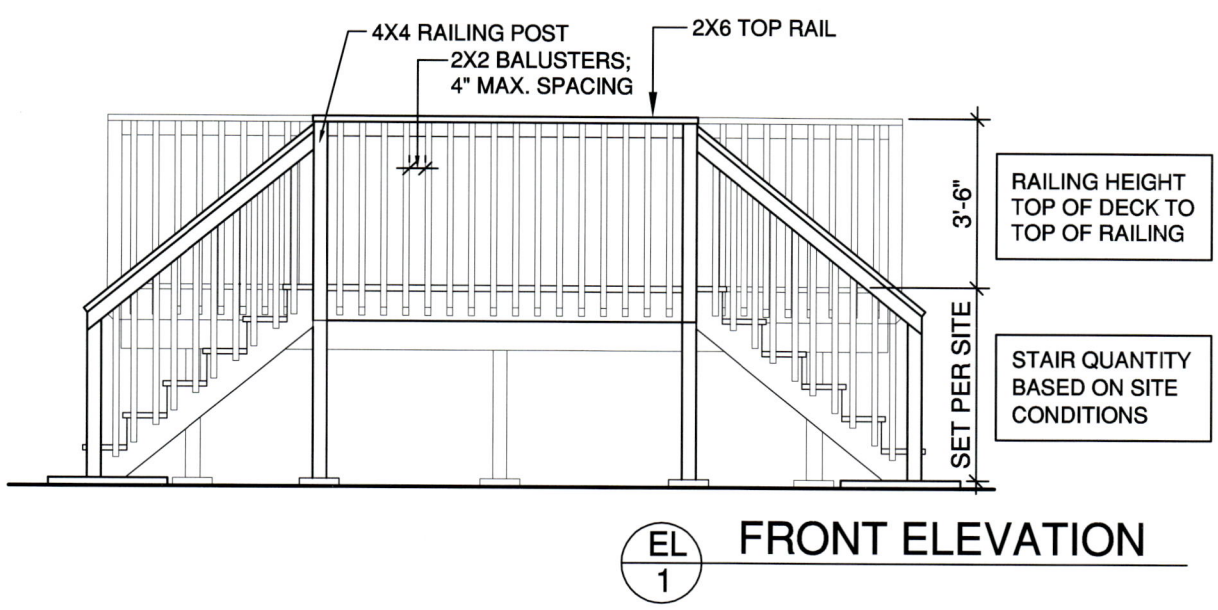

FRONT ELEVATION (EL/1)

- 4X4 RAILING POST
- 2X2 BALUSTERS; 4" MAX. SPACING
- 2X6 TOP RAIL
- 3'-6" RAILING HEIGHT TOP OF DECK TO TOP OF RAILING
- SET PER SITE — STAIR QUANTITY BASED ON SITE CONDITIONS

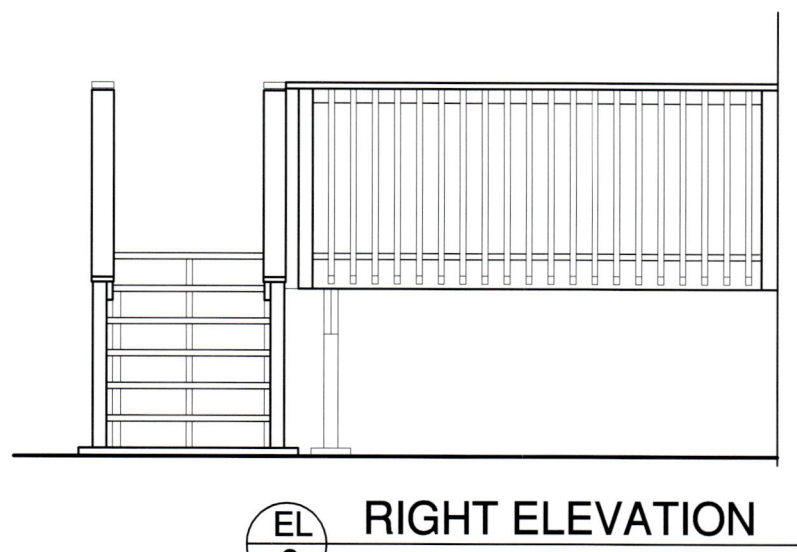

RIGHT ELEVATION (EL/2)

LEFT ELEVATION (EL/3) — REVERSE OF RIGHT ELEVATION

www.homedepot.com

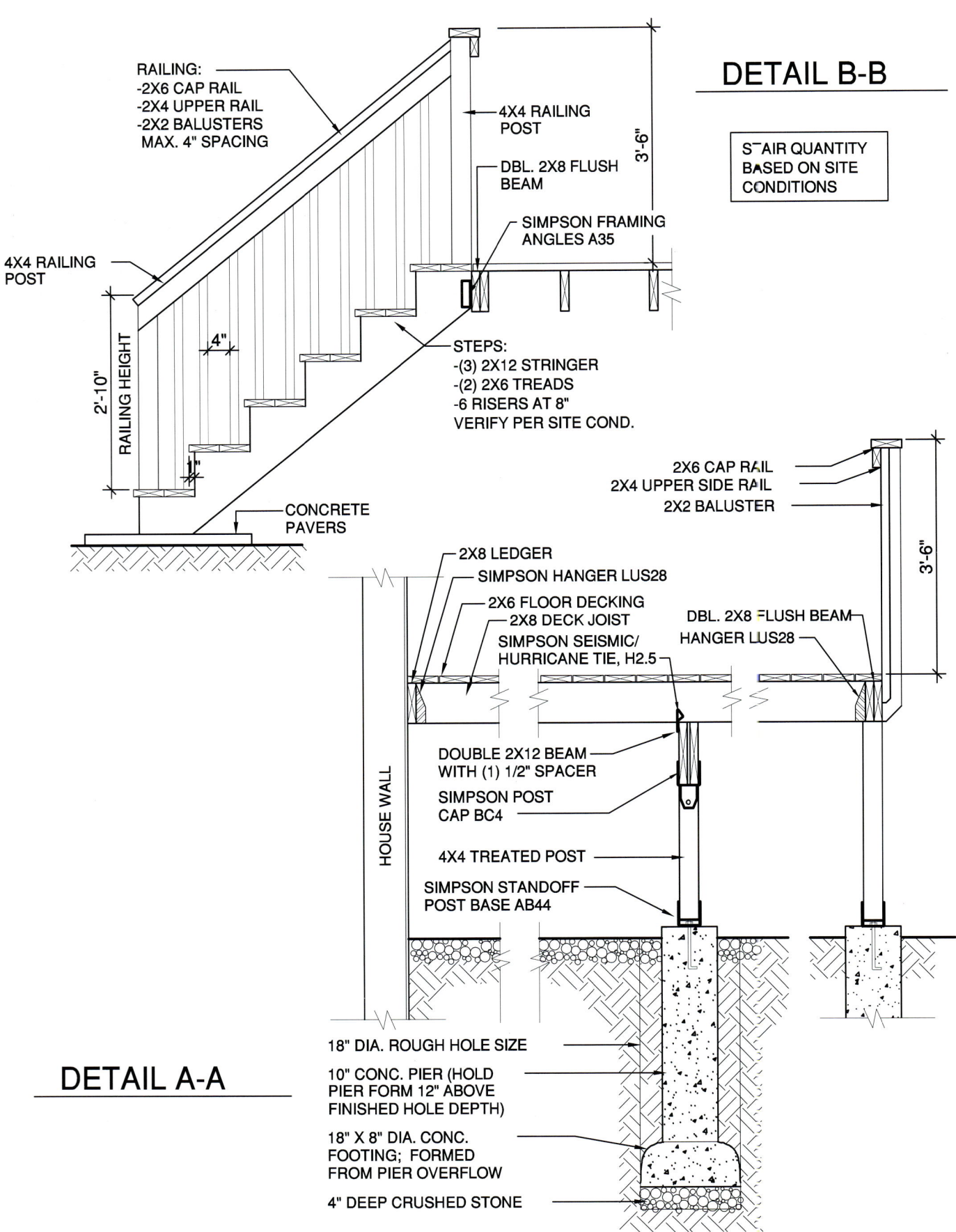

DERRICK — Material List

FOUNDATION

Item	Location	Qty	UM
60# Concrete Mix	Pier	25	BG
10"x48" Fiber Tube	Pier	5	EA
2x4 - 10' Std. & Btr.	Batterboard	5	EA
1/2"x6" Anchor Bolt/Nut/Wash.	Pier	5	EA
Post Base (ABA44)	Pier	5	EA
Crushed Gravel	Pier	10	BG
2x8 - 16' Treated	Ledger	1	EA
1x5 - 10' Zee Bar	Ledger	2	EA
5# 16d Galv. Nails	General Framing	1	EA
3/8"x4" Lag Screws	Ledger	24	EA
3/8"x1-1/2" Washer	Ledger	24	EA
10 oz. - Paintable Caulk	Ledger/Bolt	3	TB

FRAMING

Item	Location	Qty	UM
2x12 - 16' Treated	Beam	2	EA
2x8 - 8' Treated	Beam	2	EA
2x8 - 10' Treated	Joist	8	EA
2x8 - Treated	Joist	7	EA
1/2" CDX - 5 Ply Plywd.	Beam Spacer	1	EA
4x4 - 10' Treated	Post	2	EA
Post Cap (PC44-16)	Post/Beam	3	EA
5# 16d Galv. Nails	General Framing	3	EA
2x8 Joist Hanger (LUS28)	Ledger Joist	18	EA
2x8 Joist Hanger (LUS28-2)	Ledger Joist	2	EA
Hurricane Tie (H2.5)	Joist/Beam	11	EA
Framing Anchor (A34)	End/Header Joist	6	EA
1# 8d 1-1/2" Jst. Hngr. Nails	Connector	3	EA
5# 8d Ctd. Box Nails	General Framing	1	EA

FINISH/RAILING/SKIRTING

Item	Location	Qty	UM
4x4 - 10' Treated	Post	7	EA
3/8"x4" Lag Screws	Post	28	EA
3/8"x1-1/2" Washer	Post	28	EA
2x6 - 16' Treated	Decking/Stair Trd.	31	EA
1# 2-1/2" Ctd. Screws	Decking/Railing	10	EA
2x12 - 8' Treated	Stringer	6	EA
3x5 Heavy Angle (HL35)	Stringer	8	EA
5/16"x1-1/2" Lag Screws	Heavy Angle	32	EA
2x6 - 12' Treated	Cap Rail	3	EA
2x6 - 16' Treated	Cap Rail	3	EA
2x4 - 12' Treated	Side Rail	3	EA
2x4 - 16' Treated	Side Rail	3	EA
1-3/8"x1-3/8" - 4' Clr. Bev. Blstr.	Baluster	122	EA
5# 16d Galv. Nails	General Framing	2	EA
5# 8d Ctd. Box Nails	General Framing	1	EA

CHAPTER 5

THE DRAKE

HPM-1101

The angles and wide-open stairway on this deck create an interesting and unique look, while making the transition to the yard smooth and simple. Convenient built-in seating is offered on two sides, adding further value to this low-level deck.

Dimensions for this deck are 16' X 16'.

Drake

Plan View   Scale: 1/4" = 1'-0"

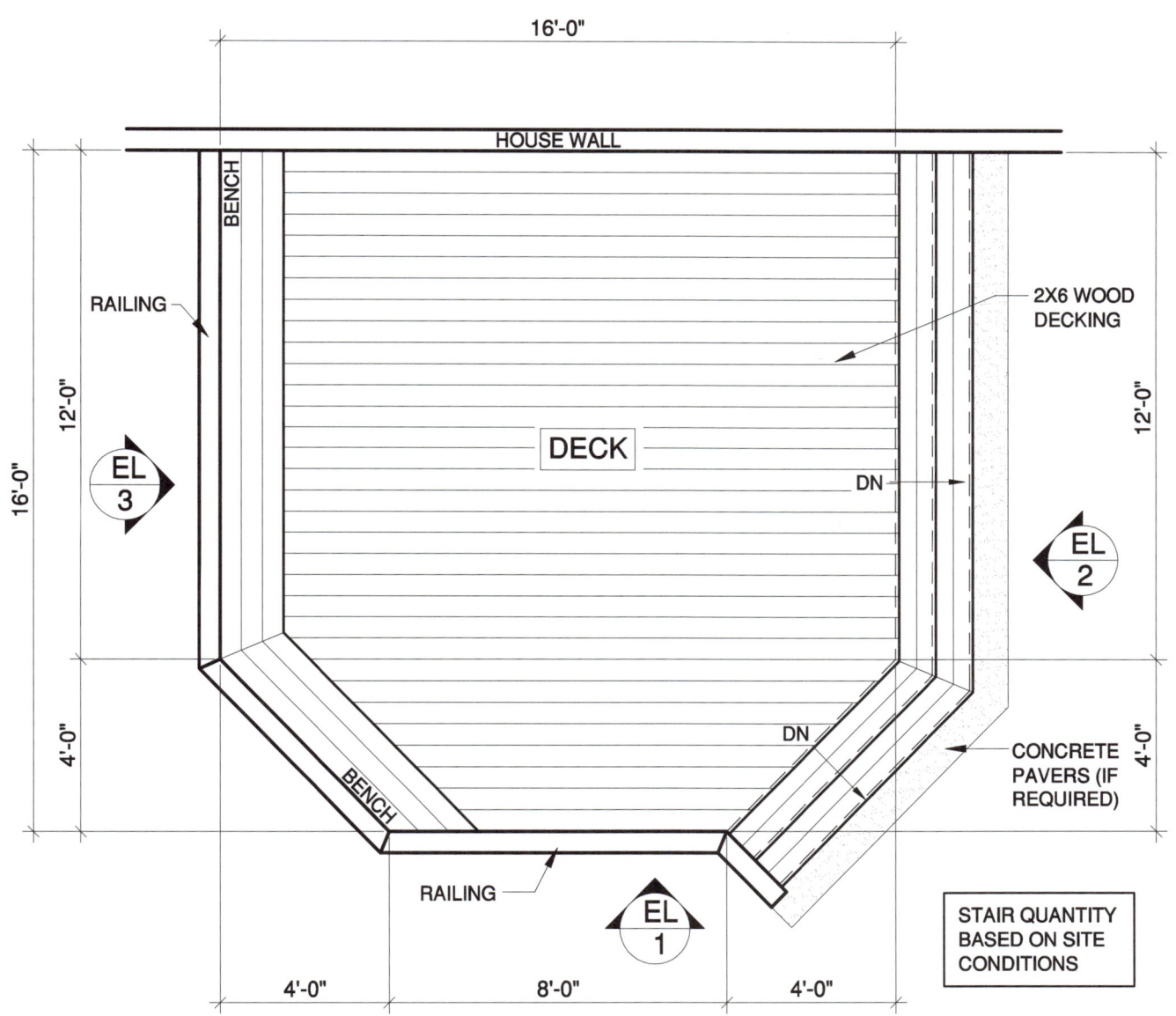

www.homedepot.com 51

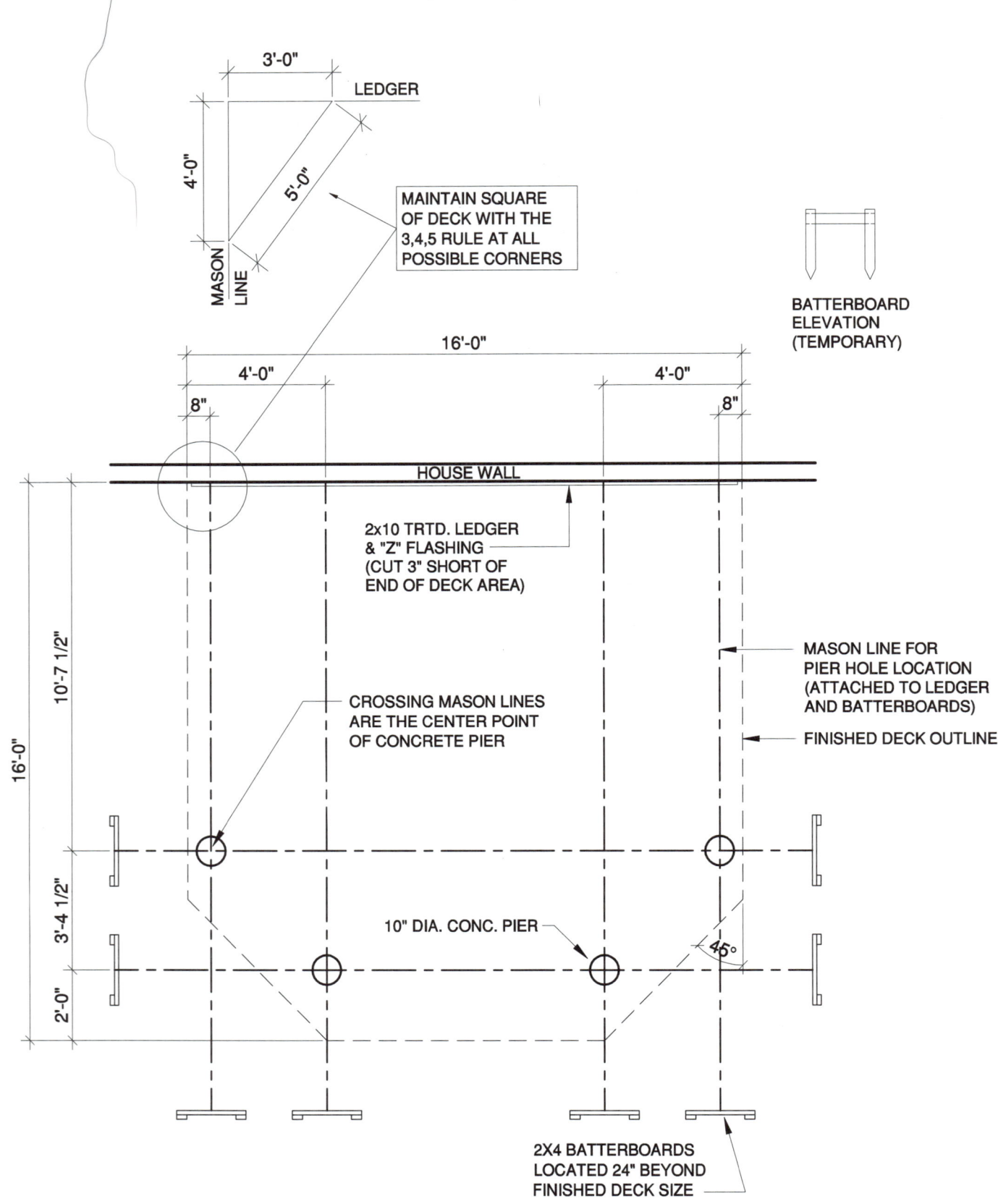

DRAKE — Framing Plan

Scale: 1/4" = 1'-0"

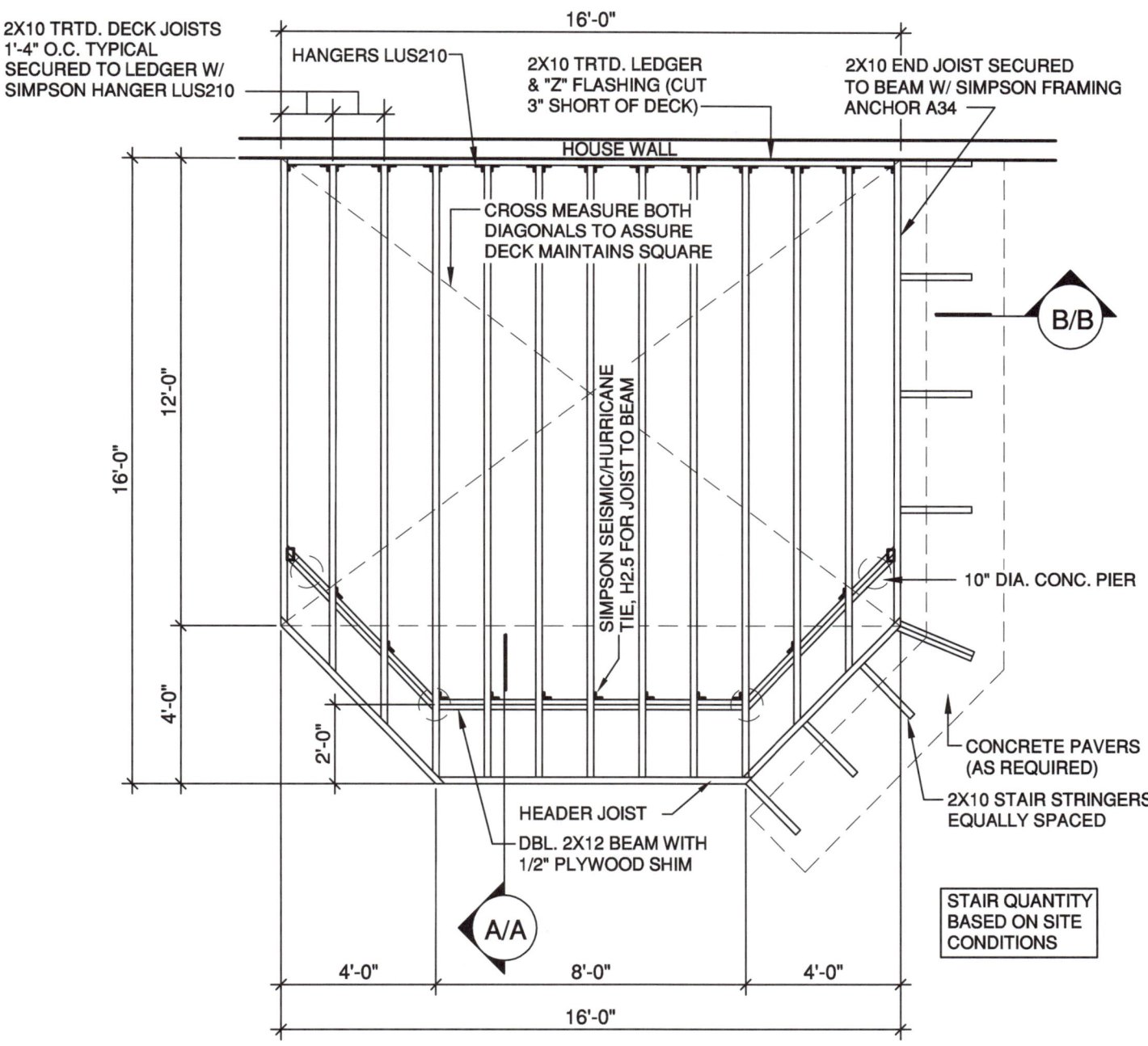

www.homedepot.com

Drake

Elevations

Scale: 1/4" = 1'-0"

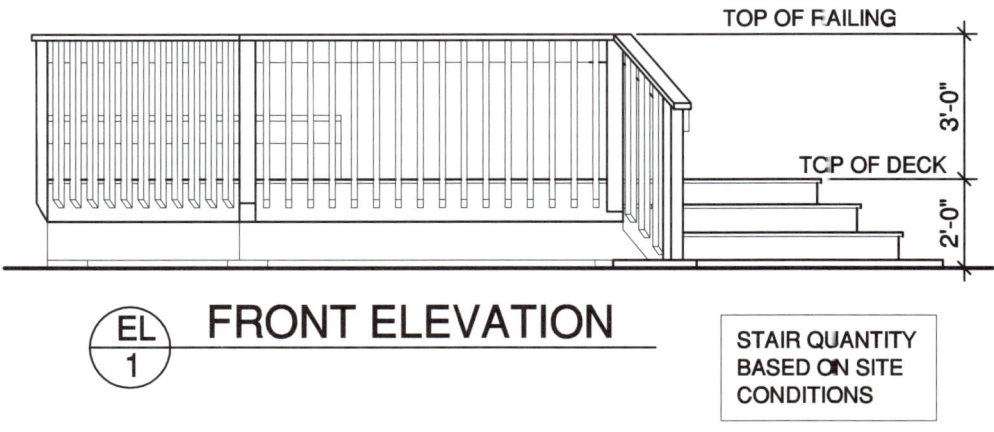

FRONT ELEVATION — EL/1

STAIR QUANTITY BASED ON SITE CONDITIONS

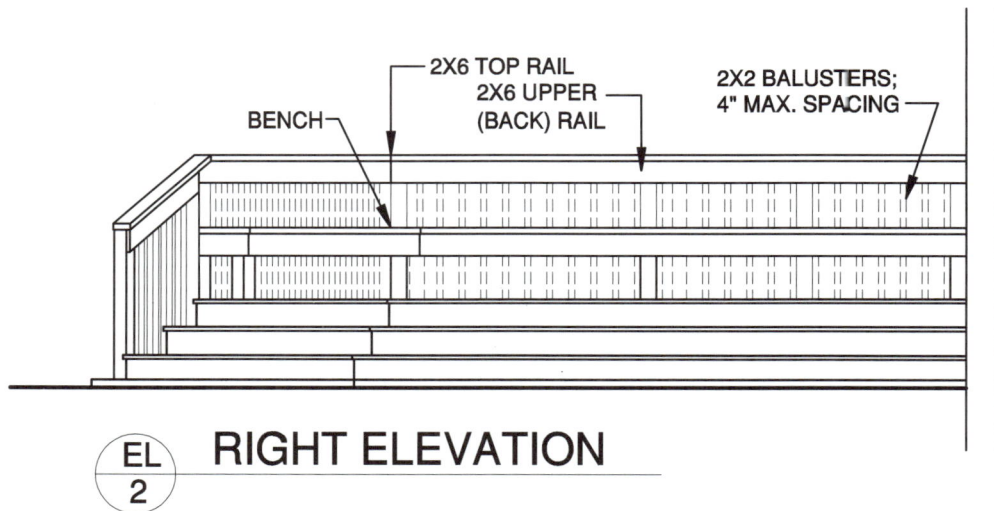

RIGHT ELEVATION — EL/2

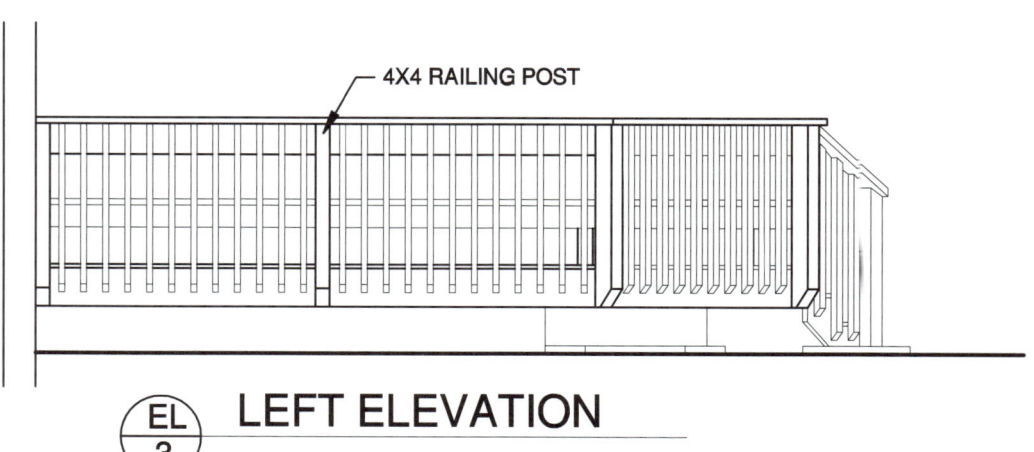

LEFT ELEVATION — EL/3

DRAKE — Details

Scale: 1/2" = 1'-0"

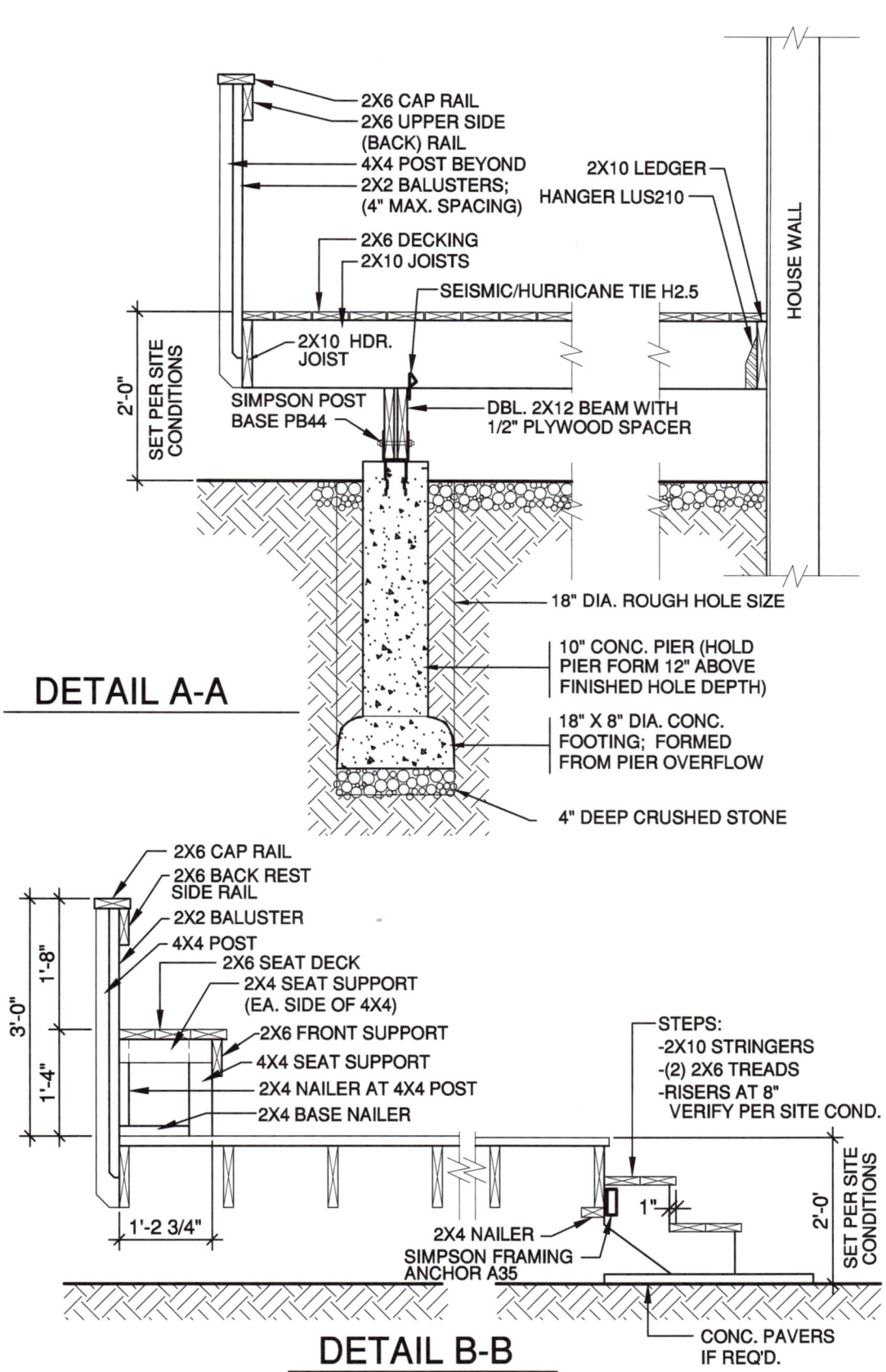

DETAIL A-A

DETAIL B-B

www.homedepot.com 55

DRAKE — Material List

FOUNDATION

Item	Location	Qty	UM
60# Concrete Mix	Pier	20	BG
10"x48" Fiber Tube	Pier	4	EA
2x4 - 10' Std. & Btr.	Batterboard	5	EA
Post Base (PB44)	Pier/Beam	6	EA
Crushed Gravel	Pier	8	BG
2x10 - 16' Treated	Ledger	1	EA
1x5 - 10' Zee Bar	Ledger	2	EA
5# 16d Galv. Nail	General Framing	1	EA
3/8"x4" Lag Screws	Ledger	24	EA
3/8"x1-1/2" Washer	Ledger	24	EA
10 oz. - Paintable Caulk	Ledger/Bolt	3	TB

FRAMING

Item	Location	Qty	UM
2x12 - 10' Treated	Beam	2	EA
2x12 - 12' Treated	Beam	2	EA
2x10 - 10' Treated	Joist	1	EA
2x10 - 12' Treated	Joist	3	EA
2x10 - 14' Treated	Joist	2	EA
2x10 - 16' Treated	Joist	9	EA
1/2" CDX - 5 Ply Plywd.	Beam	1	EA
5# 16d Galv. Nail	General Framing	3	LB
2x10 Jst. Hanger (LUS210)	Ledger Joist	11	EA
Hurricane Tie (H2.5)	Joist/Beam	11	EA
Framing Anchor (A34)	End/Header Joist	4	EA
1# 8d 1-1/2" Jst. Hngr. Nails	Connector	3	EA
5# 8d Ctd. Box Nails	General Framing	1	EA

FINISH/RAILING/SKIRTING

Item	Location	Qty	UM
4x4 - 8' Treated	Post	3	EA
3/8"x4" Lag Screws	Post	12	EA
3/8"x1-1/2" Washer	Post	12	EA
2x6 - 12' Treated	Decking	4	EA
2x6 - 16' Treated	Decking/Stair Trd.	38	EA
1# 2-1/2" Ctd. Screws	Decking/Railing	10	EA
2x10 - 16' Treated	Stringer	2	EA
3x5 Heavy Angle (HL35)	Stringer	12	EA
5/16"x1-1/2" Lag Screws	Heavy Angle	48	EA
2x6 - 16' Treated	Top/Side Rail	4	EA

ACCESSORIES

Item	Location	Qty	UM
2x6 - 8' Treated	Bench	4	EA
2x6 - 12' Treated	Bench	4	EA
2x4 - 8' Treated	Nailer	1	EA
4x4 - 10' Treated	Bench	1	EA
2x4 - 12' Treated	Bench	2	EA
2x4 - 16' Treated	Nailer	1	EA
1-3/8"x1-3/8" - 4' Clr. Bev. Blstr.	Baluster	58	EA
5# 16d Galv. Nails	General Framing	2	EA
5# 8d Ctd. Box Nails	General Framing	1	EA

CHAPTER 5

THE SCOUT

HPM-1102

Need a place to relax in the great outdoors? Build this attractive deck and enjoy your new retreat area! With its basic rectangular plan, this project is great for the beginner builder. The whole family will enjoy this addition to your home.

Dimensions for this deck are 14' X 12'.

Scout

Plan View

Scale: 1/4" = 1'-0"

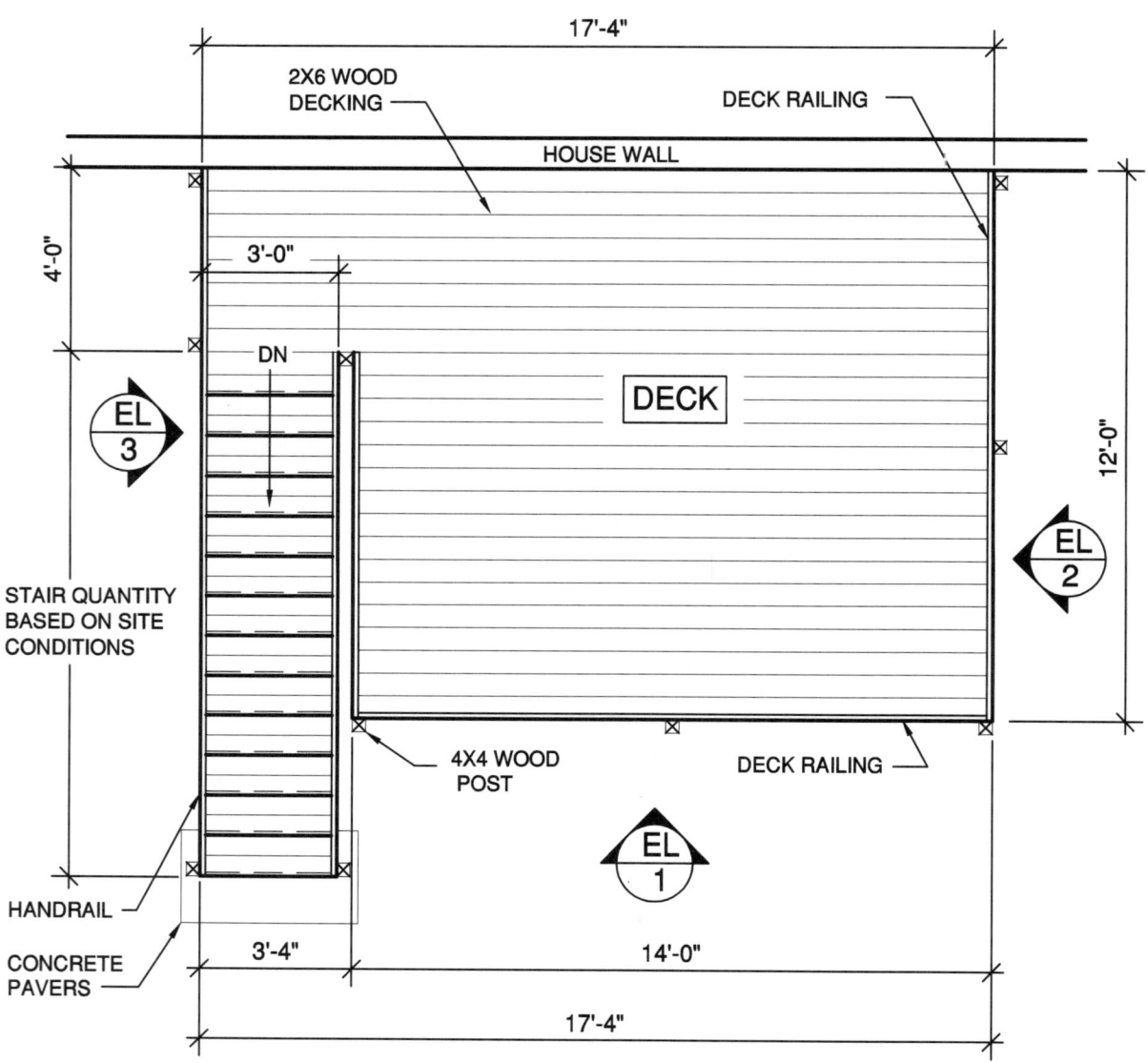

Scout — Pier Layout
Scale: 1/4" = 1'-0"

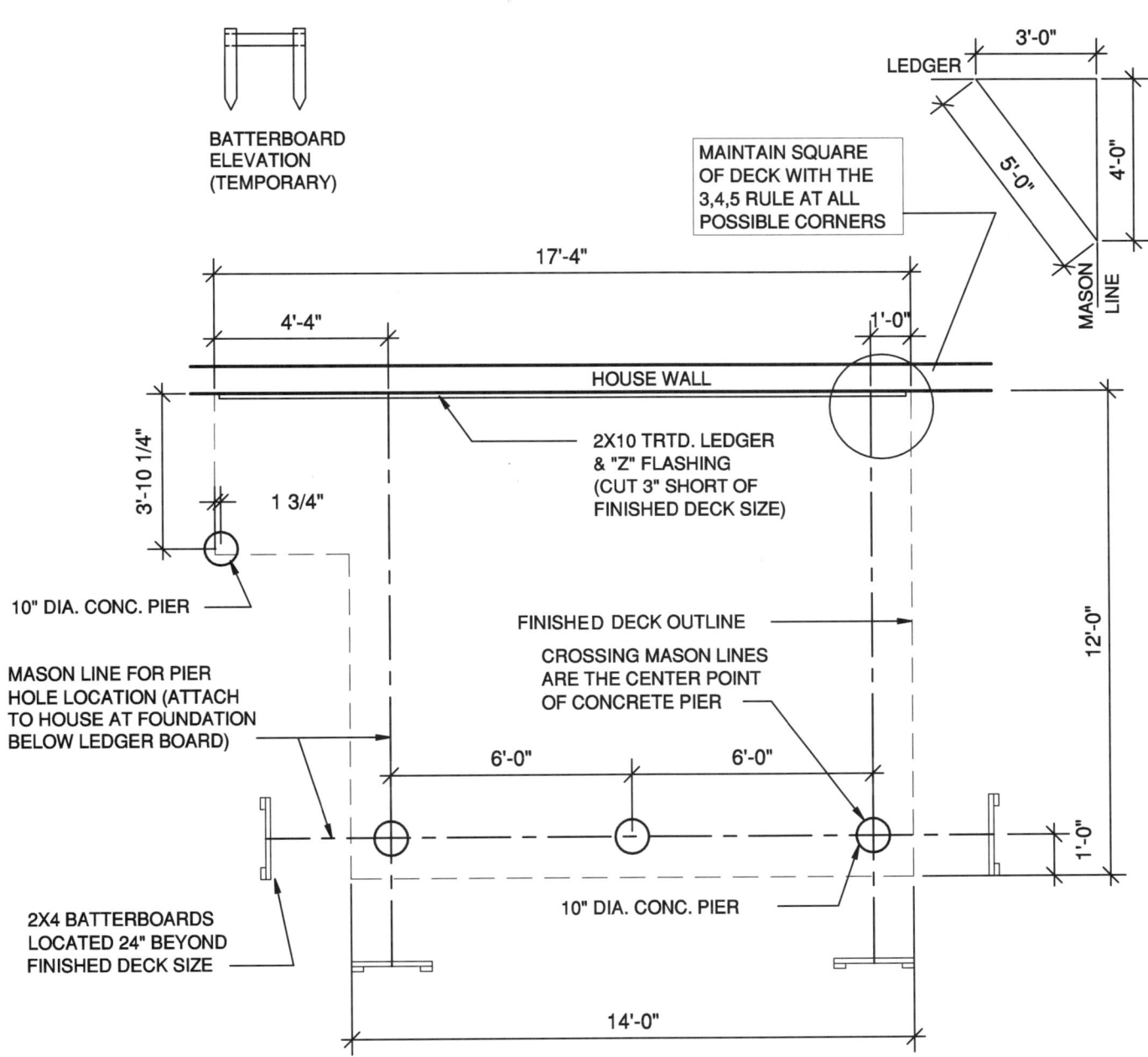

www.homedepot.com 59

Scout — Framing Plan

Scale: 1/4" = 1'-0"

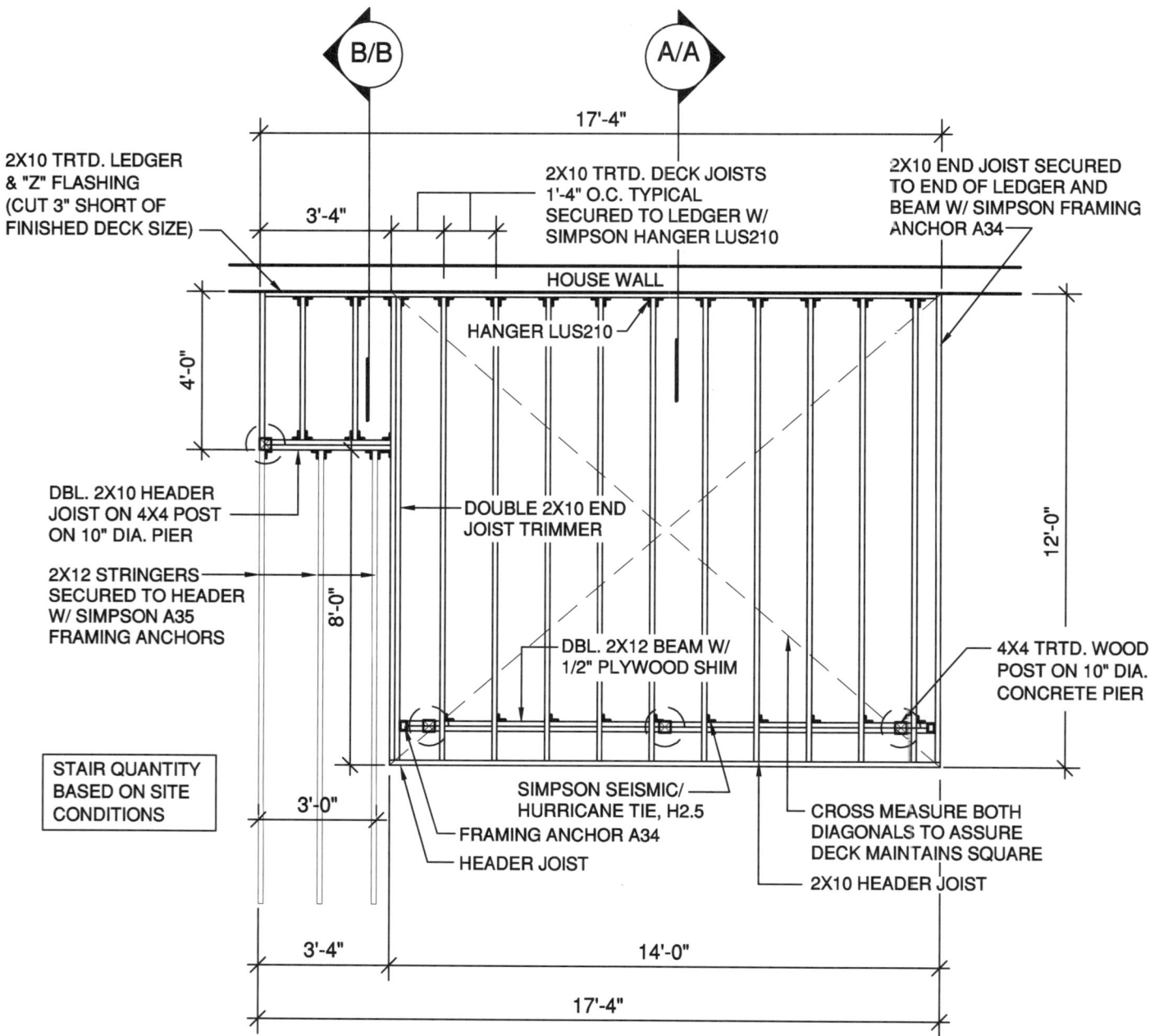

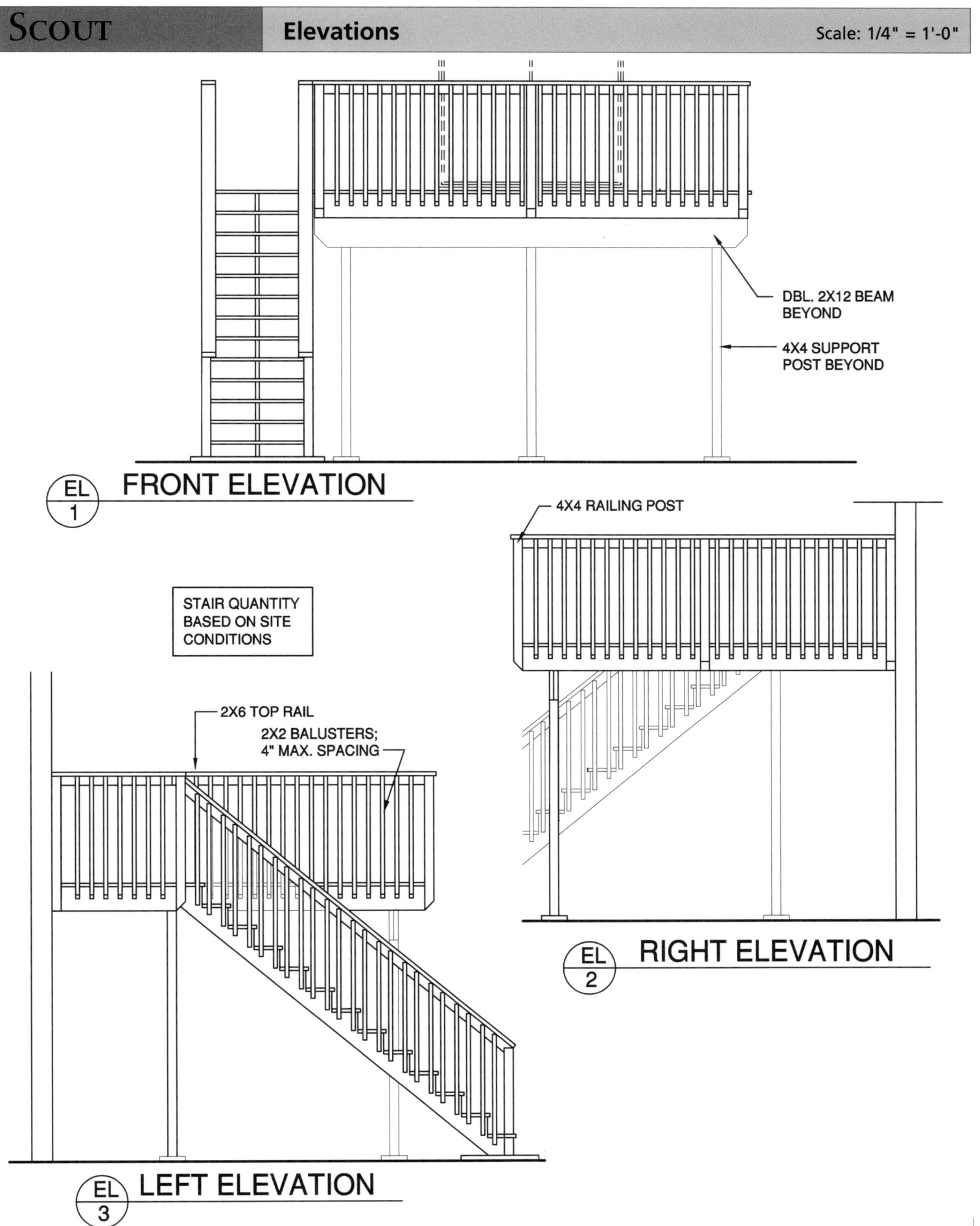

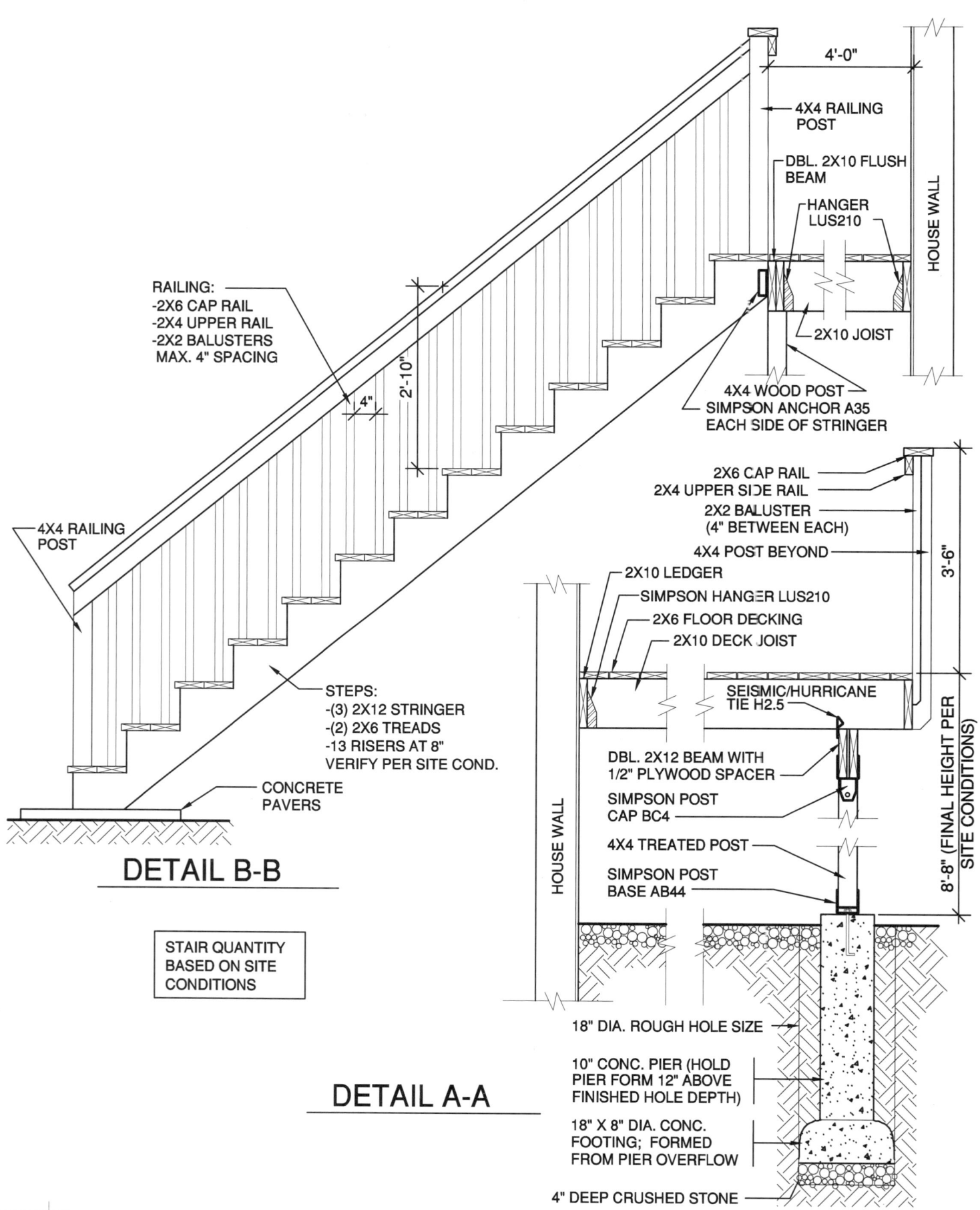

SCOUT — Material List

FOUNDATION

Item	Location	Qty	UM
60# Concrete Mix	Pier	20	BG
10x48" Fiber Tube	Pier	4	EA
2x4 - 10' Std. & Btr.	Batterboard	3	EA
1/2"x6" Anchor Bolt/Nut/Wash.	Pier	4	EA
Post Base (ABA44)	Pier	4	EA
Crushed Gravel	Pier	8	BG
2x10 - 18' Treated	Ledger	1	EA
1x5 - 10' Zee Bar	Ledger	2	EA
5# 16d Galv. Nails	General Framing	1	EA
3/8"x4" Lag Screws	Ledger	28	EA
3/8"x1-1/2" Washer	Ledger	28	EA
10 oz. - Paintable Caulk	Ledger/Bolt	3	TB

FRAMING

Item	Location	Qty	UM
2x12 - 14' Treated	Beam	2	EA
2x10 - 12' Treated	Jst./Flush Beam	15	EA
2x10 - 14' Treated	Header Joist	1	EA
1/2" CDX - 5 Ply Plywd.	Beam Spacer	1	EA
4x4 - 10' Treated	Post	4	EA
Post Cap (PC44-16)	Post/Beam	3	EA
5# 16d Galv. Nail	General Framing	3	EA
2x10 Jst. Hanger (LUS210)	Ledger Joist	14	EA
2x10 Jst. Hanger (LUS210-2)	Ledger Joist	2	EA
Hurricane Tie (H2.5)	Joist/Beam	10	EA
Framing Anchor (A34)	End/Header Joist	7	EA
1# 8d 1-1/2" Jst. Hngr. Nails	Connector	3	EA
5# 8d Ctd. Box Nails	General Framing	1	EA

FINISH/RAILING/SKIRTING

Item	Location	Qty	UM
4x4 - 10' Treated	Post	5	EA
3/8"x4" Lag Screws	Post	20	EA
3/8"x1-1/2" Washer	Post	20	EA
2x6 - 12' Treated	Decking/Stair Trd.	12	EA
2x6 - 16' Treated	Decking/Stair Trd.	16	EA
1# 2-1/2" Ctd. Screws	Decking/Railing	10	EA
2x12 - 16' Treated	Stringer	3	EA
3x5 Heavy Angle (HL35)	Stringer	5	EA
5/16"x1-1/2" Lag Screws	Heavy Angle	20	EA
2x6 - 12' Treated	Cap Rail	1	EA
2x6 - 16' Treated	Cap Rail	4	EA
2x4 - 12' Treated	Side Rail	1	EA
2x4 - 16' Treated	Side Rail	4	EA
1-3/8"x1-3/8" - 4' Clr. Bev. Blstr.	Baluster	132	EA
5# 16d Galv. Nails	General Framing	2	EA
5# 8d Ctd. Box Nails	General Framing	1	EA

CHAPTER 5

THE DURVIN

HPM-1103

Do you have an empty corner between the walls of your home and/or garage? This deck makes efficient use of unused outdoor space while creating a cozy and comfortable outdoor getaway. A wind buffer and a source of shade are other advantages of the two-sided deck.

Dimensions for this deck are 16' X 16'.

Durvin — Plan View

Scale: 1/4" = 1'-0"

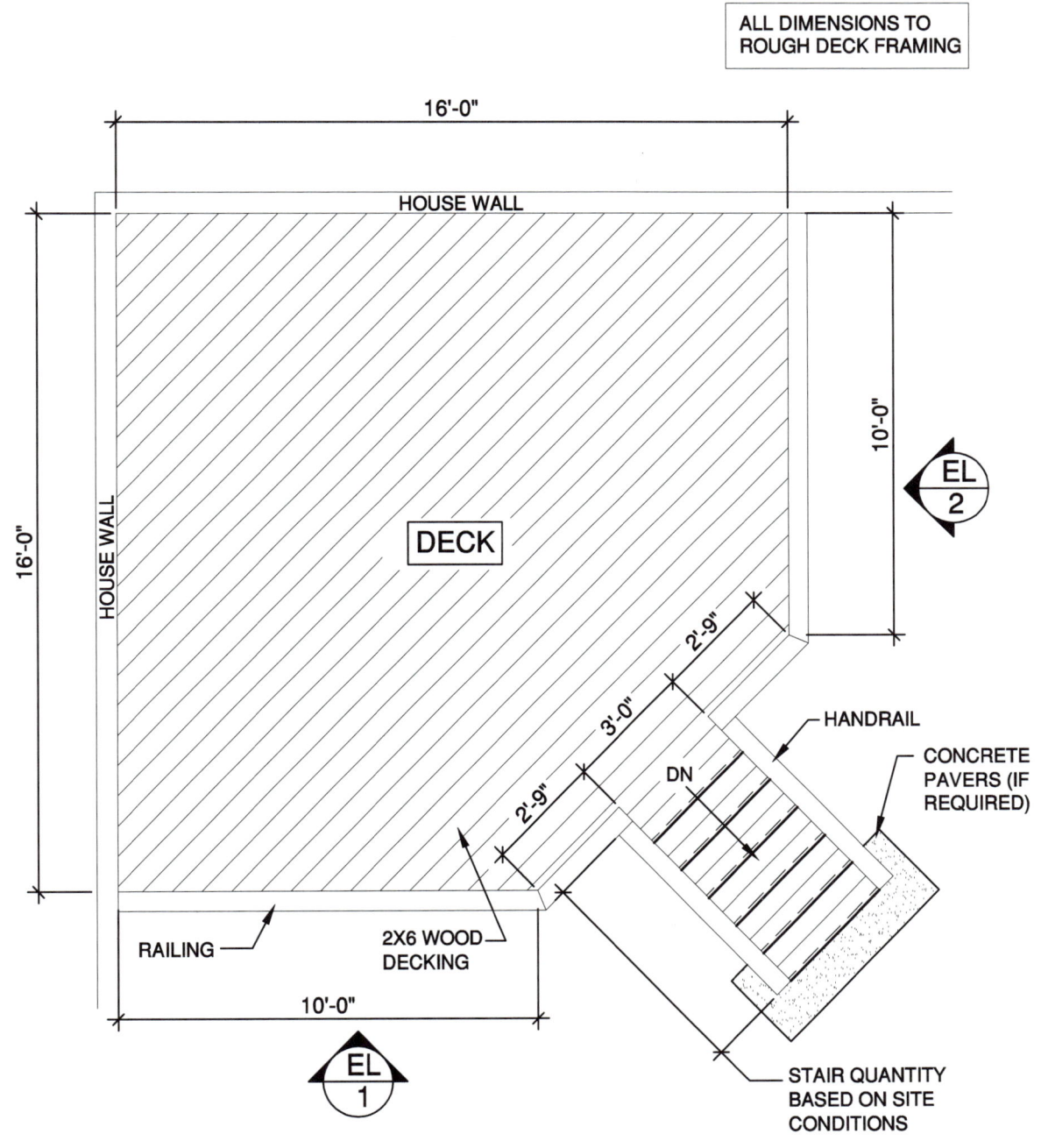

www.homedepot.com 65

Durvin
Pier Layout
Scale: 1/4" = 1'-0"

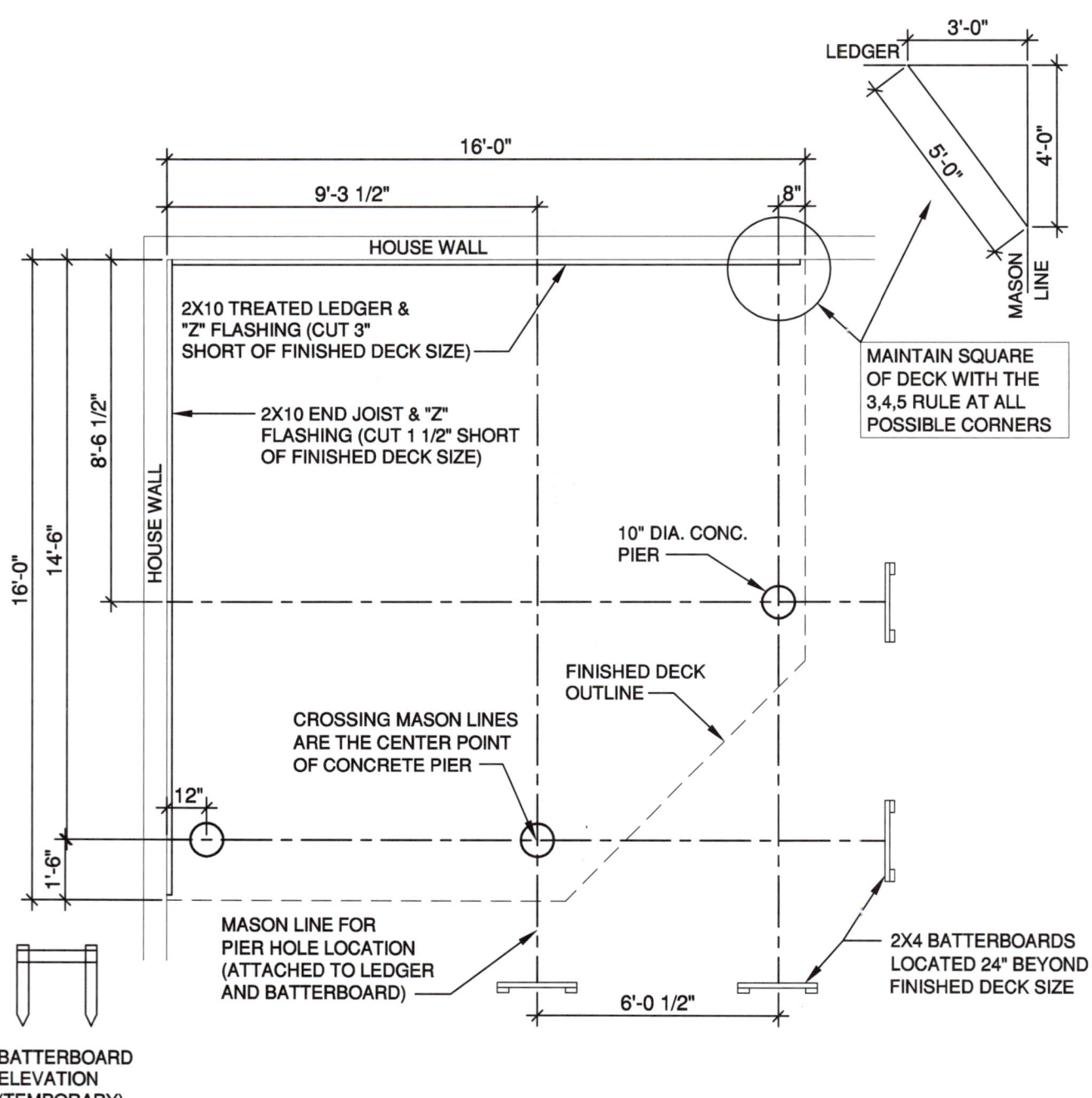

Durvin — Framing Plan

Scale: 1/4" = 1'-0"

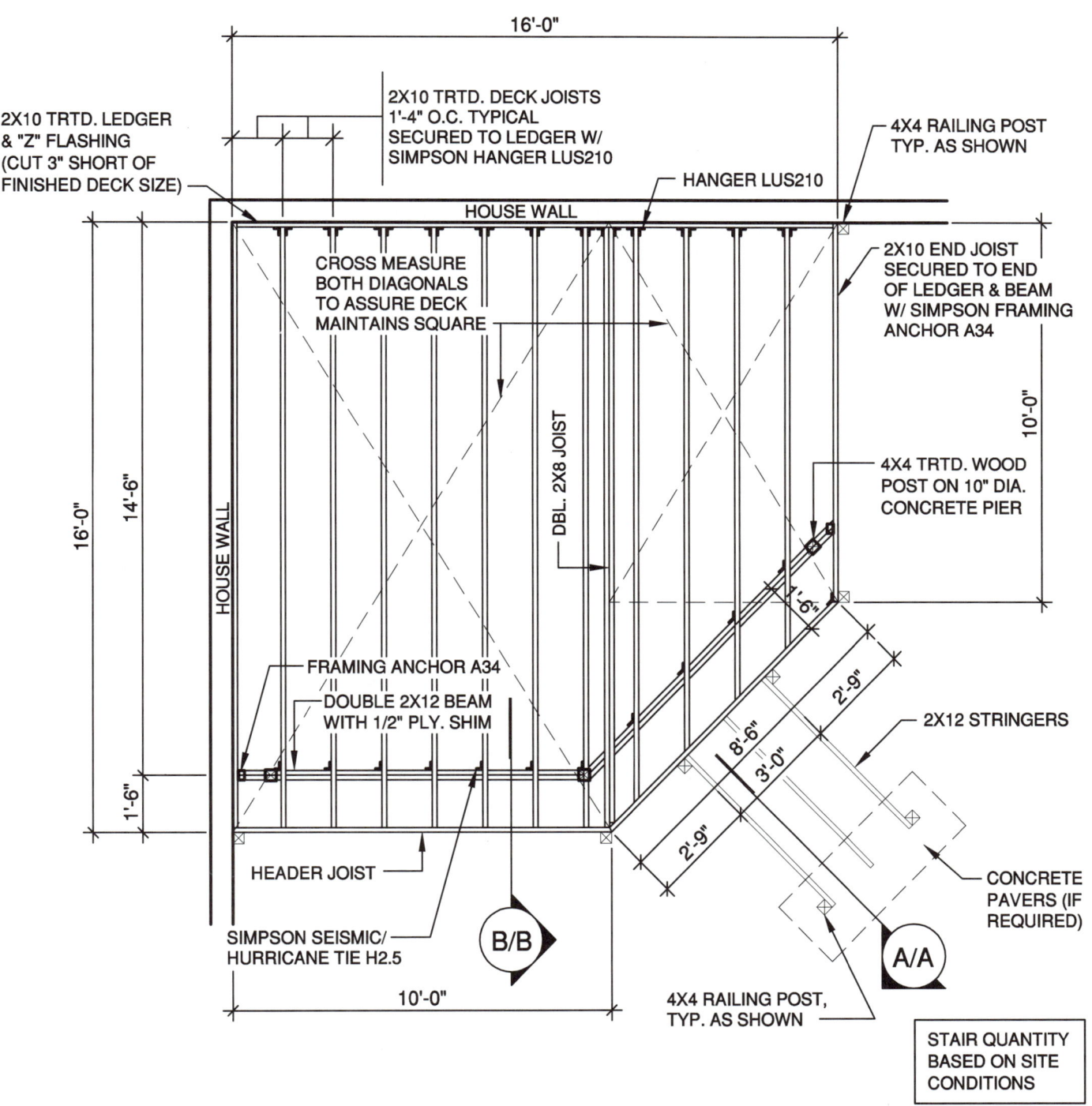

www.homedepot.com

Durvin — Elevations

Scale: 1/4" = 1'-0"

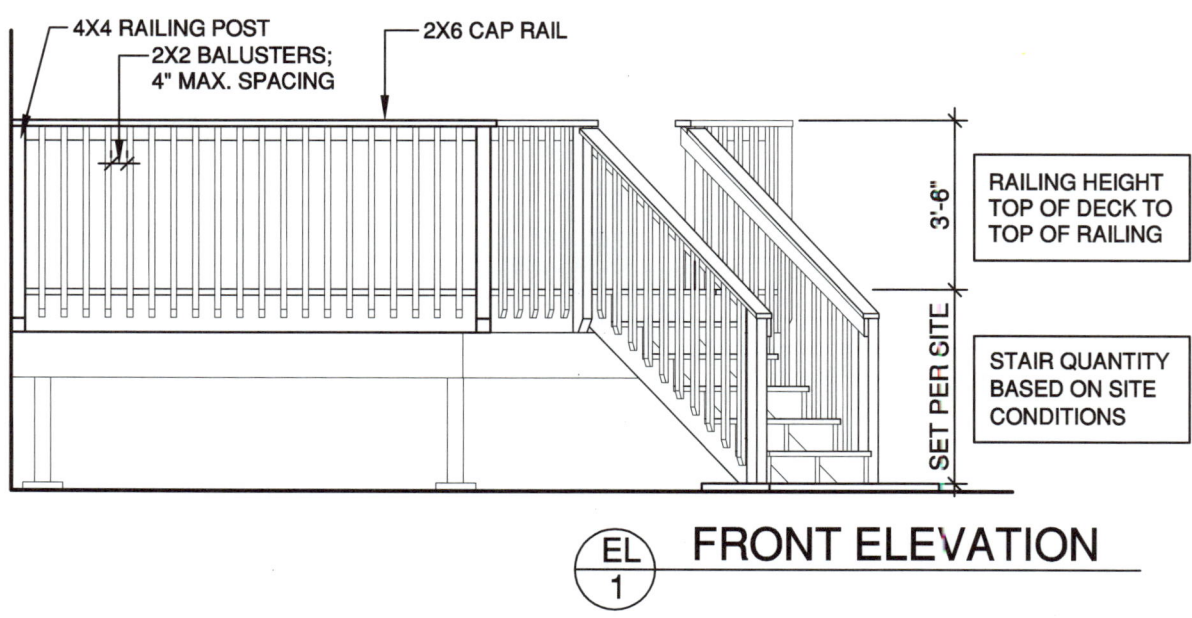

- 4X4 RAILING POST
- 2X2 BALUSTERS; 4" MAX. SPACING
- 2X6 CAP RAIL
- 3'-6" RAILING HEIGHT TOP OF DECK TO TOP OF RAILING
- SET PER SITE — STAIR QUANTITY BASED ON SITE CONDITIONS

EL 1 — FRONT ELEVATION

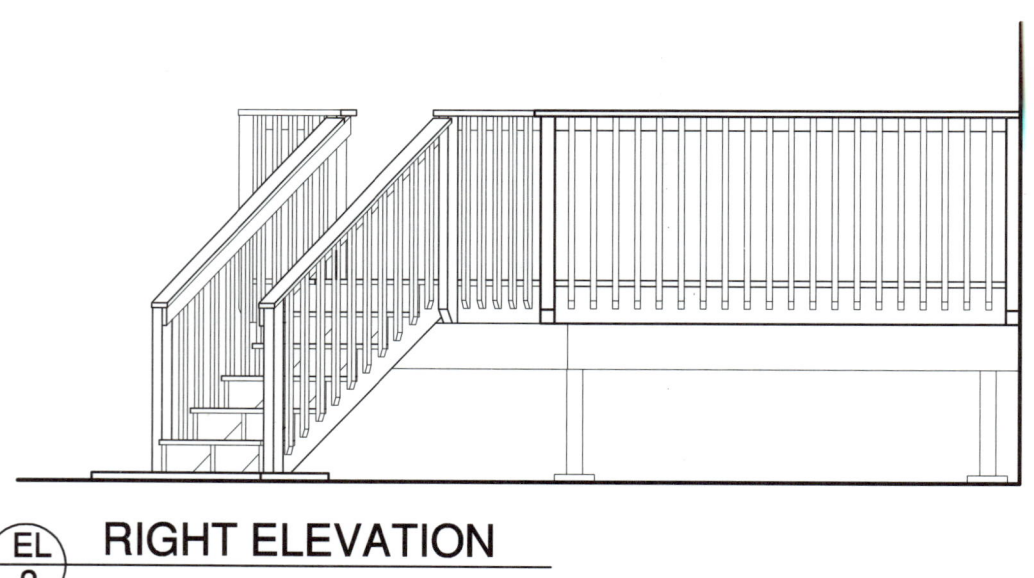

EL 2 — RIGHT ELEVATION

Durvin Details

Scale: 1/2" = 1'-0"

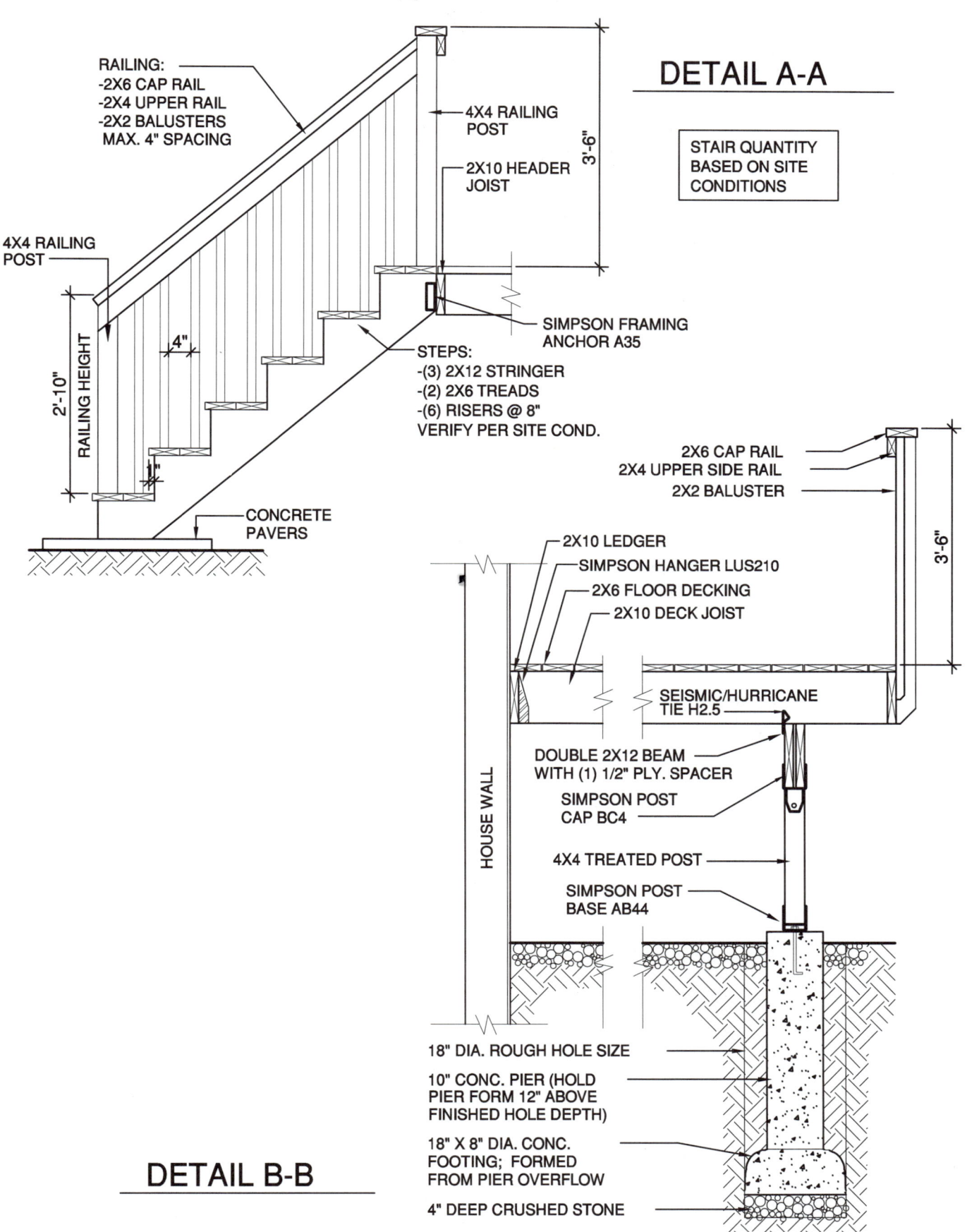

www.homedepot.com 69

DURVIN — Material List

FOUNDATION

Item	Location	Qty	UM
60# Concrete Mix	Pier	15	BG
10"x48" Fiber Tube	Pier	3	EA
2x4 - 10' Std. & Btr.	Batterboard	3	EA
1/2"x6" Anchor Bolt/Nut/Wash.	Pier	3	EA
Post Base (ABA44)	Pier	3	EA
Crushed Gravel	Pier	6	BG
2x10 - 16' Treated	Ledger	2	EA
1x5 - 10' Zee Bar	Ledger	4	EA
5# 16d Galv. Nails	General Framing	5	LB
3/8"x4" Lag Screws	Ledger	48	EA
3/8"x1-1/2" Washer	Ledger	48	EA
10 oz. - Paintable Caulk	Ledger/Bolt	4	TB

FRAMING

Item	Location	Qty	UM
2x12 - 10' Treated	Beam	4	EA
2x10 - 10' Treated	Header/End Joist	3	EA
2x10 - 12' Treated	Joist	1	EA
2x10 - 14' Treated	Joist	2	EA
2x10 - 16' Treated	Joist/Blocking	12	EA
1/2" CDX - 5 Ply Plywd.	Beam Spacer	1	EA
4x4 - 12' Treated	Post	1	EA
4x4 Post Cap (PC44-16)	Post/Beam	3	EA
5# 6d Galv. Finish Nails	General Framing	3	EA
2x10 Jst. Hanger (LUS210)	Ledger Joist	11	EA
2x10 Jst. Hanger (LUS210-2)	Ledger Joist	1	EA
Hurricane Tie (H2.5)	Joist/Beam	12	EA
Framing Anchor (A34)	End/Header Joist	5	EA
1# 8d 1-1/2" Jst. Hngr. Nails	Connector	3	EA
5# 8d Ctd. Box Nails	General Framing	1	EA

FINISH/RAILING/SKIRTING

Item	Location	Qty	UM
4x4 - 10' Treated	Post	4	EA
3/8"x4" Lag Screws	Post	16	EA
3/8"x1-1/2" Washer	Post	16	EA
2x6 - 12' Treated	Decking/Stair Tread	26	EA
2x6 - 16' Treated	Decking/Stair Tread	20	EA
1# 2-1/2" Ctd. Screws	Decking/Railing	10	EA
2x12 - 8' Treated	Stringer	3	EA
3x5 Heavy Angle (HL35)	Stringer	6	EA
5/16"x1-1/2" Lag Screws	Heavy Angle	24	EA
2x6 - 12' Treated	Top Rail	4	EA
2x4 - 12' Treated	Side Rail	4	EA
1-3/8"x1-3/8" - 4' Clr. Bev. Blstr.	Baluster	74	EA
5# 16d Galv. Nails	General Framing	2	EA
5# 8d Ctd. Box Nails	General Framing	1	EA

CHAPTER 5

THE DORCHESTER

HPM-1105

This dynamic octagonal deck is an exciting focal point when added to a home. Two staircases exit the deck for convenient access to both sides of the yard; this is exceptionally useful if the grade below the deck is steep or angular.

Dimensions for this deck are 16' X 16'.

Dorchester — Plan View

Scale: 1/4" = 1'-0"

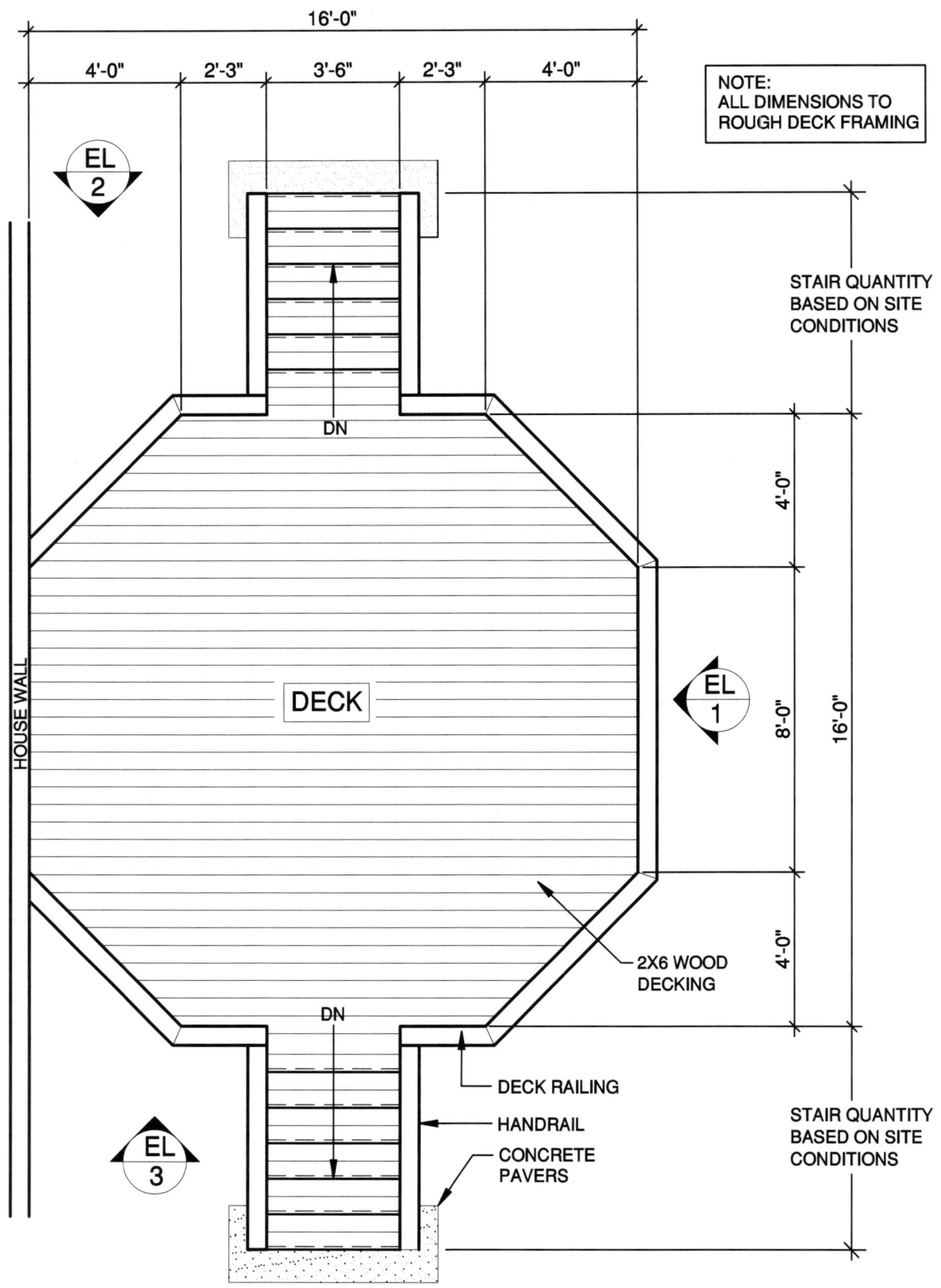

NOTE: ALL DIMENSIONS TO ROUGH DECK FRAMING

STAIR QUANTITY BASED ON SITE CONDITIONS

2X6 WOOD DECKING
DECK RAILING
HANDRAIL
CONCRETE PAVERS

STAIR QUANTITY BASED ON SITE CONDITIONS

DORCHESTER — Pier Layout

Scale: 1/4" = 1'-0"

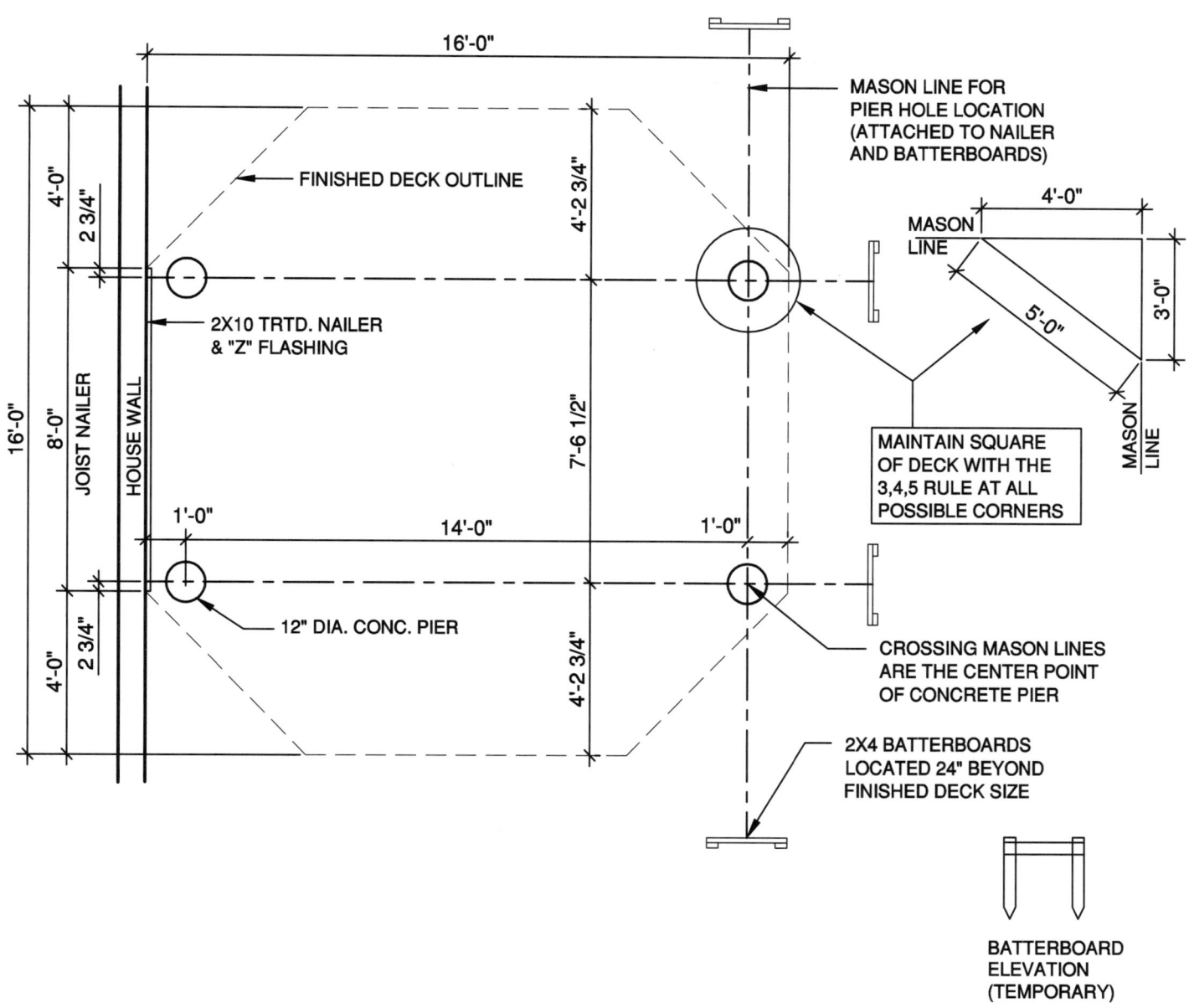

www.homedepot.com 73

DORCHESTER — Framing Plan

Scale: 1/4" = 1'-0"

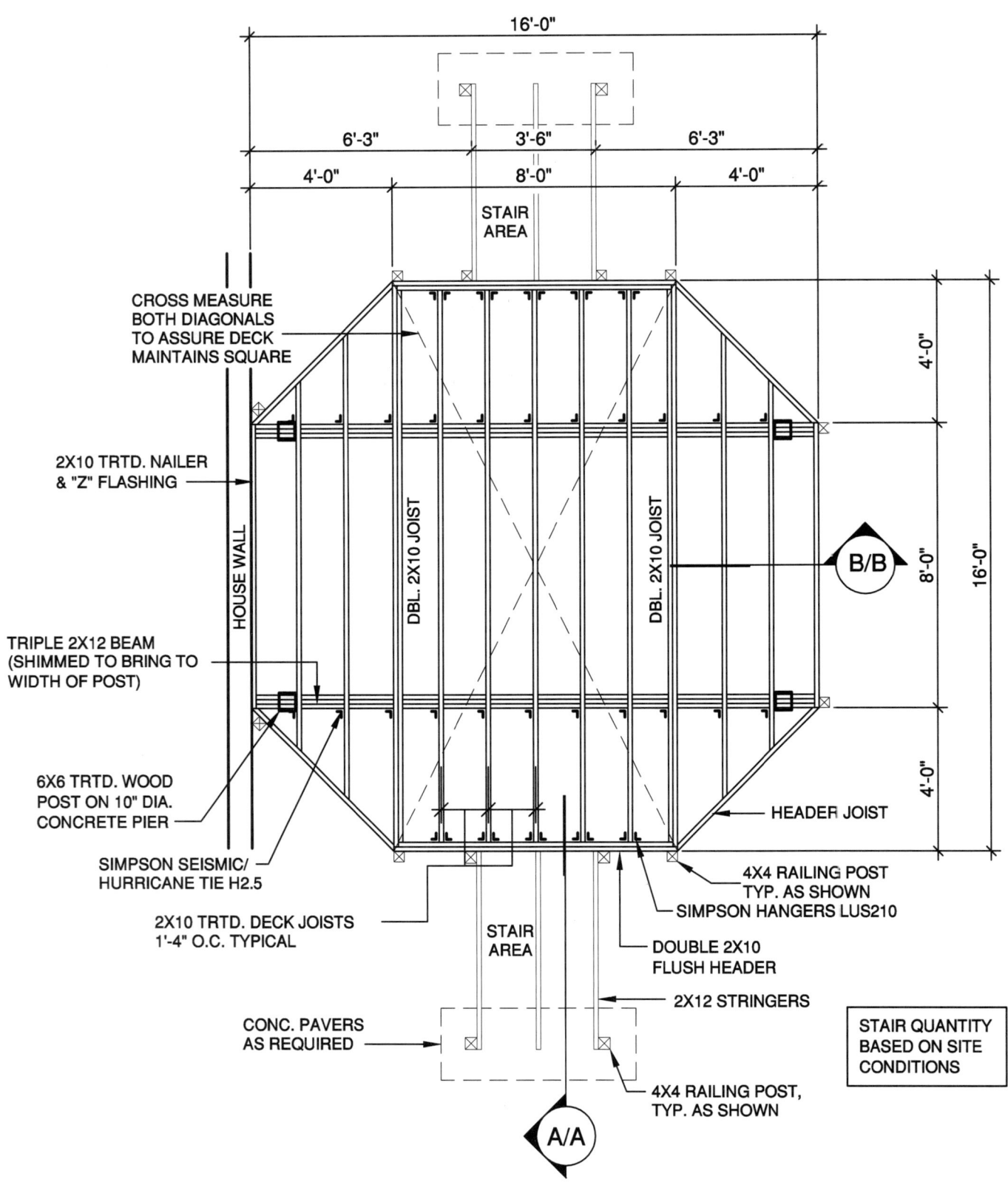

STAIR QUANTITY BASED ON SITE CONDITIONS

74 www.DreamIt-BuildIt.com

DORCHESTER | Elevations

Scale: 1/4" = 1'-0"

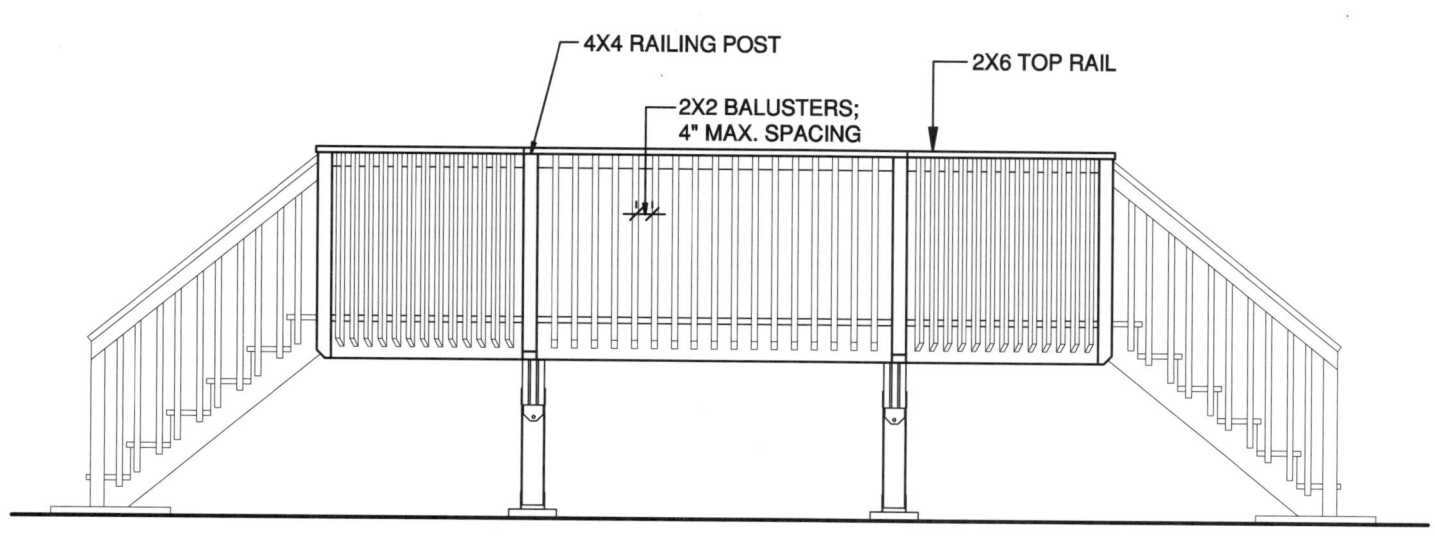

FRONT ELEVATION (EL/1)

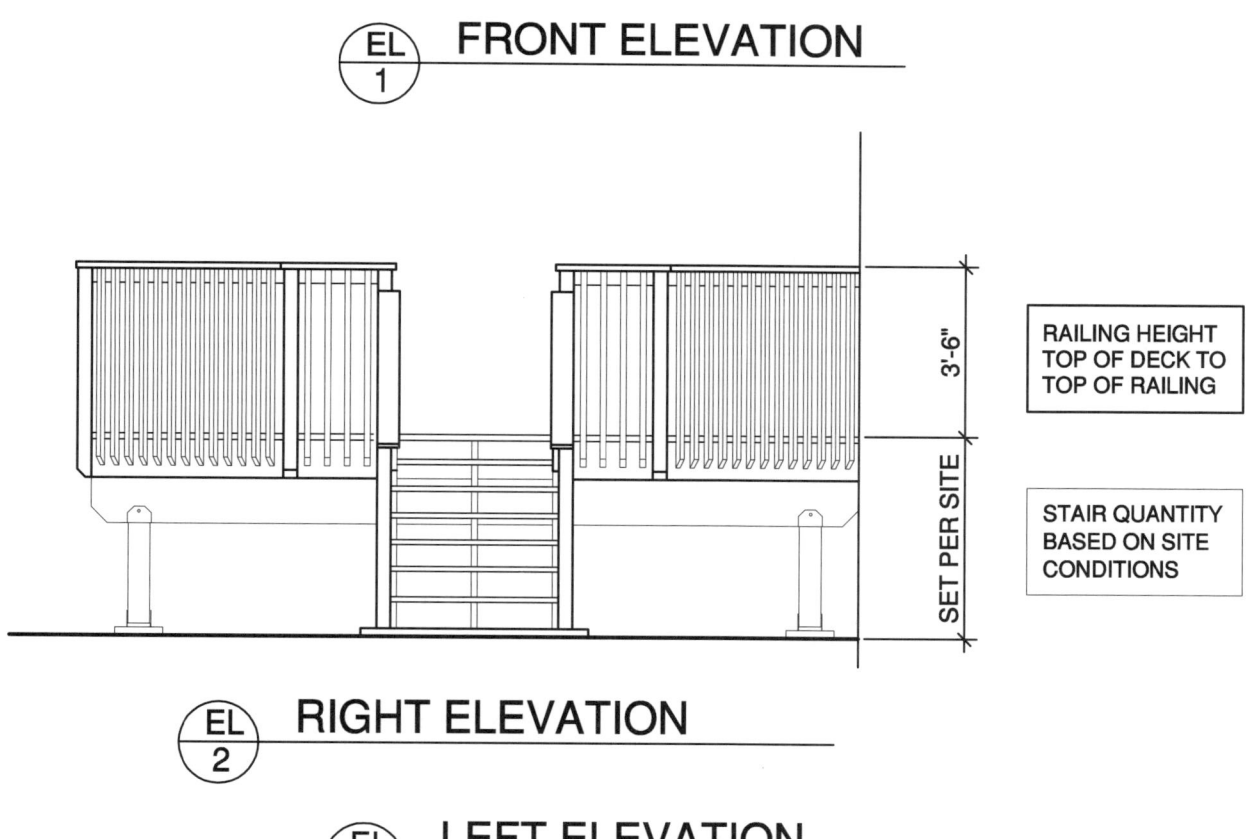

RIGHT ELEVATION (EL/2)

LEFT ELEVATION (EL/3)
REVERSE OF RIGHT ELEVATION

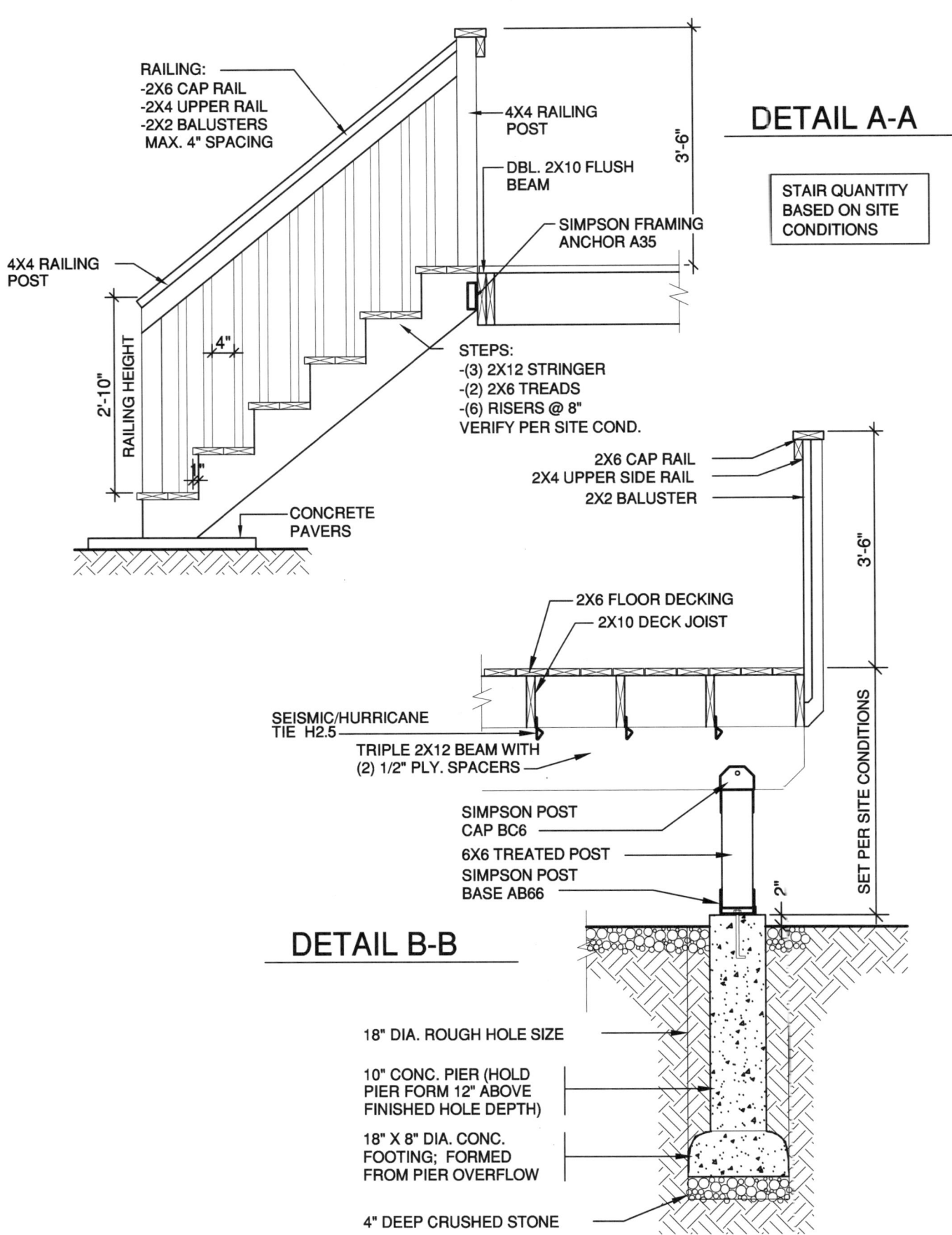

DORCHESTER — Material List

FOUNDATION

Item	Location	Qty	UM
60# Concrete Mix	Pier	20	BG
10"x48" Fiber Tube	Pier	4	EA
2x4 - 10' Std. & Btr.	Batterboard	3	EA
1/2"x6" Anchor Bolt/Nut/Wash.	Pier	4	EA
Post Base (ABA66)	Pier	4	EA
Crushed Gravel	Pier	8	BG
2x10 - 8' Treated	Ledger	1	EA
1x5 - 10' Zee Bar	Ledger	1	EA
5# 16d Galv. Nails	General Framing	1	EA
3/8"x4" Lag Screws	Ledger	10	EA
3/8"x1-1/2" Washer	Ledger	10	EA
10 oz. - Paintable Caulk	Ledger/Bolt	3	TB

FRAMING

Item	Location	Qty	UM
2x12 - 16' Treated	Beam	6	EA
2x10 - 16' Treated	Joist	9	EA
2x10 - 14' Treated	Joist	2	EA
2x10 - 12' Treated	Joist	4	EA
2x10 - 8' Treated	Joist	5	EA
1/2" CDX - 5 Ply Plywd.	Beam	2	EA
6x6 - 8' Treated	Post	2	EA
Post Cap (PC66-16)	Post/Beam	4	EA
5# 16d Galv. Nails	General Framing	3	EA
2x10 Jst. Hngr. (LUS210)	Header Joist	10	EA
Hurricane Tie (H2.5)	Joist/Beam	22	EA
1# 8d 1-1/2" Hanger Nails	Connector	3	EA
5# 8d Zinc Ctd. Box Nails	General Framing	1	EA

FINISH/RAILING/SKIRTING

Item	Location	Qty	UM
4x4 - 10' Treated	Post	8	EA
3/8"x4" Lag Screws	Post	32	EA
3/8"x1-1/2" Washer	Post	32	EA
2x6 - 12' Treated	Decking/Stair Tread	15	EA
2x6 - 16' Treated	Decking	32	EA
1# 2-1/2" Ctd. Screws	Decking/Railing	10	EA
2x12 - 8' Treated	Stringer	6	EA
3x5 Heavy Angle (HL35)	Stringer	12	EA
5/16"x1-1/2" Lag Screws	Heavy Angle	48	EA
2x6 - 16' Treated	Cap Rail	2	EA
2x6 - 10' Treated	Cap Rail	5	EA
2x4 - 16' Treated	Side Rail	2	EA
2x4 - 10' Treated	Side Rail	5	EA
1-3/8"x1-3/8" - 4' Clr. Bev. Blstr.	Baluster	132	EA
5# 16d Galv. Nails	General Framing	2	EA
5# 8d Ctd. Box Nails	General Framing	1	EA

CHAPTER 5

DESIGN BY DEKBRANDS

THE PORTSIDE

PSD-24

Surrounding your above-ground pool with a deck gives it a finished appearance. The versatile frame construction of this deck is available for any size above-ground pool and cuts in half the time and cost of conventional deck construction. The stairway and surrounding railing make access to the pool easy and safe for all ages.

Dimensions for this deck are 3'-3" wide around a pool that is 24' in diameter.

PORTSIDE — Plan View

Scale: 1/4" = 1'-0"

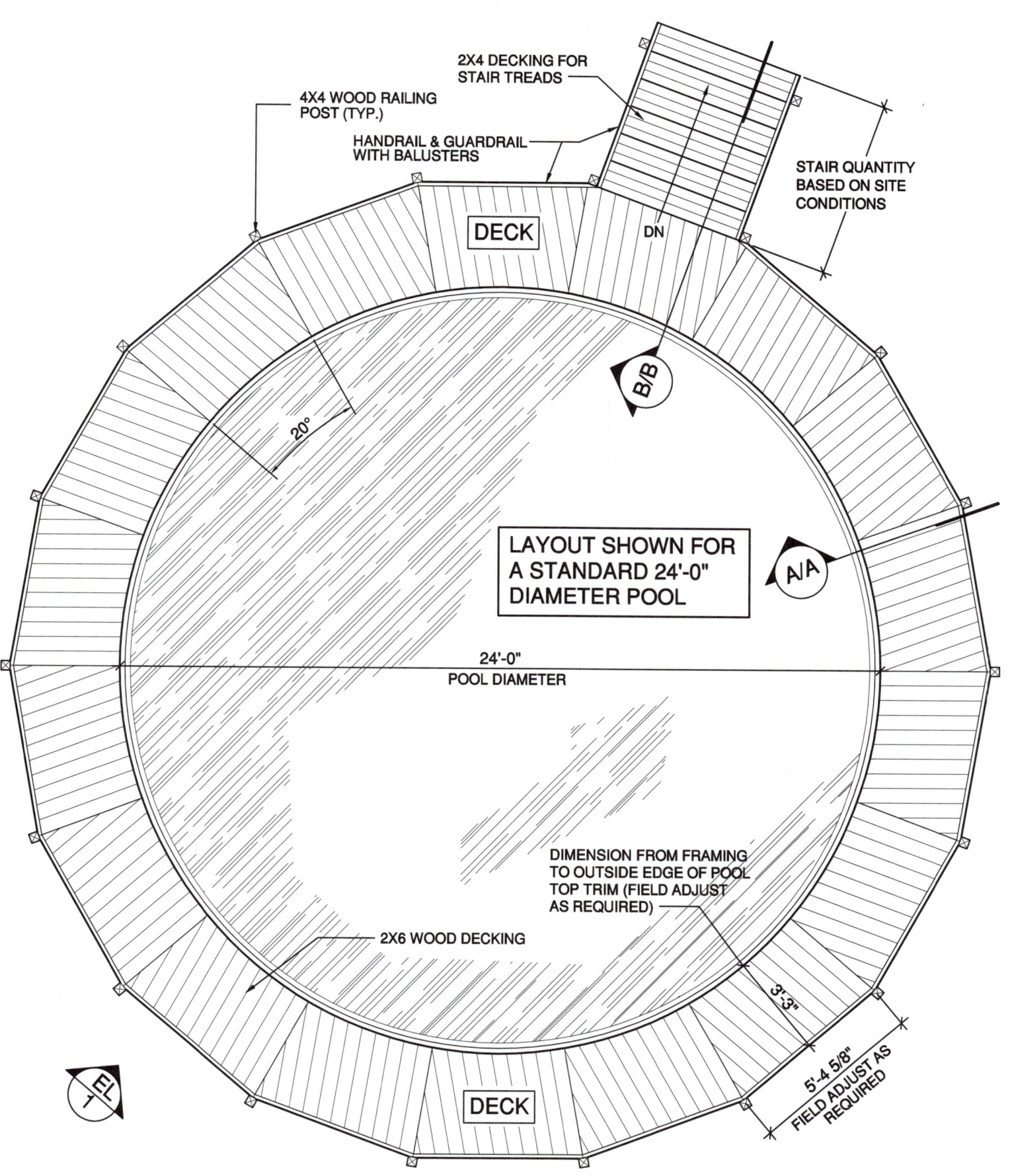

- 4X4 WOOD RAILING POST (TYP.)
- 2X4 DECKING FOR STAIR TREADS
- HANDRAIL & GUARDRAIL WITH BALUSTERS
- STAIR QUANTITY BASED ON SITE CONDITIONS
- DECK
- DN
- 20°
- LAYOUT SHOWN FOR A STANDARD 24'-0" DIAMETER POOL
- 24'-0" POOL DIAMETER
- DIMENSION FROM FRAMING TO OUTSIDE EDGE OF POOL TOP TRIM (FIELD ADJUST AS REQUIRED)
- 2X6 WOOD DECKING
- 3'-3"
- 5'-4 5/8" FIELD ADJUST AS REQUIRED
- DECK

www.homedepot.com 79

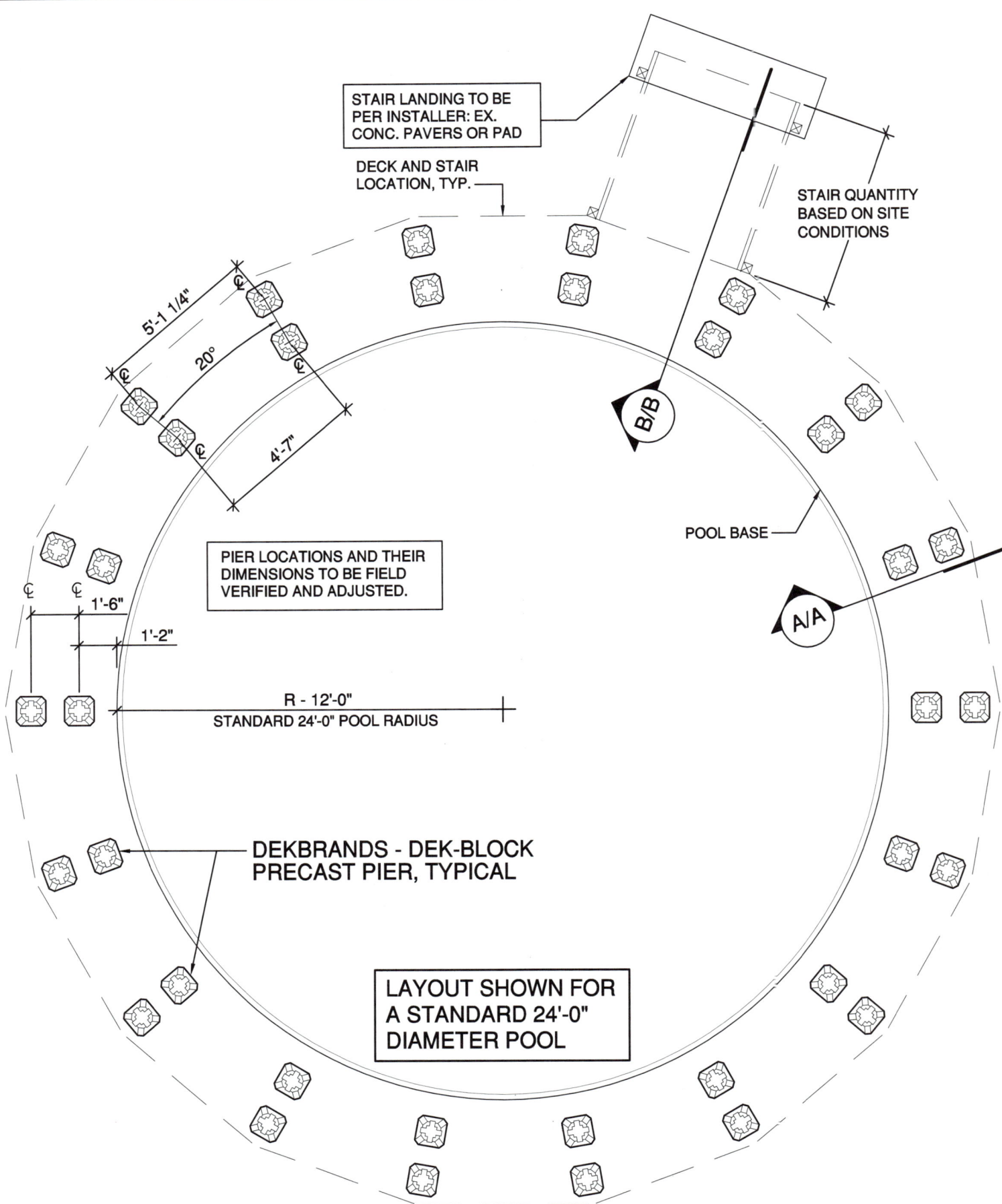

PORTSIDE — Framing Plan

Scale: 1/4" = 1'-0"

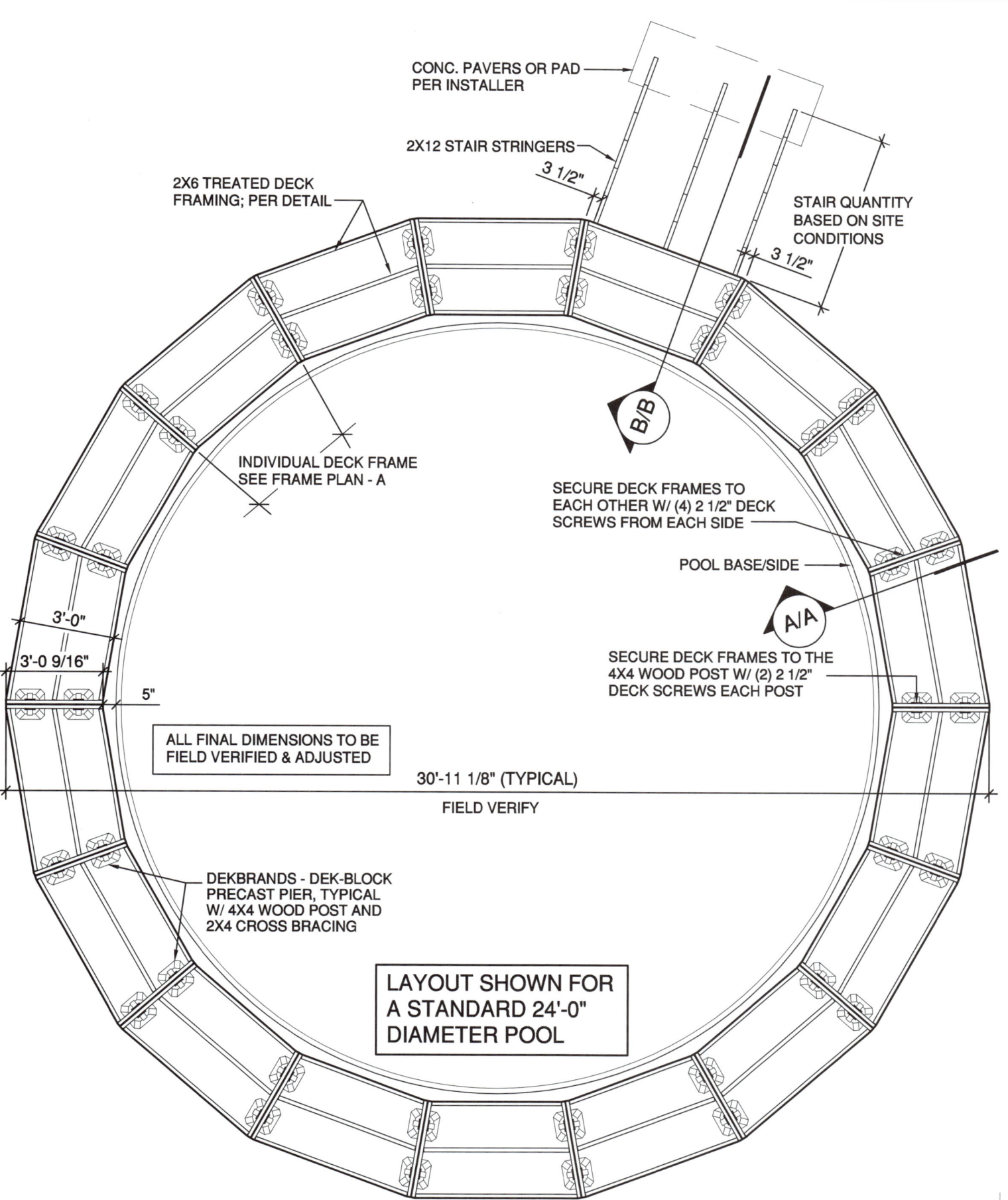

PORTSIDE — Elevation and Details

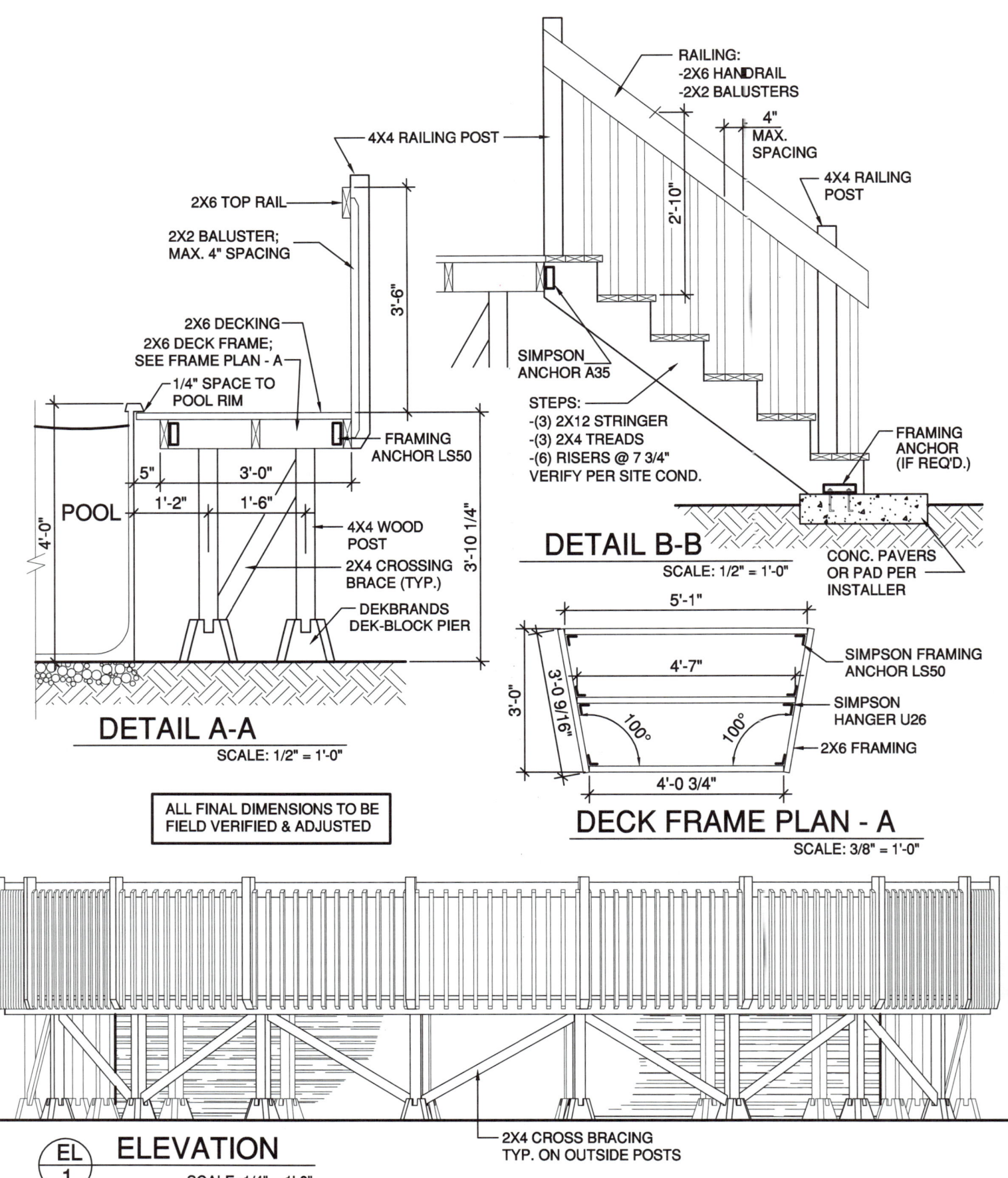

PORTSIDE — Material List

FOUNDATION

Item	Location	Qty	UM
Dek-Block Pier	Pier	36	EA

FRAMING

Item	Location	Qty	UM
4x4 - 12' Treated	Post	9	EA
2x4 - 10' Treated	Cross Bracing	18	EA
2x6 - 10' Treated	Deck Frame	11	EA
2x6 - 14' Treated	Deck Frame	18	EA
2x6 Joist Hanger (LUS26)	Ledger Joist	36	EA
Framing Anchor (A35)	Deck Frame	72	EA
1# 8d 1-1/2" Hanger Nails	Connector	3	EA
5# 8d Ctd. Box Nails	General Framing	1	EA
5# 16d Galv. Nails	General Framing	3	EA

FINISH/RAILING/SKIRTING

Item	Location	Qty	UM
4x4 - 10' Treated	Post	10	EA
3/8"x4" Lag Screws	Post	40	EA
3/8"x1-1/2" Washer	Post	40	EA
2x6 - 8' Treated	Top Rail	19	EA
2x6 - 8' Treated	Decking/Tread	87	EA
1# 2-1/2" Ctd. Screws	Decking/Railing	216	EA
2x12 - 8' Treated	Stringer	3	EA
3x5 Heavy Angle (HL35)	Stringer	6	EA
5/16"x1-1/2" Lag Screws	Heavy Angle	24	EA
1-3/8"x1-3/8" - 4' Clr. Bev. Blstr.	Baluster	245	EA
2x4 - 16' Treated	Tread	6	EA
5# 16d Galv. Nails	General Framing	2	EA
5# 8d Ctd. Box Nails	General Framing	1	EA

CHAPTER 5

THE RIDGEVIEW

HPM-1109

This wraparound deck has an interesting and appealing design. The main deck, with wide planters at either end, steps down to a smaller landing with a third built-in planter. Two stairways allow for convenient access, exit and traffic flow. The Ridgeview is an appealing sight from every angle!

Dimensions for this deck are 24' X 20'.

Ridgeview — Plan View

Scale: 1/4" = 1'-0"

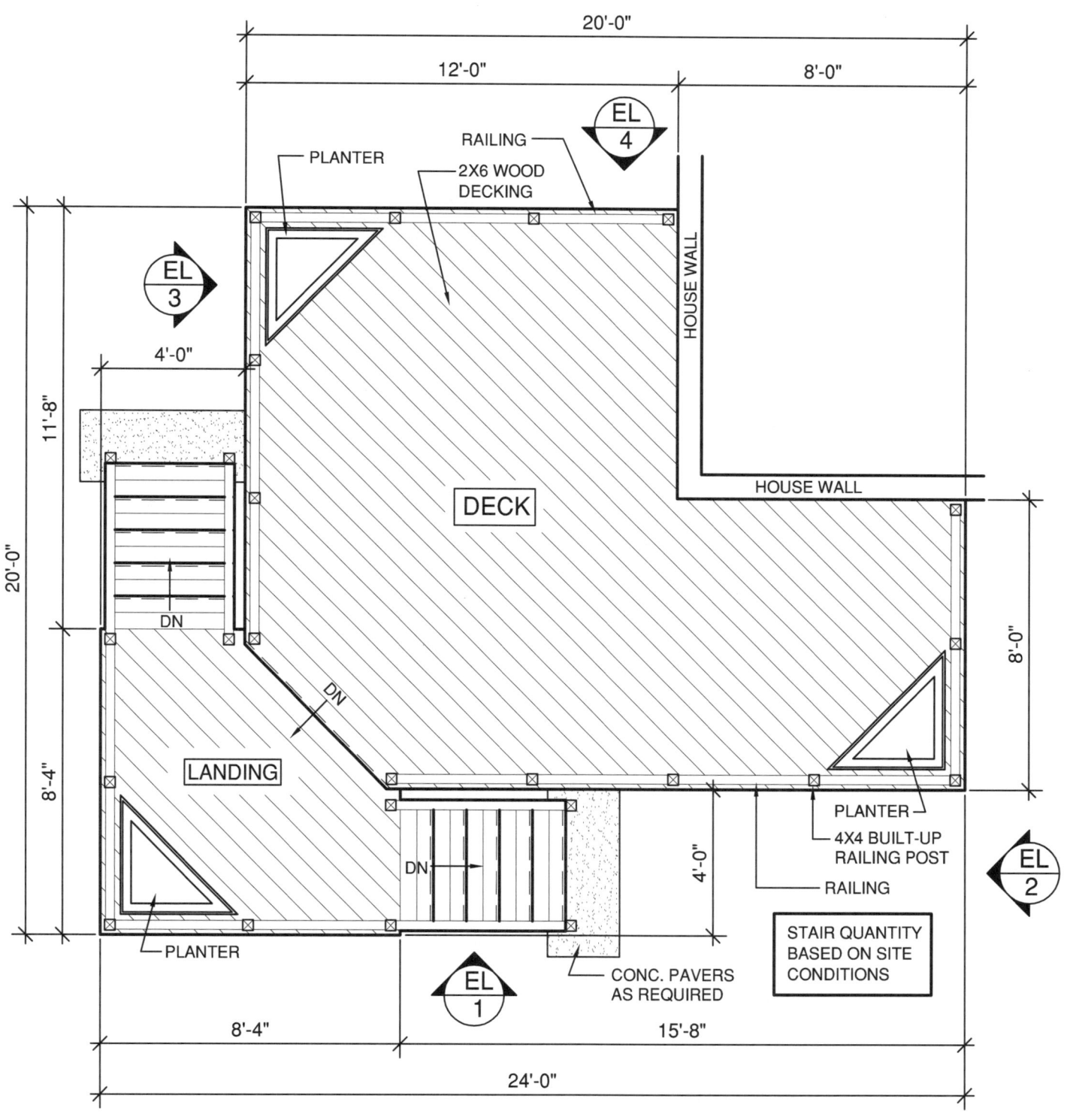

www.homedepot.com

Ridgeview — Pier Layout

Scale: 1/4" = 1'-0"

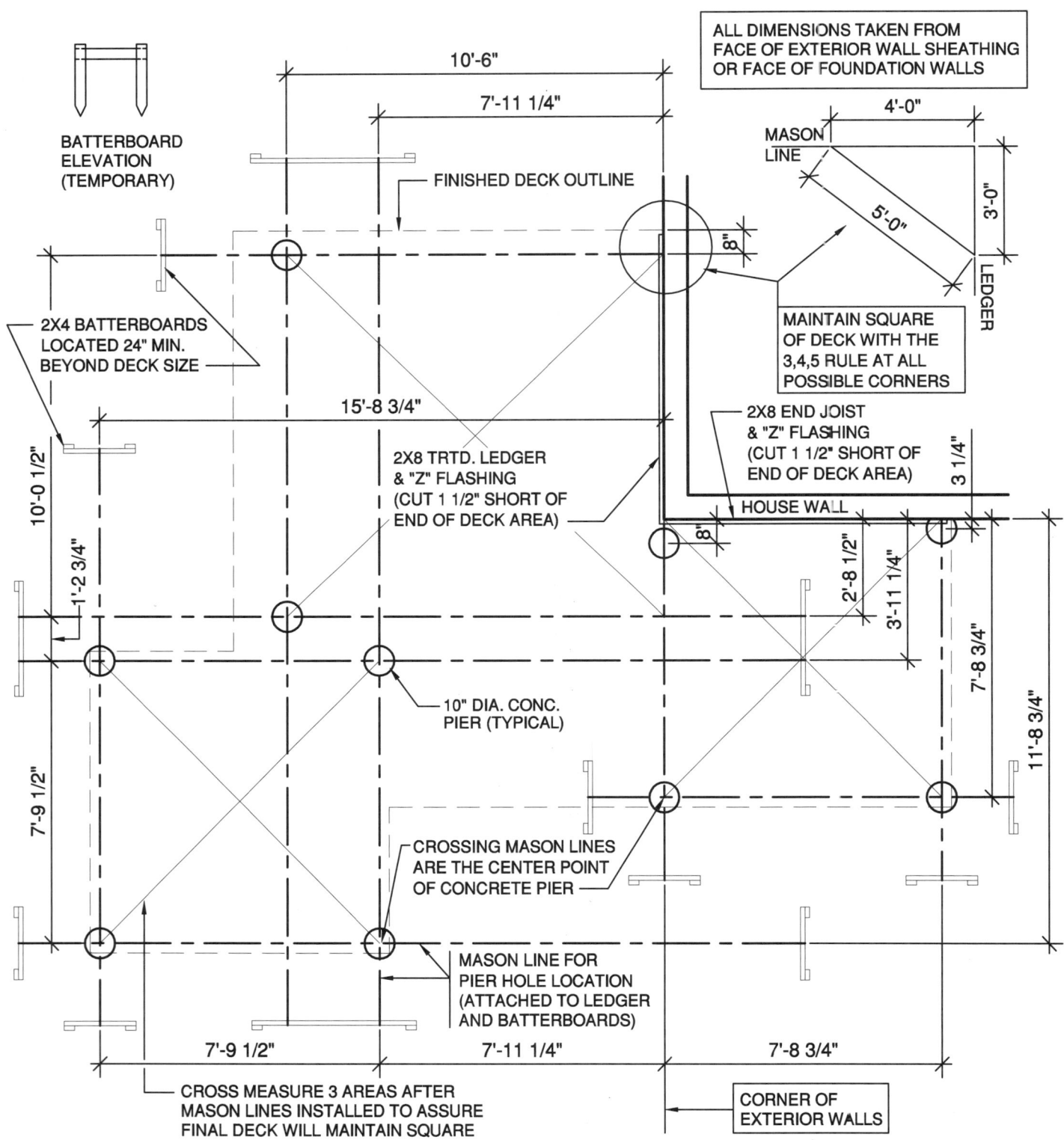

86 www.DreamIt-BuildIt.com

Ridgeview — Framing Plan

Scale: 1/4" = 1'-0"

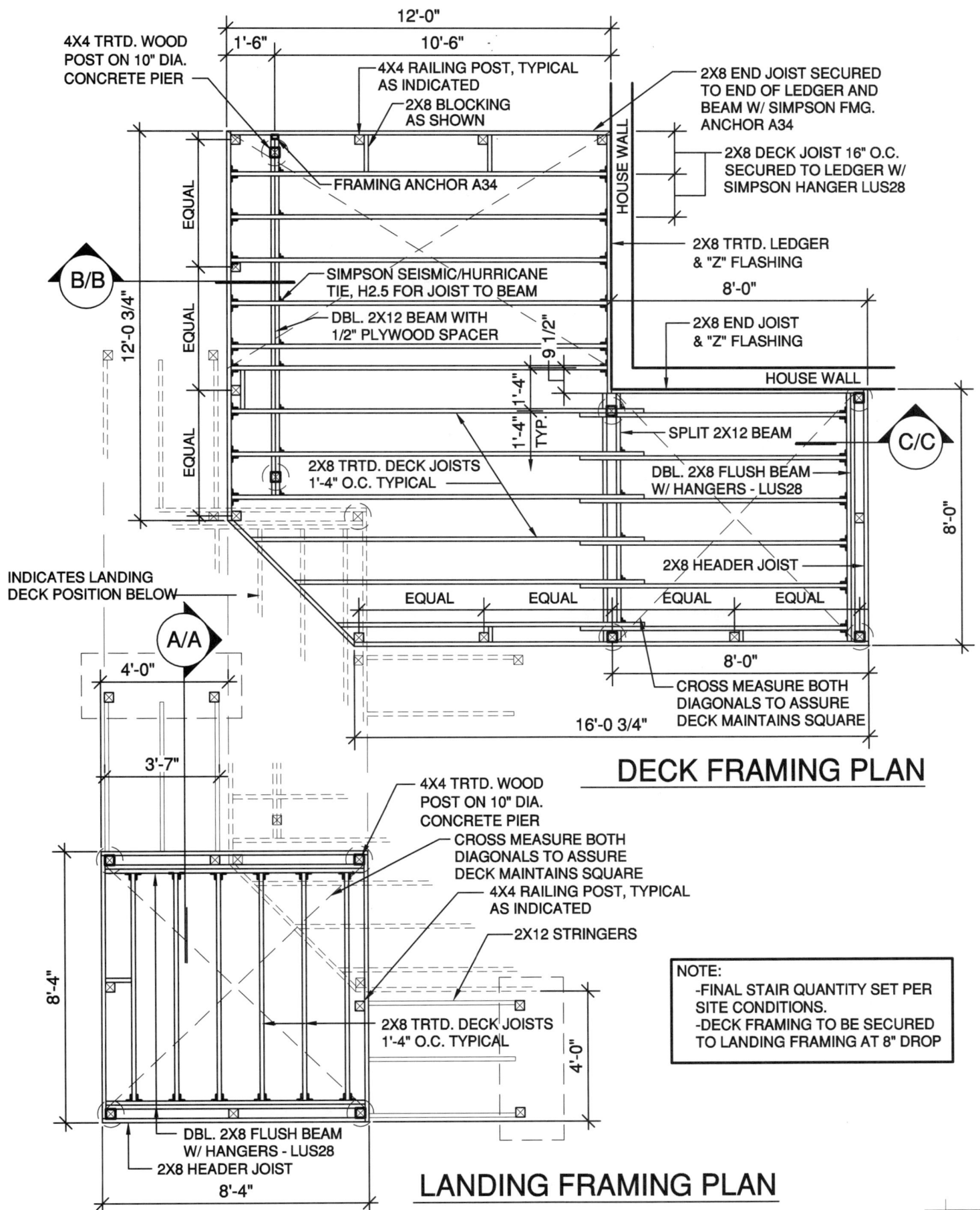

DECK FRAMING PLAN

LANDING FRAMING PLAN

NOTE:
- FINAL STAIR QUANTITY SET PER SITE CONDITIONS.
- DECK FRAMING TO BE SECURED TO LANDING FRAMING AT 8" DROP

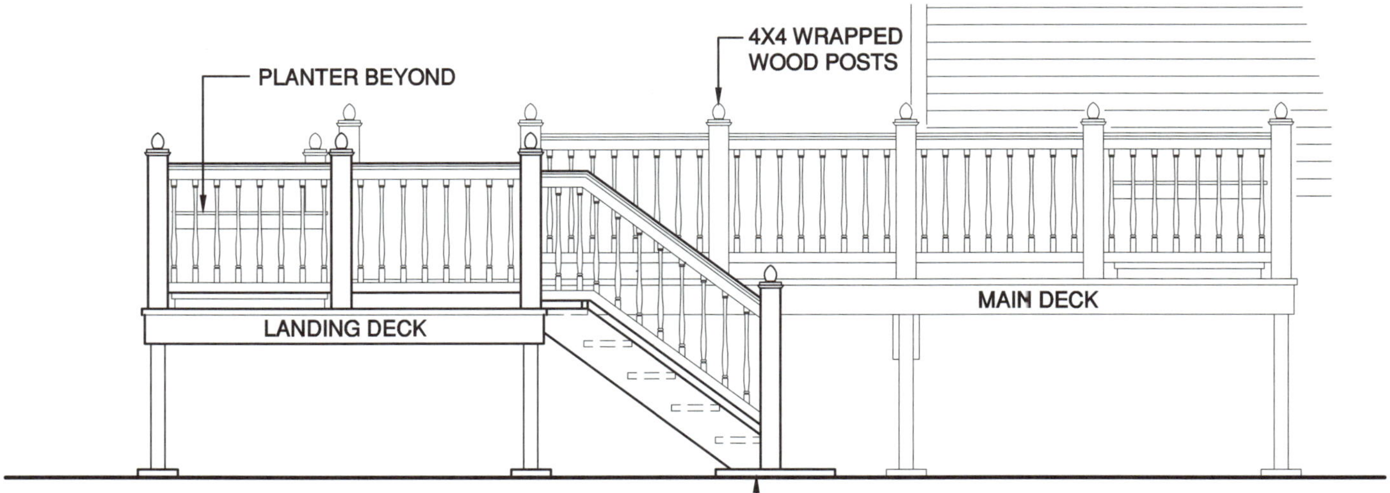

Ridgeview
Elevations and Details

FRONT ELEVATION
SCALE: 1/4" = 1'-0"

Labels: PLANTER BEYOND; 4X4 WRAPPED WOOD POSTS; LANDING DECK; MAIN DECK; CONCRETE PAVERS AS REQUIRED

STAIR QUANTITY BASED ON SITE CONDITIONS

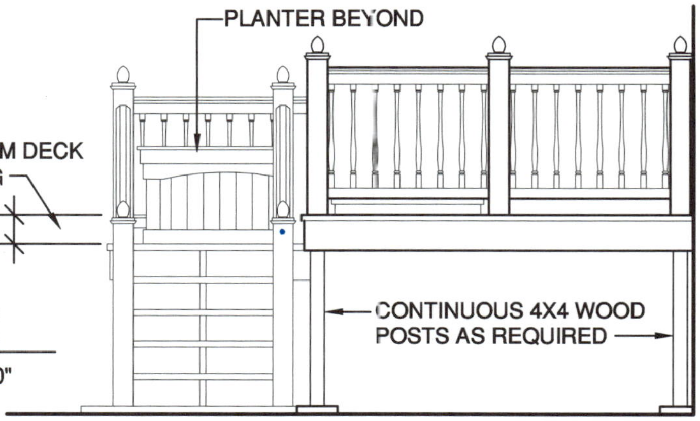

RIGHT ELEVATION
SCALE: 1/4" = 1'-0"

Labels: PLANTER BEYOND; 1 STEP FROM DECK TO LANDING; 7 1/4"; CONTINUOUS 4X4 WOOD POSTS AS REQUIRED

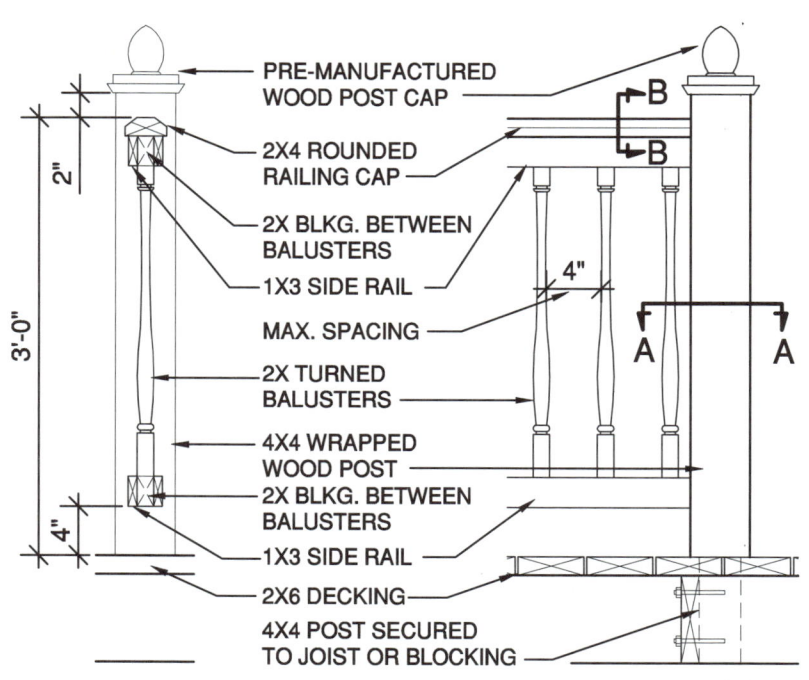

Labels: PRE-MANUFACTURED WOOD POST CAP; 2X4 ROUNDED RAILING CAP; 2X BLKG. BETWEEN BALUSTERS; 1X3 SIDE RAIL; 4" MAX. SPACING; 2X TURNED BALUSTERS; 4X4 WRAPPED WOOD POST; 2X BLKG. BETWEEN BALUSTERS; 1X3 SIDE RAIL; 2X6 DECKING; 4X4 POST SECURED TO JOIST OR BLOCKING; 2"; 3'-0"; 4"

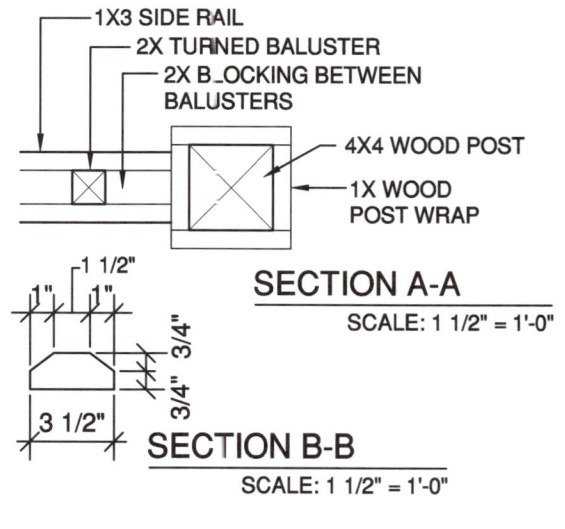

SECTION A-A
SCALE: 1 1/2" = 1'-0"

Labels: 1X3 SIDE RAIL; 2X TURNED BALUSTER; 2X BLOCKING BETWEEN BALUSTERS; 4X4 WOOD POST; 1X WOOD POST WRAP

SECTION B-B
SCALE: 1 1/2" = 1'-0"

Dimensions: 1 1/2"; 1"; 1"; 3/4"; 3/4"; 3 1/2"

RAILING DETAILS
SCALE: 3/4" = 1'-0"

Ridgeview — Elevation and Detail

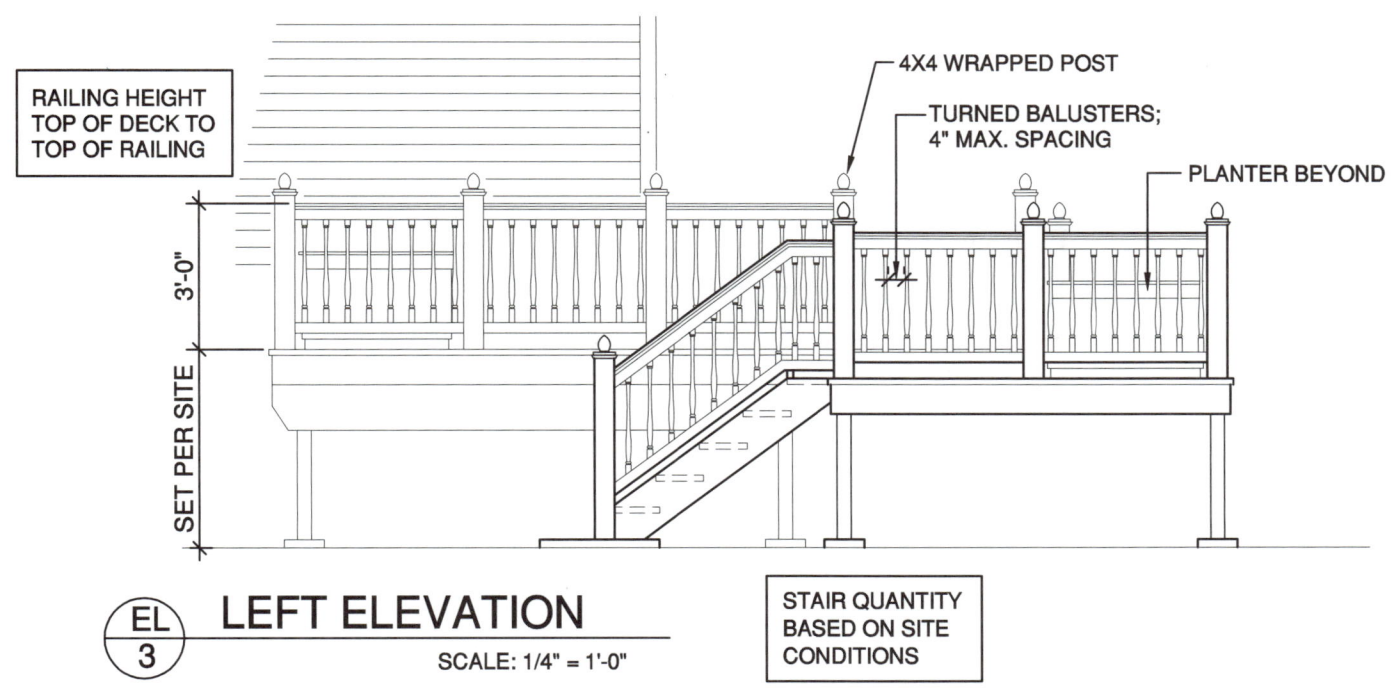

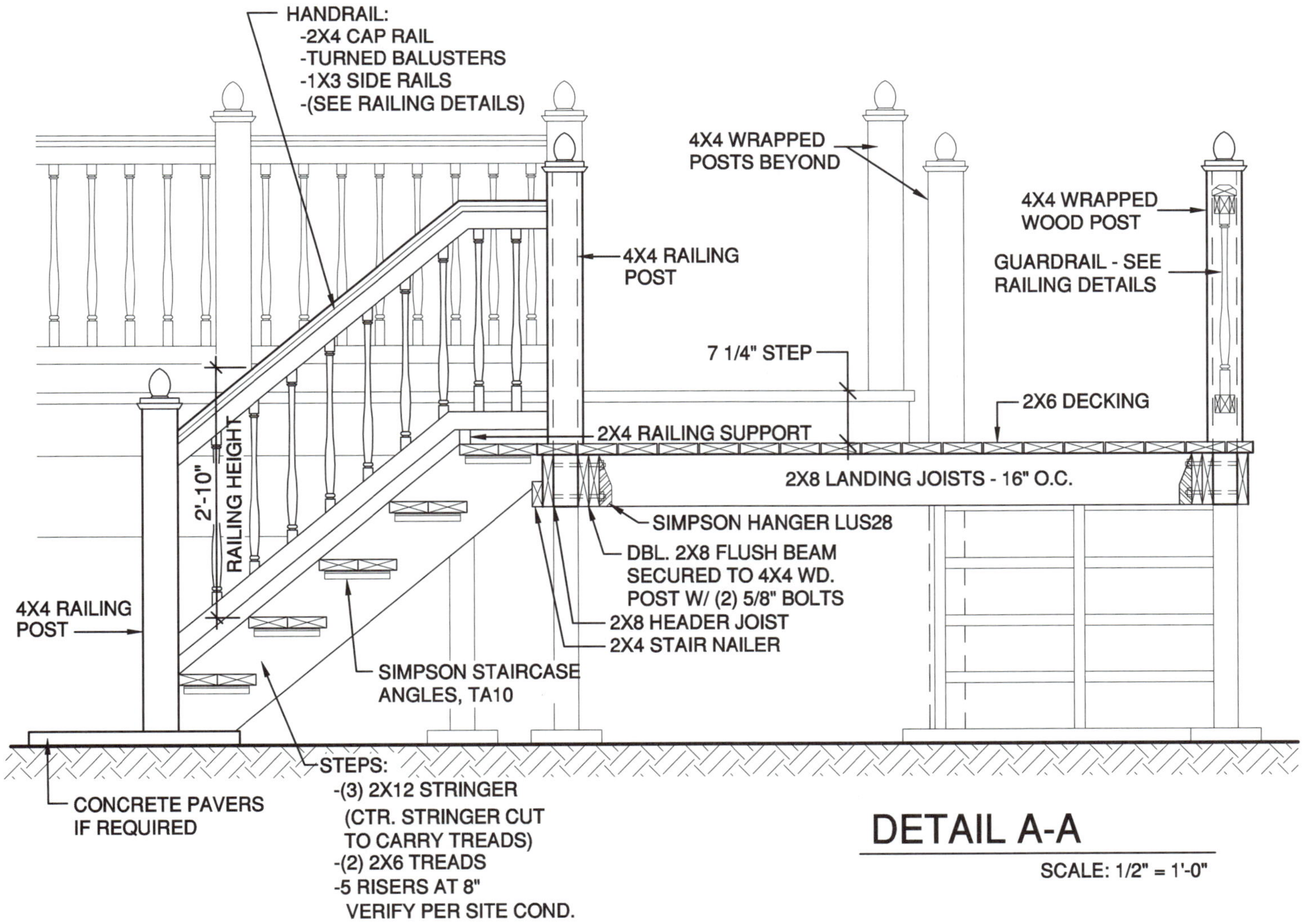

RIDGEVIEW — Elevation and Detail

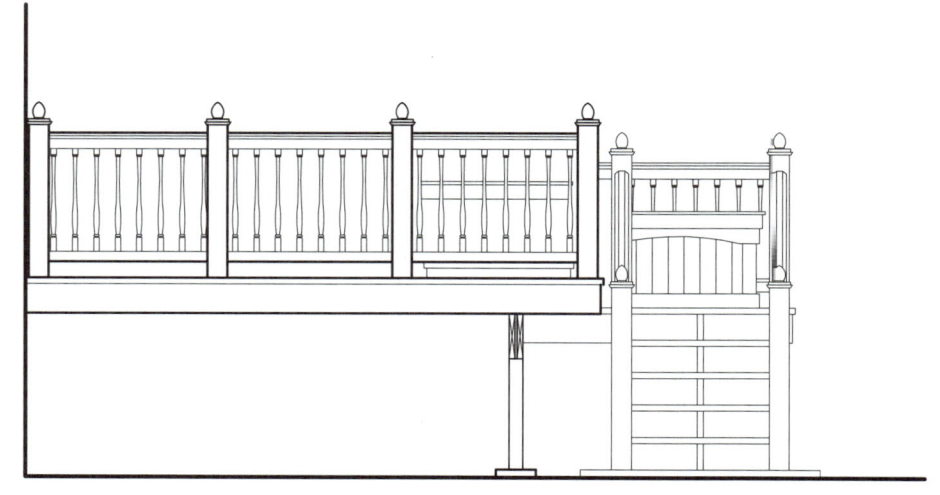

REAR ELEVATION
SCALE: 1/4" = 1'-0"

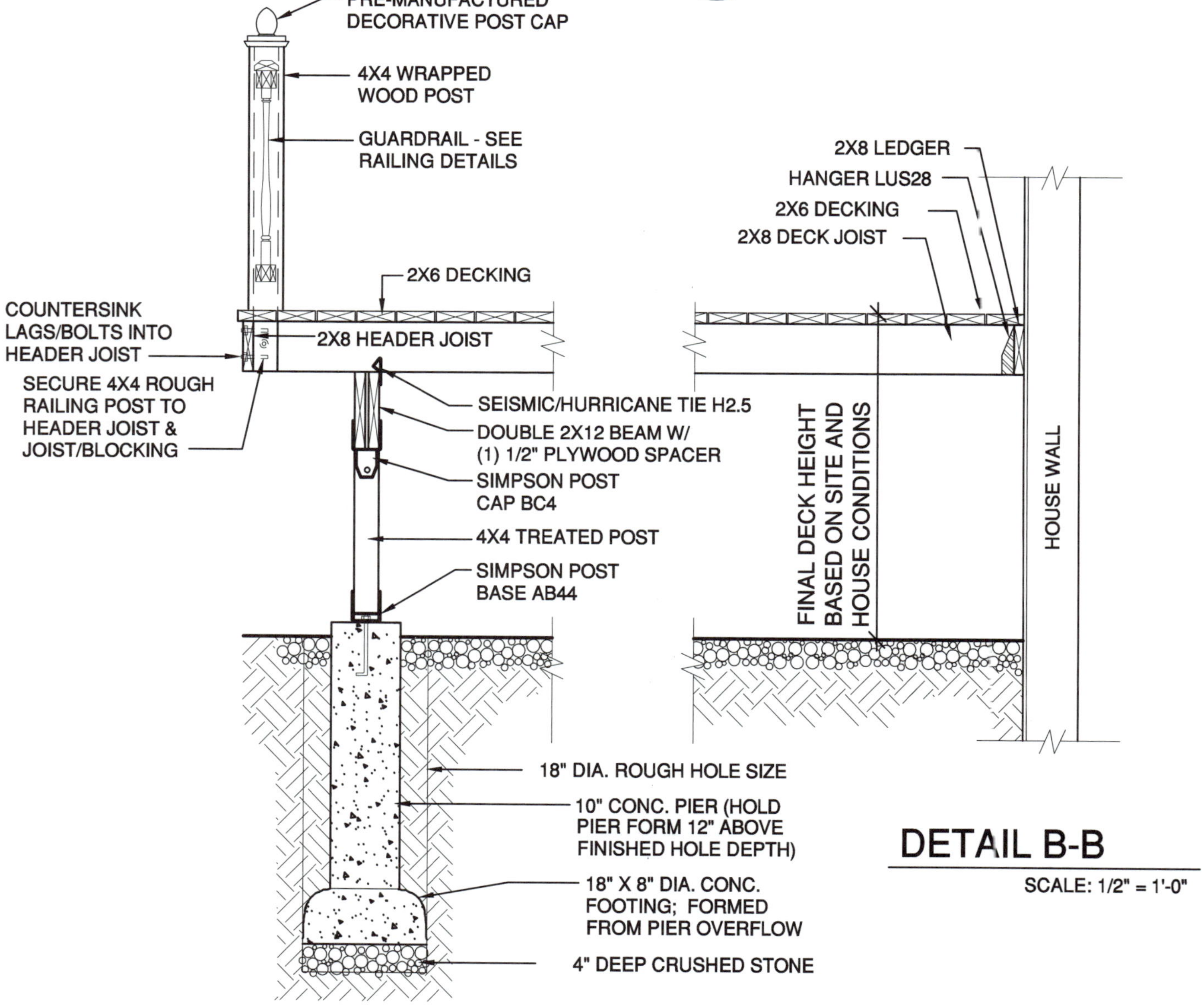

DETAIL B-B
SCALE: 1/2" = 1'-0"

Callouts:
- PRE-MANUFACTURED DECORATIVE POST CAP
- 4X4 WRAPPED WOOD POST
- GUARDRAIL - SEE RAILING DETAILS
- 2X8 LEDGER
- HANGER LUS28
- 2X6 DECKING
- 2X8 DECK JOIST
- 2X6 DECKING
- COUNTERSINK LAGS/BOLTS INTO HEADER JOIST
- 2X8 HEADER JOIST
- SECURE 4X4 ROUGH RAILING POST TO HEADER JOIST & JOIST/BLOCKING
- SEISMIC/HURRICANE TIE H2.5
- DOUBLE 2X12 BEAM W/ (1) 1/2" PLYWOOD SPACER
- SIMPSON POST CAP BC4
- 4X4 TREATED POST
- SIMPSON POST BASE AB44
- FINAL DECK HEIGHT BASED ON SITE AND HOUSE CONDITIONS
- HOUSE WALL
- 18" DIA. ROUGH HOLE SIZE
- 10" CONC. PIER (HOLD PIER FORM 12" ABOVE FINISHED HOLE DEPTH)
- 18" X 8" DIA. CONC. FOOTING; FORMED FROM PIER OVERFLOW
- 4" DEEP CRUSHED STONE

www.DreamIt-BuildIt.com

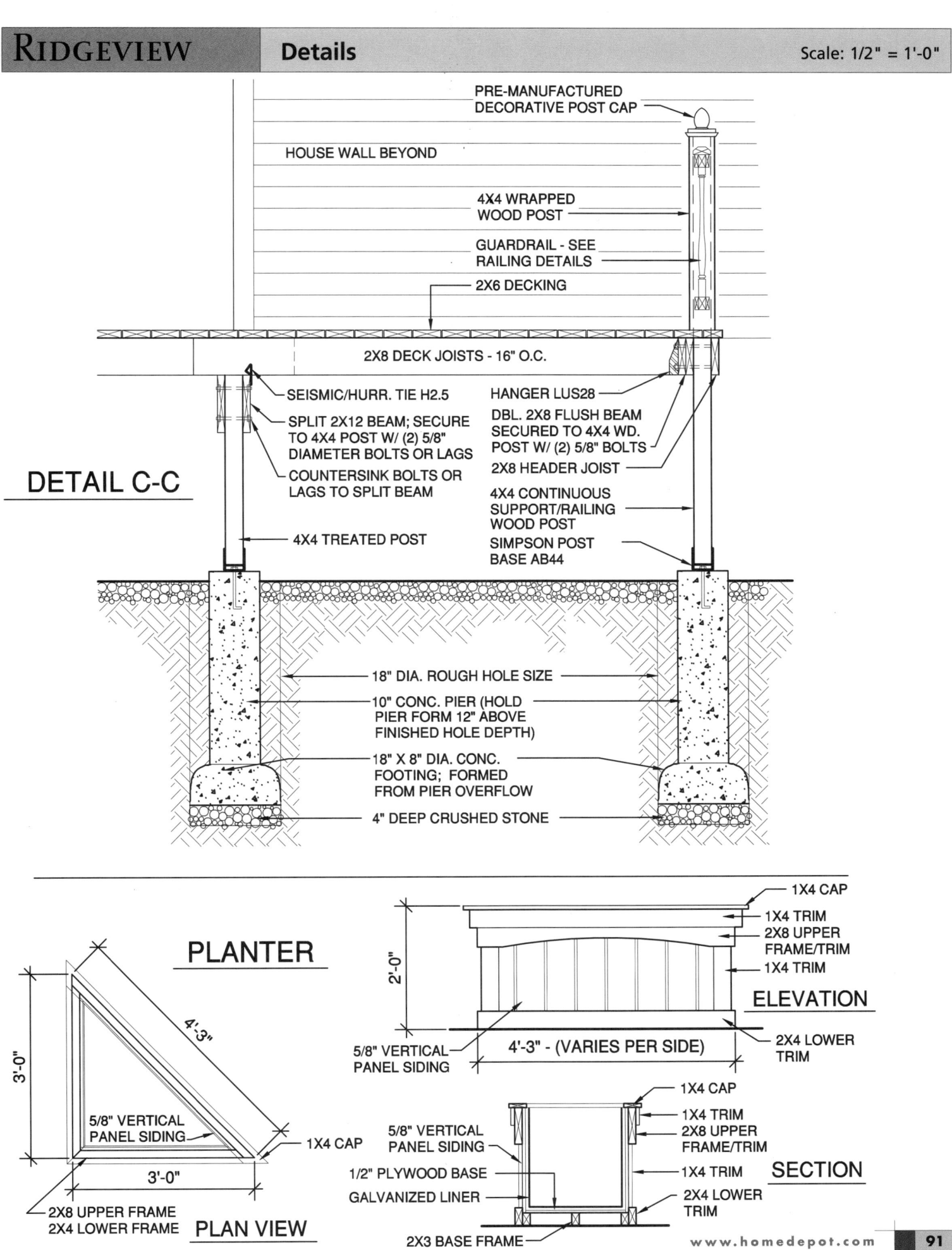

RIDGEVIEW — Material List

FOUNDATION

Item	Location	Qty	UM
60# Concrete Mix	Pier	50	BG
10"x48" Fiber Tube	Pier	10	EA
2x4 - 10' Std. & Btr.	Batterboard	9	EA
1/2"x6" Anchor Bolt/Nut/Wash.	Pier	10	EA
Post Base (ABA44)	Pier	10	EA
Crushed Gravel	Pier	20	BG
2x8 - 8' Treated	Ledger	2	EA
1x5 - 10' Zee Bar	Ledger	2	EA
5# 16d Galv. Nails	General Framing	1	EA
3/8"x4" Lag Screws	Ledger	22	EA
3/8"x1-1/2" Washer	Ledger	22	EA
10 oz. - Paintable Caulk	Ledger/Bolt	3	TB

FRAMING

Item	Location	Qty	UM
2x12 - 8' Treated	Beam	2	EA
2x12 - 12' Treated	Beam	2	EA
2x8 - 8' Treated	Flush Bm./Jst.	17	EA
2x8 - 10' Treated	Flush Bm./Jst.	10	EA
2x8 - 12' Treated	Joist	8	EA
2x8 - 14' Treated	Joist/Blocking	8	EA
1/2" CDX - 5 Ply Plywd.	Beam	1	EA
4x4 - 8' Treated	Post	8	EA
Post Cap (PC44-16)	Post/Beam	2	EA
5# 16d Galv. Nails	General Framing	3	EA
2x8 Joist Hanger (LUS28)	Ledger Joist	32	EA
Hurricane Tie (H2.5)	Joist/Beam	15	EA
Framing Anchor (A34)	End/Header Joist	5	EA
1# 8d 1-1/2" Hanger Nails	Connector	3	EA
5# 8d Ctd. Box Nails	General Framing	1	EA
5/8"x7" Lag Bolt/Nut/Wash.	Split Beam	4	EA
5/8"x9" Lag Bolt/Nut/Wash.	Flush Beam	12	EA

FINISH/RAILING/SKIRTING

Item	Location	Qty	UM
4x4 - 8' Treated	Post	10	EA
3/8"x4" Lag Screws	Post	38	EA
3/8"x1-1/2" Washer	Post	38	EA
2x6 - 12' Treated	Decking/Stair Trd.	40	EA
2x6 - 16' Treated	Decking/Stair Trd.	30	EA
1# 2-1/2" Ctd. Screw	Decking/Railing	10	EA
2x12 - 8' Treated	Stringer	6	EA
3x5 Heavy Angle (HL35)	Stringer	12	EA
5/16"x1-1/2" Lag Screws	Heavy Angle	48	EA
2x6 - 8' Treated	Cap Rail	12	EA
1x3 - 8' Treated	Side Rail	48	EA
2x3 - 8' Treated	Blstr. Blocking	24	EA
1-3/8"x1-3/8" - 3' Trnd. Blstr.	Baluster	178	EA
2x4 - 8' Treated	Stair Nailer	2	EA
5# 16d Galv. Nails	General Framing	2	EA
5# 8d Ctd. Box Nails	General Framing	1	EA
1x4 - 8' Treated	Post Wrap	25	EA
1x6 - 8' Treated	Post Wrap	25	EA
Wood Post Cap	Post	25	EA
1x4 - 12' Treated	Planter	9	EA
2x3 - 14' Treated	Planter	3	EA
2x4 - 12' Treated	Planter	3	EA
2x8 - 12' Treated	Planter	3	EA
5/8" T1-11 Siding	Planter	3	EA

CHAPTER 5

THE TACKLEBERRY

HPM-1112

A freestanding deck creates a welcoming retreat in your backyard, as well as a great outdoor addition to your home. Lattice around the perimeter of this deck offers some privacy and shade. Two unique triangular planting boxes anchor the deck in opposite corners.

Dimensions for this deck are 16' X 16'.

TACKLEBERRY — Plan View

Scale: 1/4" = 1'-0"

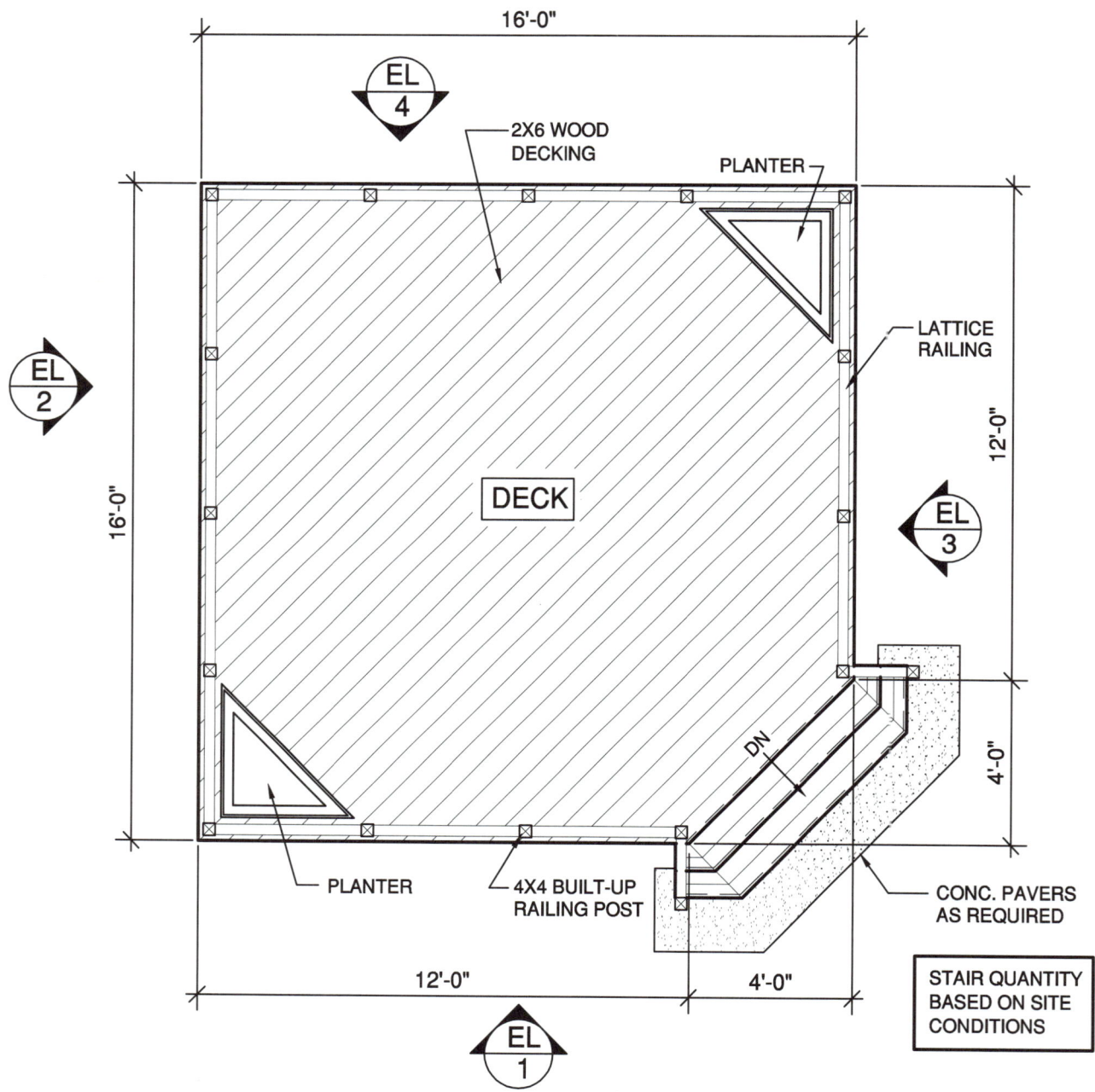

TACKLEBERRY — Pier Layout

Scale: 1/4" = 1'-0"

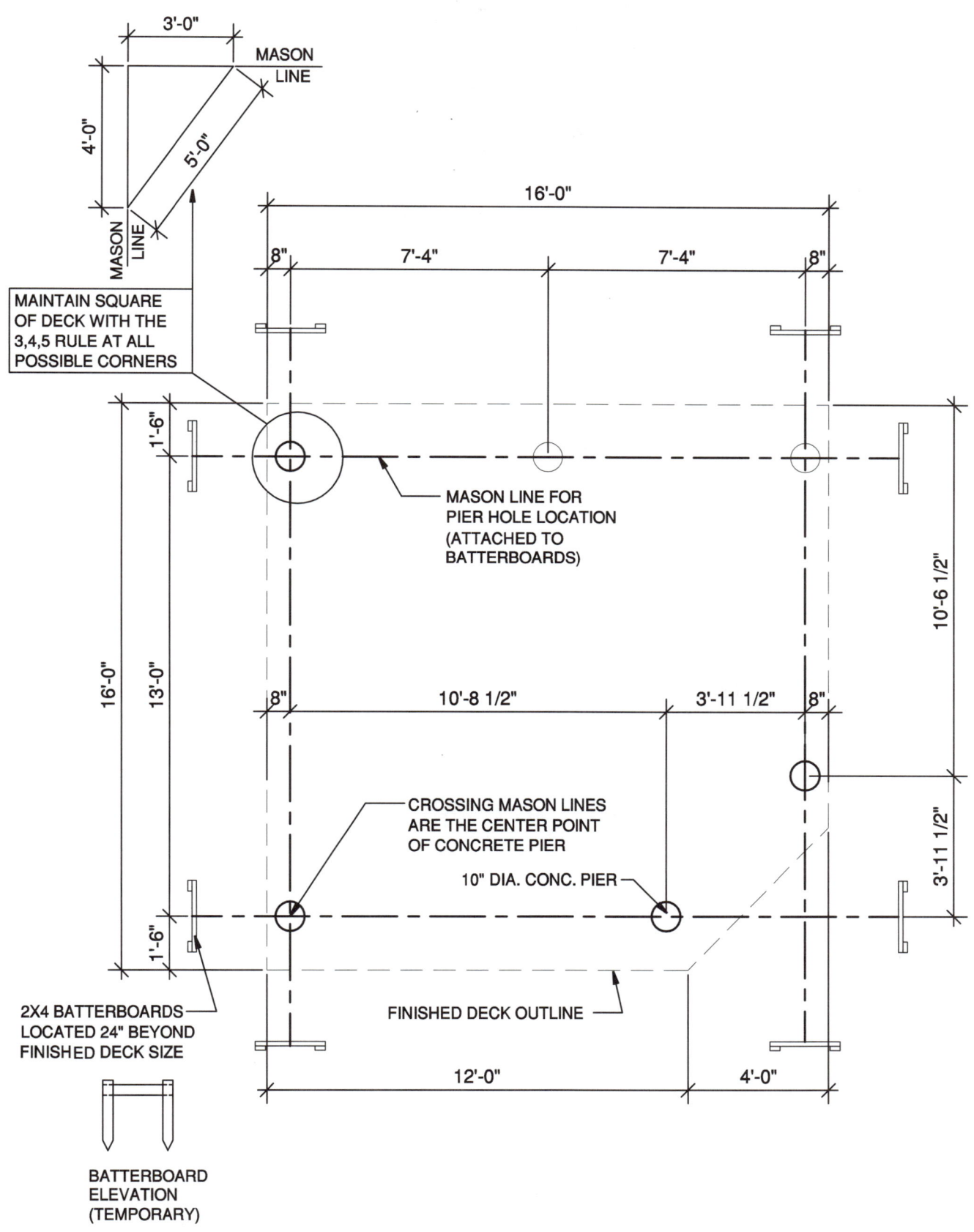

www.homedepot.com 95

TACKLEBERRY — Framing Plan

Scale: 1/4" = 1'-0"

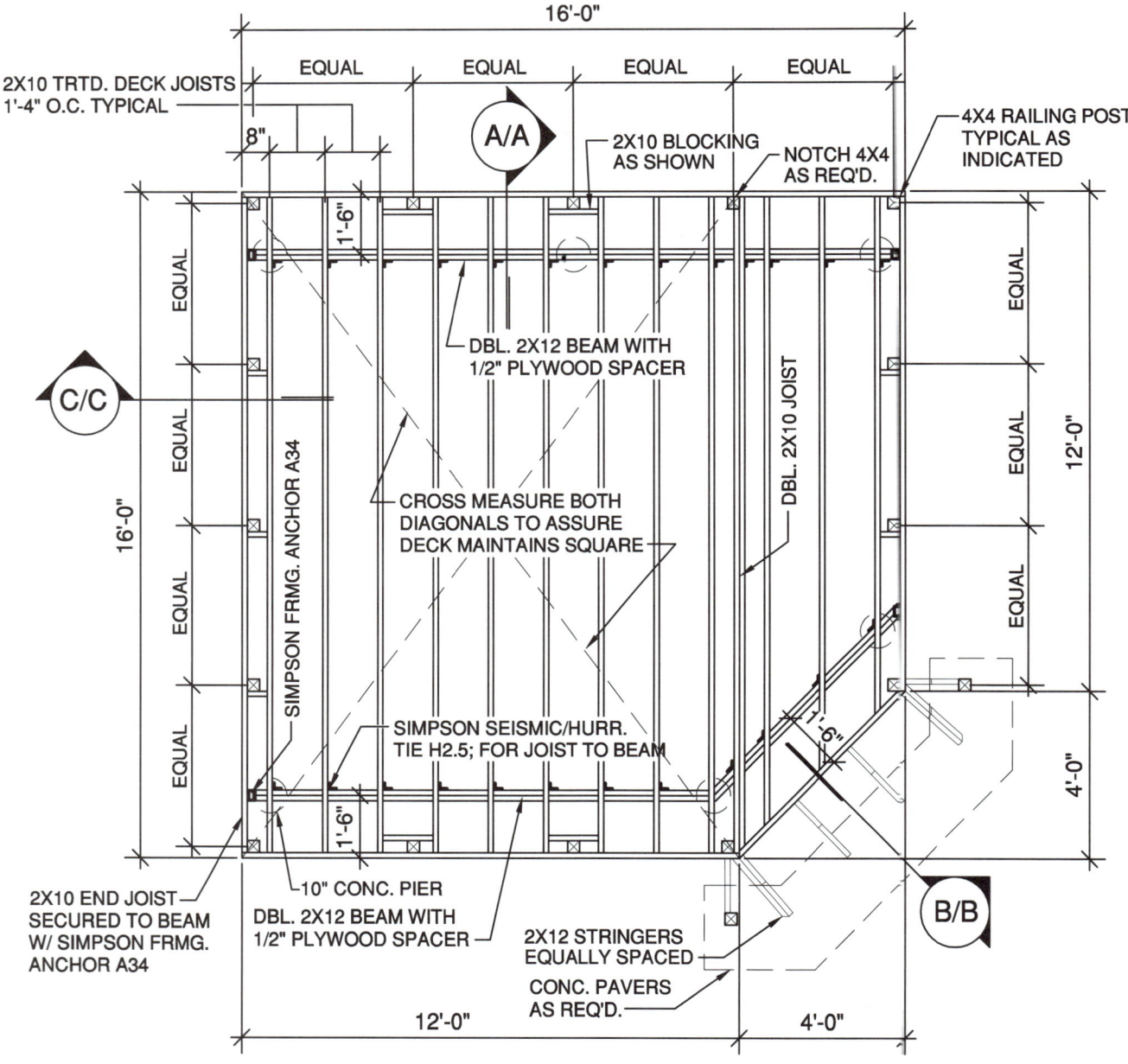

96 www.DreamIt-BuildIt.com

TACKLEBERRY — Elevations

Scale: 1/4" = 1'-0"

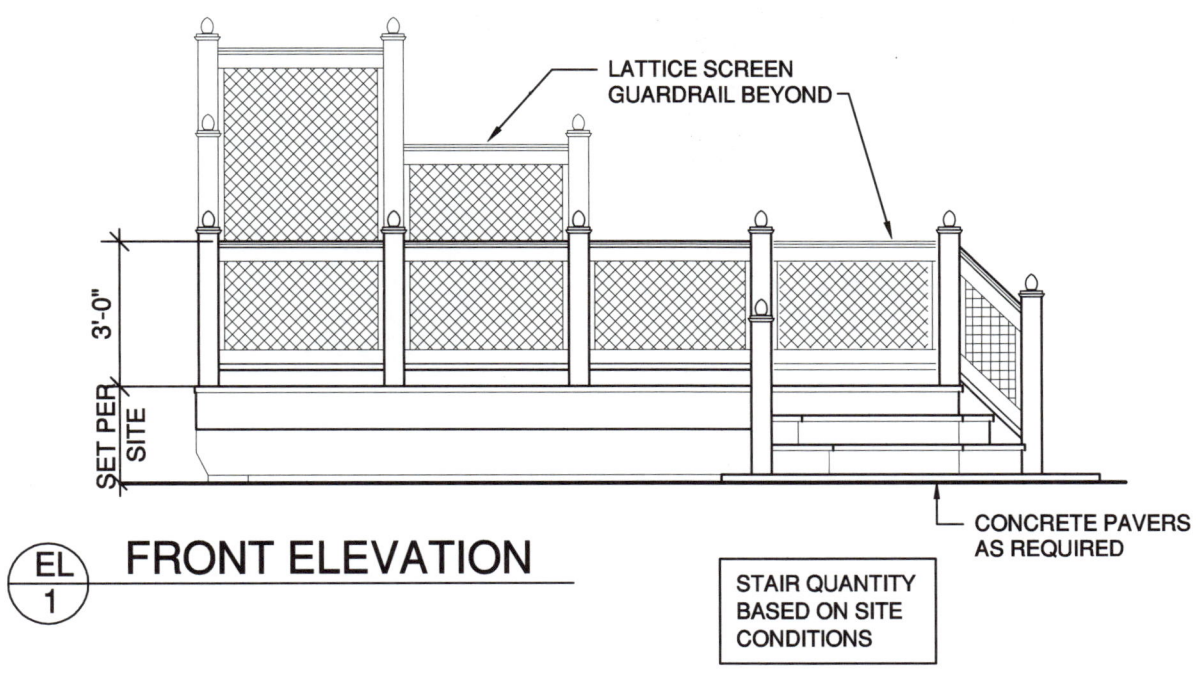

FRONT ELEVATION — EL 1

- LATTICE SCREEN GUARDRAIL BEYOND
- CONCRETE PAVERS AS REQUIRED
- STAIR QUANTITY BASED ON SITE CONDITIONS
- 3'-0" SET PER SITE

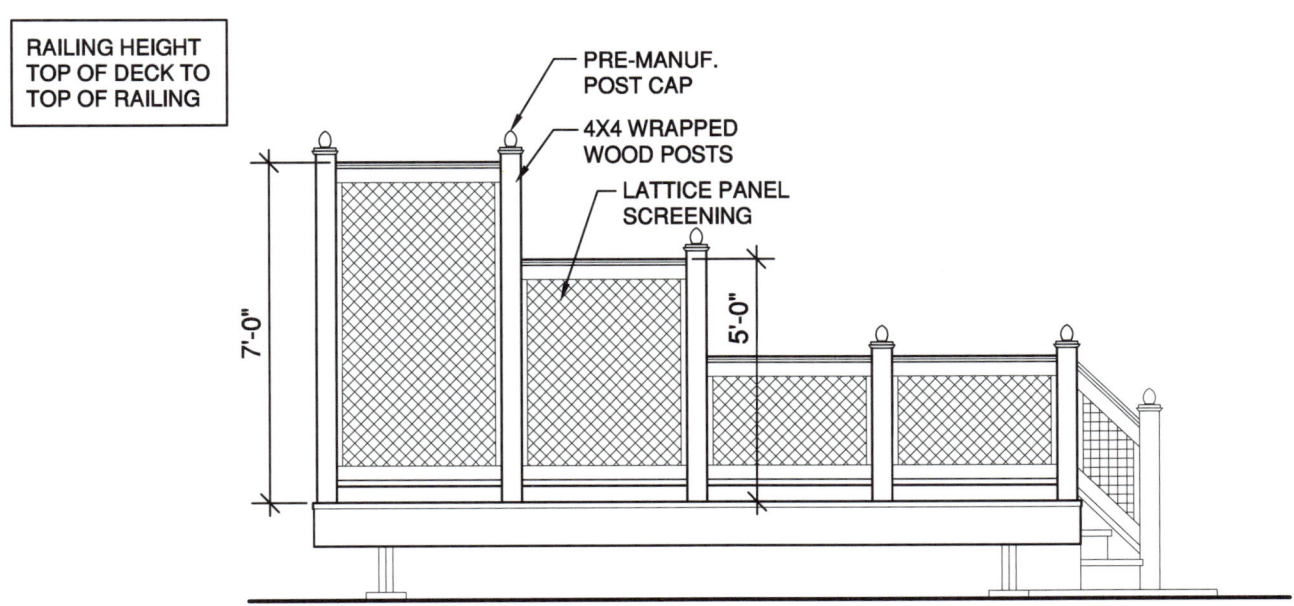

LEFT ELEVATION — EL 2

- RAILING HEIGHT TOP OF DECK TO TOP OF RAILING
- PRE-MANUF. POST CAP
- 4X4 WRAPPED WOOD POSTS
- LATTICE PANEL SCREENING
- 7'-0"
- 5'-0"

www.homedepot.com

Tackleberry — Elevations

Scale: 1/4" = 1'-0"

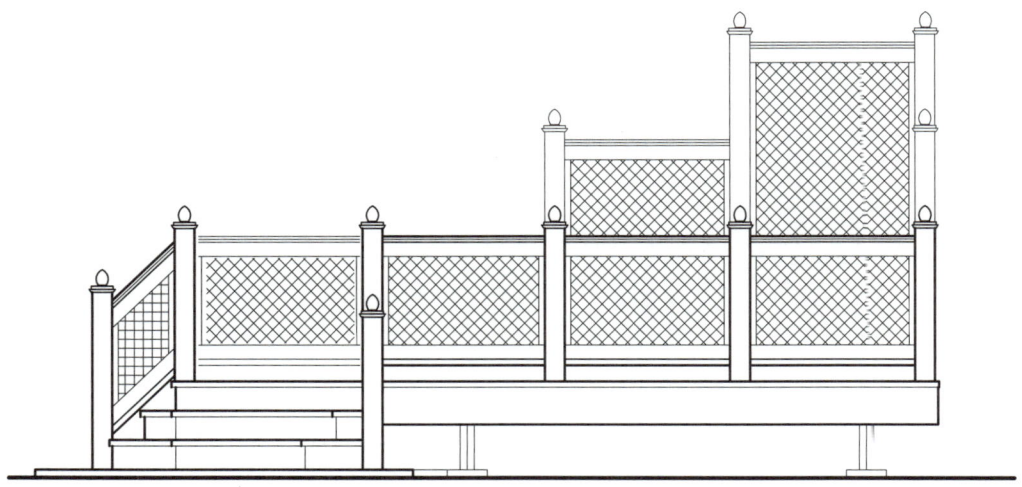

RIGHT ELEVATION (EL/3)

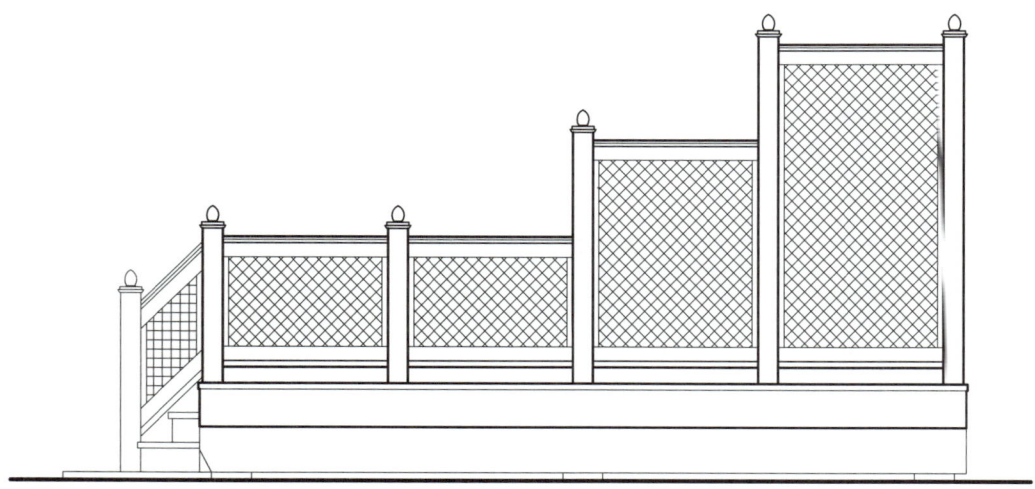

REAR ELEVATION (EL/4)

TACKLEBERRY — Details

Scale: 1/2" = 1'-0"

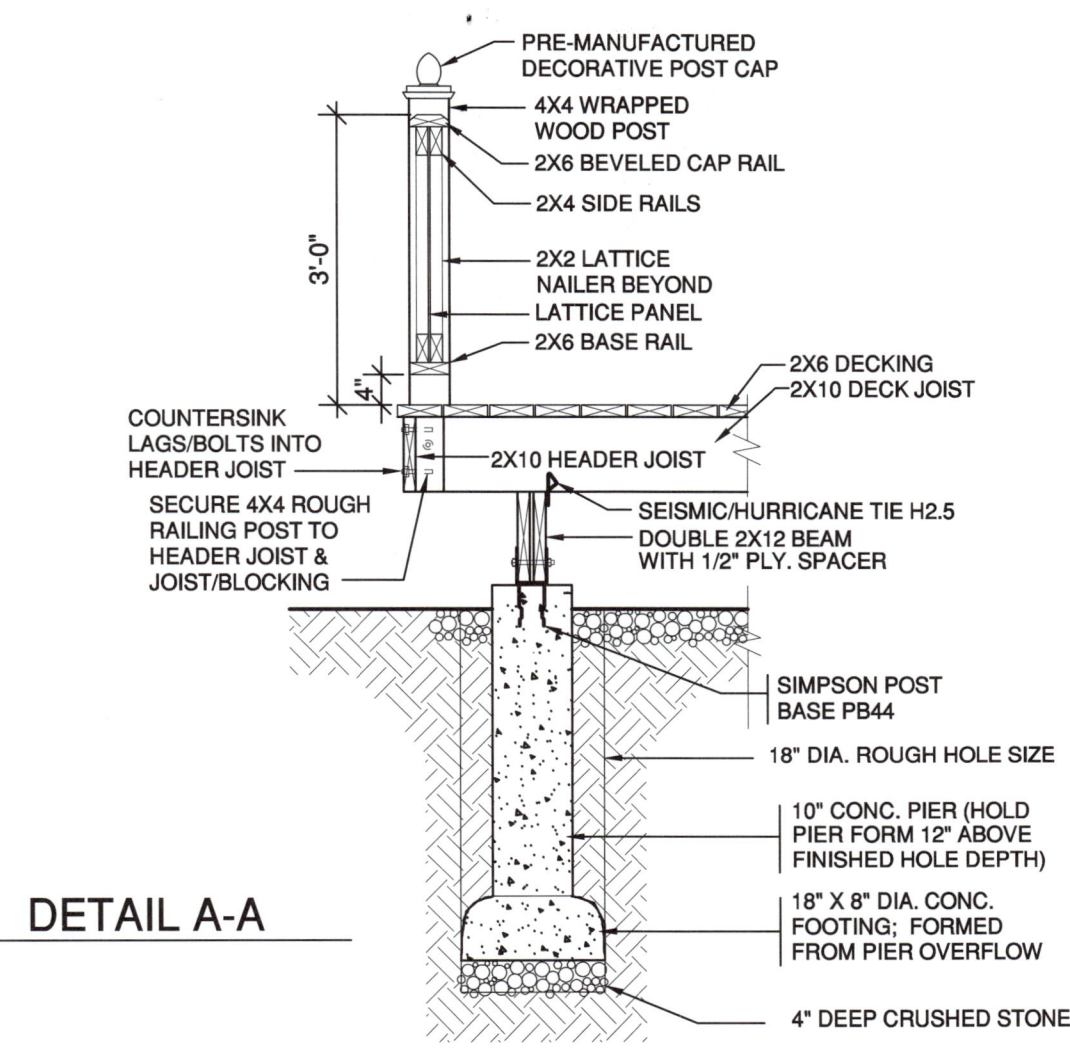

DETAIL A-A

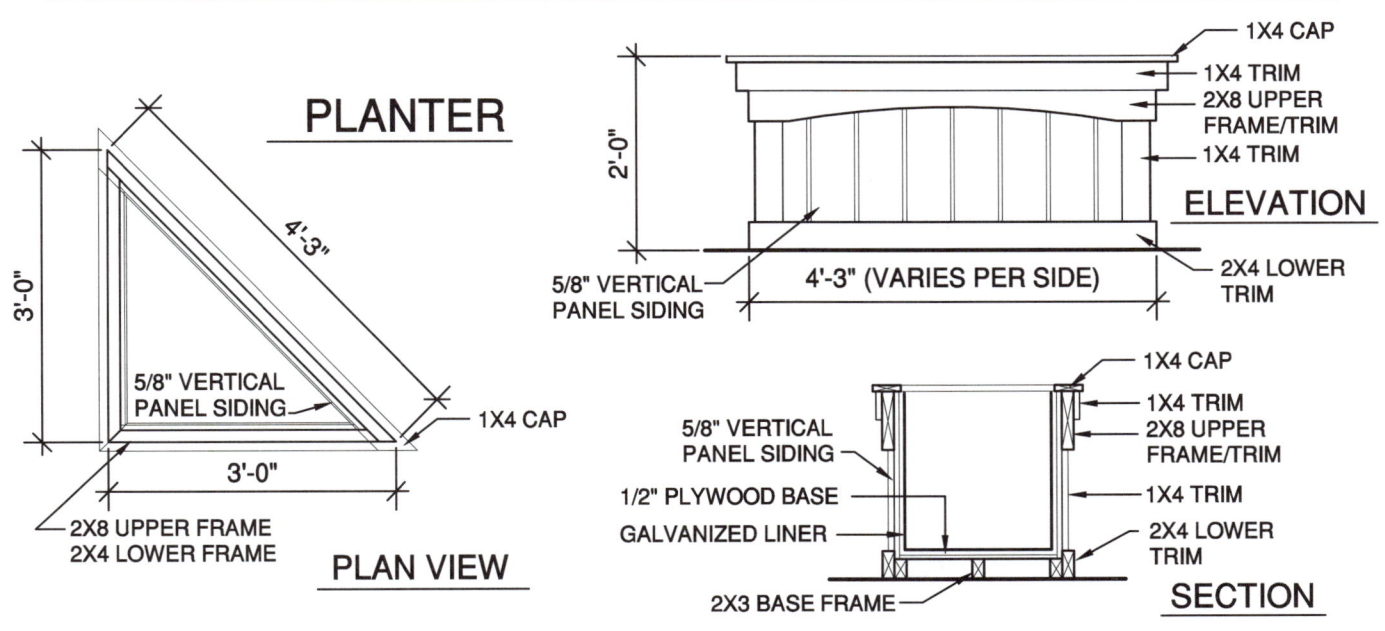

PLANTER — PLAN VIEW — ELEVATION — SECTION

www.homedepot.com

TACKLEBERRY Details

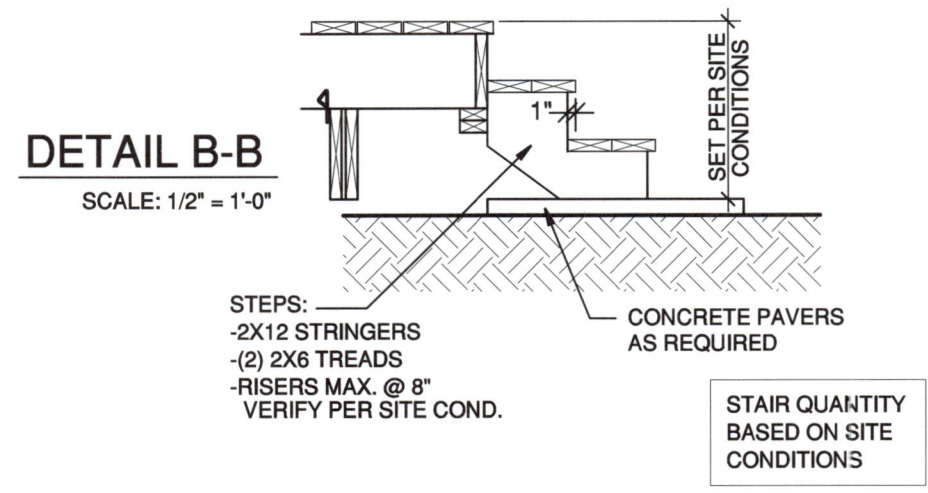

DETAIL B-B
SCALE: 1/2" = 1'-0"

STEPS:
- 2X12 STRINGERS
- (2) 2X6 TREADS
- RISERS MAX. @ 8" VERIFY PER SITE COND.

CONCRETE PAVERS AS REQUIRED

STAIR QUANTITY BASED ON SITE CONDITIONS

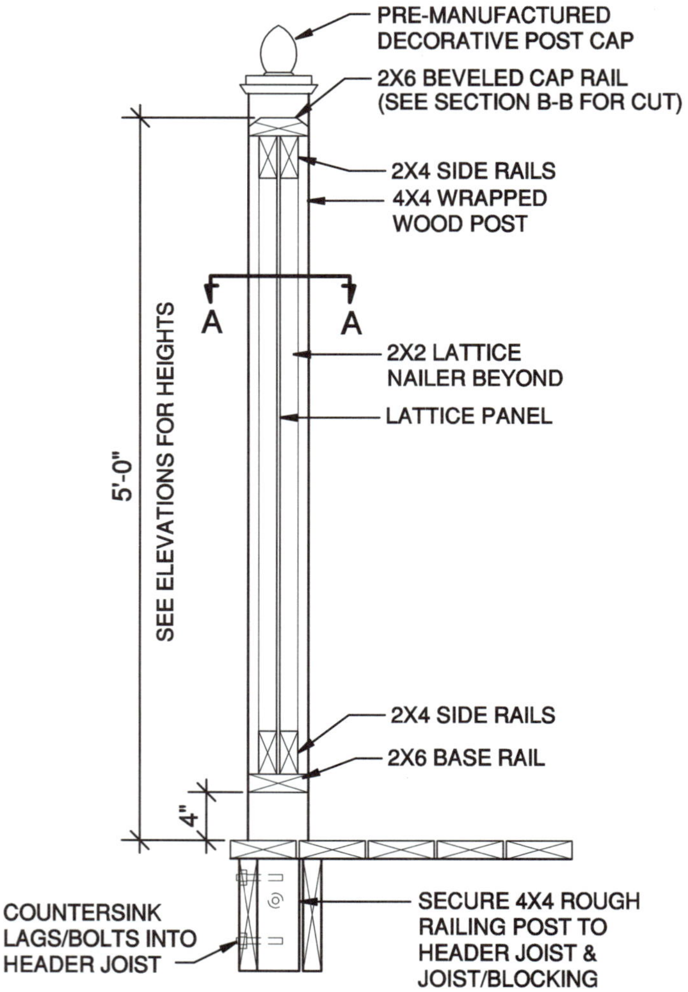

- PRE-MANUFACTURED DECORATIVE POST CAP
- 2X6 BEVELED CAP RAIL (SEE SECTION B-B FOR CUT)
- 2X4 SIDE RAILS
- 4X4 WRAPPED WOOD POST
- 2X2 LATTICE NAILER BEYOND
- LATTICE PANEL
- 2X4 SIDE RAILS
- 2X6 BASE RAIL
- COUNTERSINK LAGS/BOLTS INTO HEADER JOIST
- SECURE 4X4 ROUGH RAILING POST TO HEADER JOIST & JOIST/BLOCKING

5'-0" SEE ELEVATIONS FOR HEIGHTS

4"

DETAIL C-C
SCALE: 3/4" = 1'-0"

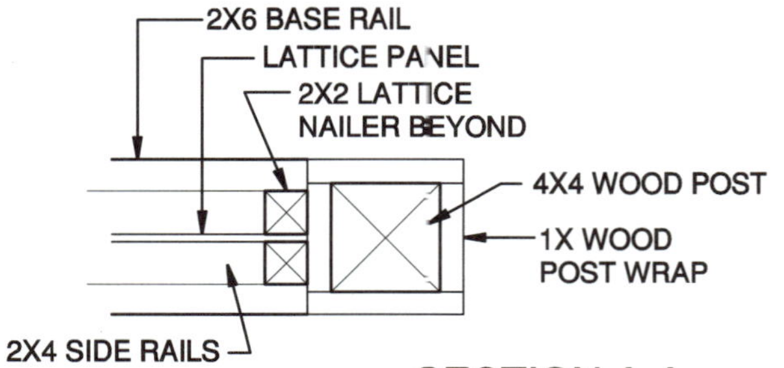

- 2X6 BASE RAIL
- LATTICE PANEL
- 2X2 LATTICE NAILER BEYOND
- 4X4 WOOD POST
- 1X WOOD POST WRAP
- 2X4 SIDE RAILS

SECTION A-A
SCALE: 1 1/2" = 1'-0"

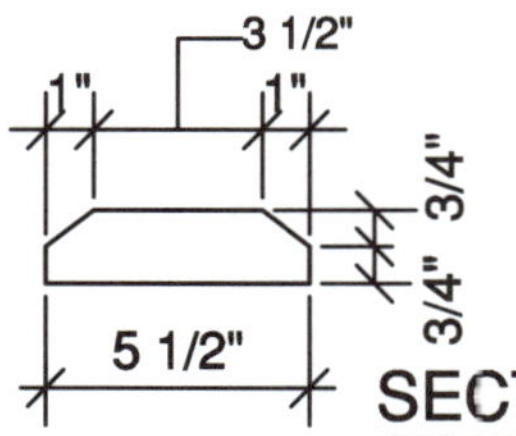

3 1/2"
1" 1"
3/4"
3/4"
5 1/2"

SECTION B-B
SCALE: 1 1/2" = 1'-0"

RAILING/SCREEN DETAILS

TACKLEBERRY — Material List

FOUNDATION

Item	Location	Qty	UM
60# Concrete Mix	Pier	30	BG
10"x48" Fiber Tube	Pier	6	EA
2x4 - 10' Std. & Btr.	Batterboard	5	EA
Post Base (PB44)	Pier	7	EA
Crushed Gravel	Pier	12	BG
5# 16d Galv. Nails	General Framing	1	EA

FRAMING

Item	Location	Qty	UM
2x12 - 12' Treated	Beam	2	EA
2x12 - 14' Treated	Beam	1	EA
2x12 - 16' Treated	Beam	2	EA
2x10 - 12' Treated	Joist	3	EA
2x10 - 14' Treated	Joist	2	EA
2x10 - 16' Treated	Joist/Blocking	16	EA
1/2" CDX - 5 Ply Plywd.	Beam Spacer	2	EA
5# 16d Galv. Nails	General Framing	3	EA
Hurricane Tie (H2.5)	Joist/Beam	26	EA
Angle Bracket (A34)	End Joist/Beam	7	EA
1# 8d 1-1/2" Hanger Nails	Connector	3	EA
5# 8d Ctd. Box Nails	General Framing	1	EA

FINISH/RAILING/SKIRTING

Item	Location	Qty	UM
4x4 - 10' Treated	Post	10	EA
3/8"x4" Lag Screws	Post	17	EA
3/8"x1-1/2" Washer	Post	17	EA
2x6 - 12' Treated	Decking/Stair Trd.	26	EA
2x6 - 16' Treated	Decking/Stair Trd.	20	EA
1# 2-1/2" Ctd. Screws	Decking/Railing	10	EA
2x12 - 12' Treated	Stringer	2	EA
3x5 Heavy Angle (HL35)	Stringer	10	EA
5/16"x1-1/2" Lag Screws	Heavy Angle	40	EA
2x4 - 12' Treated	Stair Stringer Nailer	2	EA
2x6 - 8' Treated	Cap/Base Rail	14	EA
2x4 - 8' Treated	Side Rail	28	EA
2x2 - 8' Treated	Lattice Nailer	8	EA
Post Cap	Post	17	EA
Garden Weave Lattice	Screen	7	EA
5# 16d Galv. Nails	General Framing	2	EA
5# 8d Ctd. Box Nails	General Framing	1	EA
1x4 - 8' Treated	Post Wrap	29	EA
1x6 - 8' Treated	Post Wrap	29	EA
1x4 - 12' Treated	Planter	6	EA
2x3 - 14' Treated	Planter	2	EA
2x4 - 12' Treated	Planter	2	EA
2x8 - 12' Treated	Planter	2	EA
1/2" Plywood Base	Planter	1	EA
5/8" T1-11 Siding	Planter	2	EA

CHAPTER 5

THE IRONDALE

HPM-1113

This wraparound octagonal deck nestles itself around an outside corner of your home and is ideal when a traditional side or rear deck won't work. Its 21-ft. diameter provides adequate space for a variety of seasonal accessories and activities. The angled stairway makes access to the yard quick and easy.

Dimensions for this deck are 21' X 21'.

Irondale — Plan View

Scale: 1/4" = 1'-0"

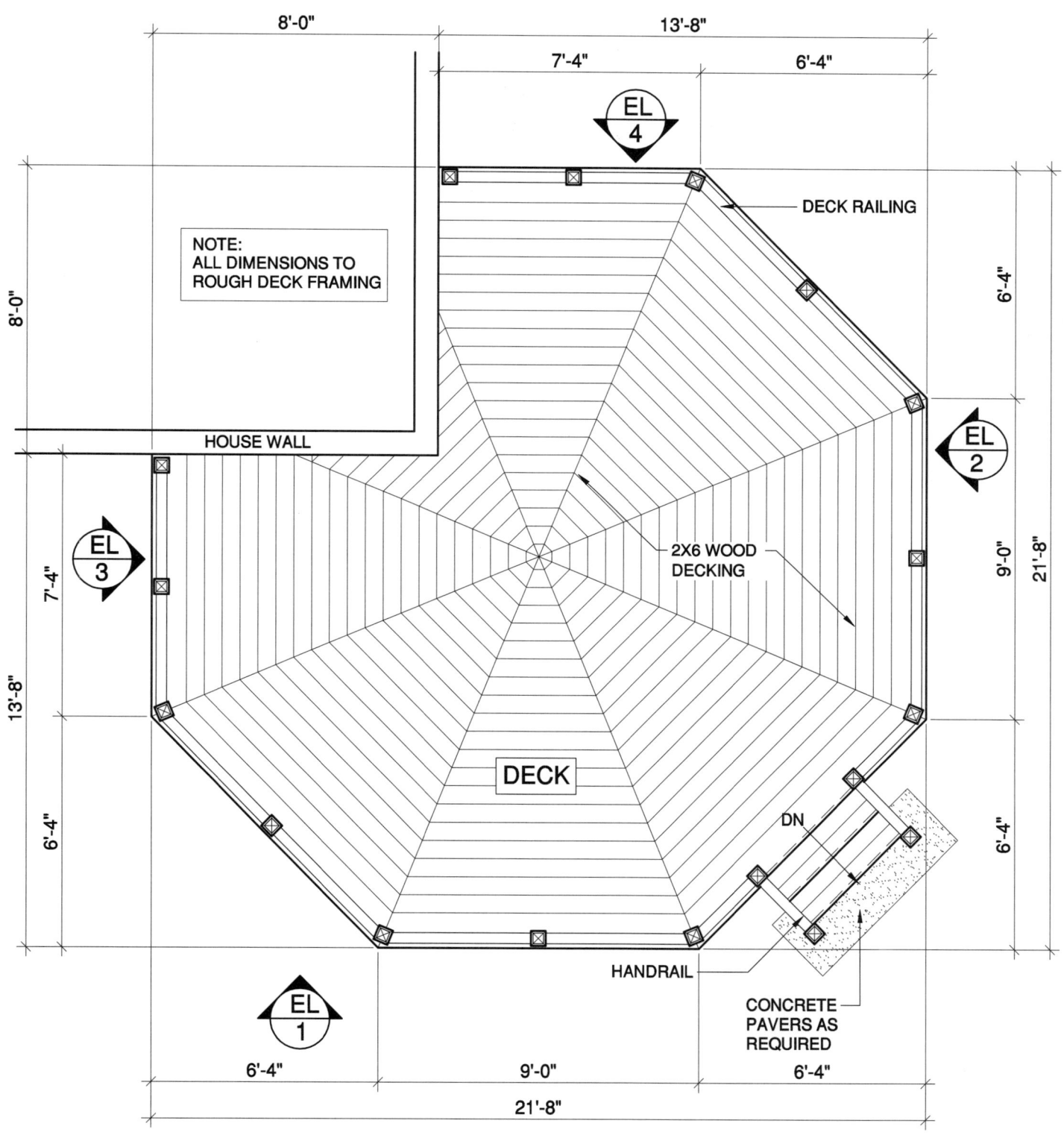

www.homedepot.com 103

IRONDALE — Pier Layout

Scale: 1/4" = 1'-0"

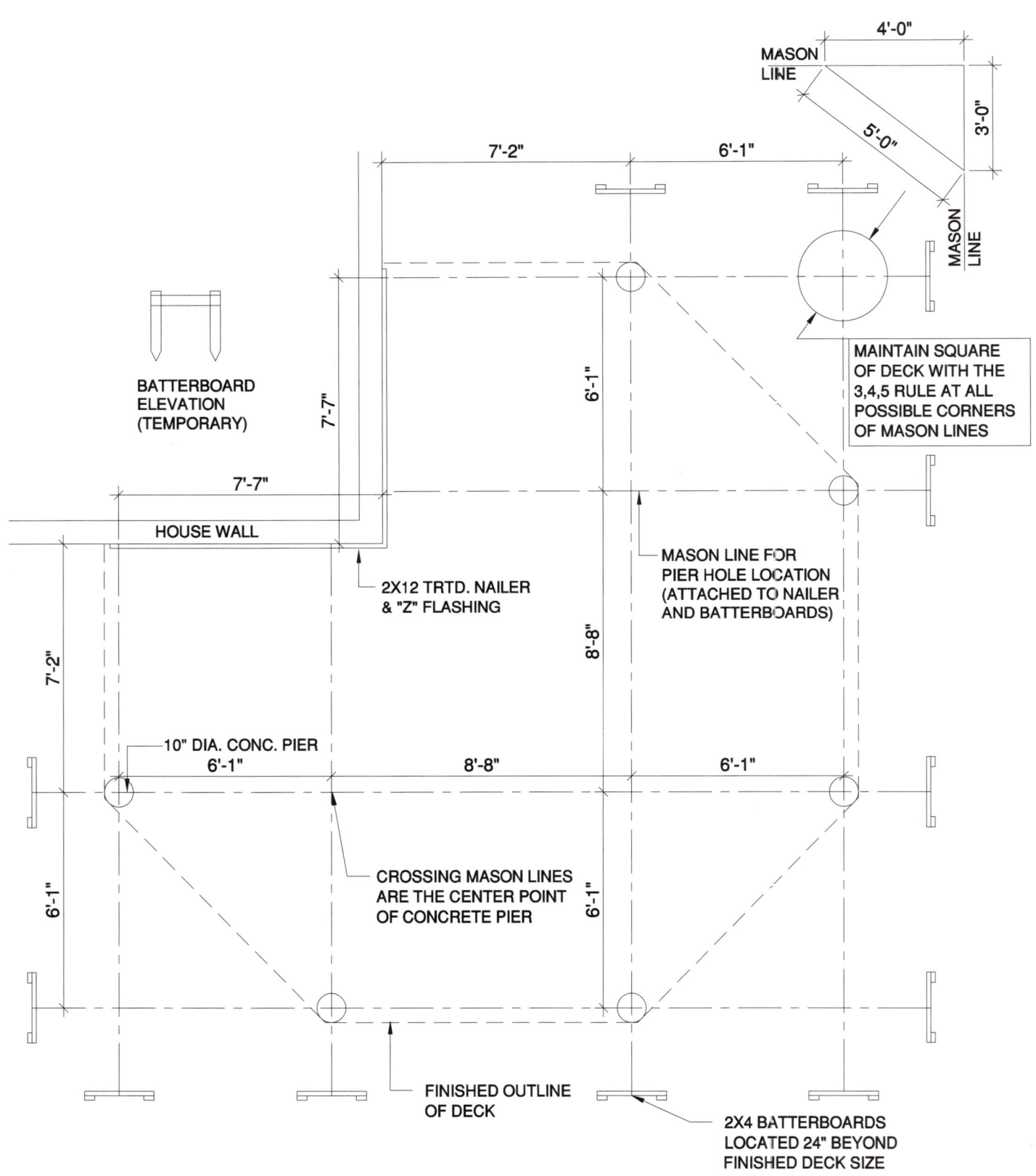

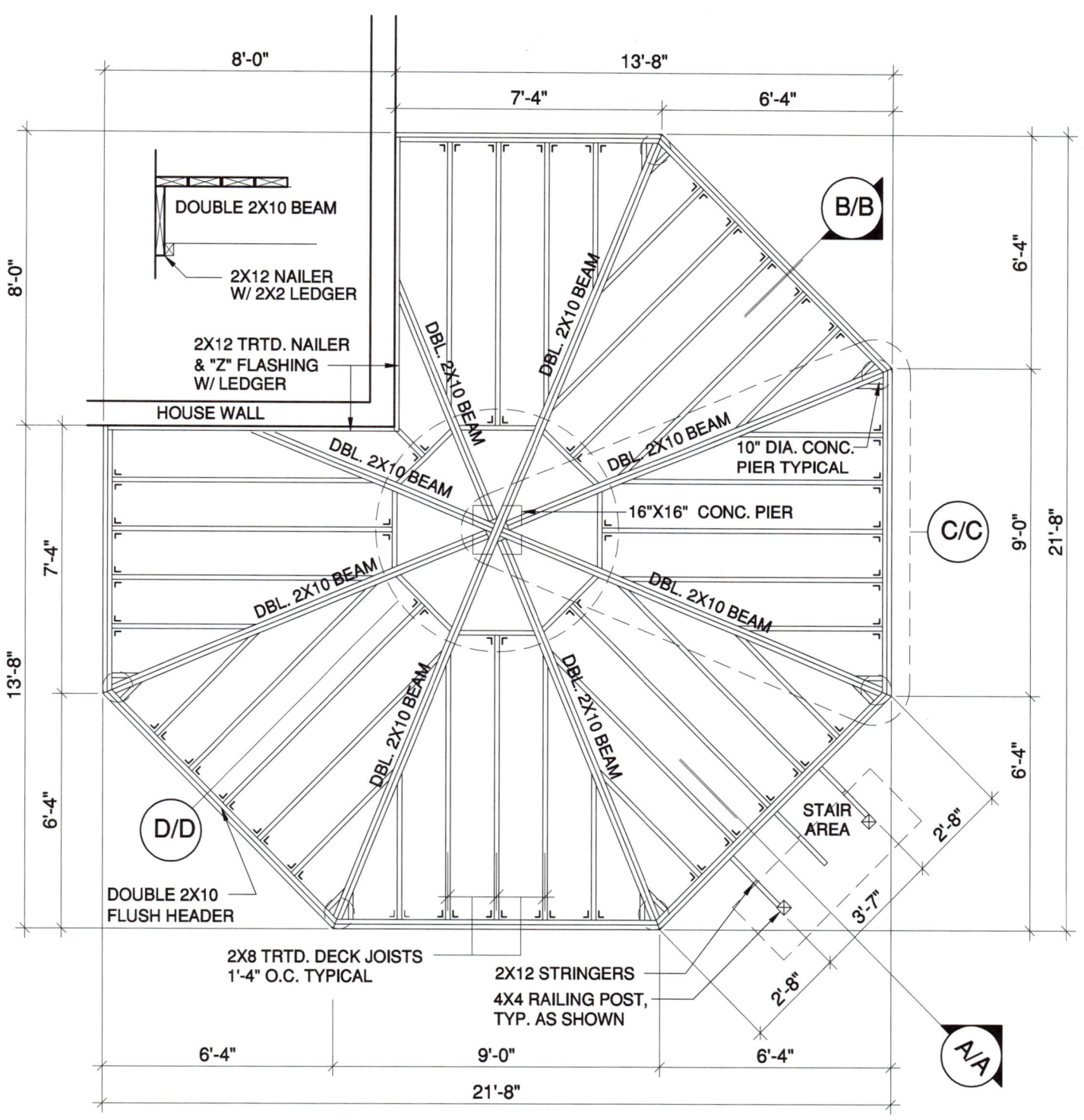

Irondale — Framing Plan

Scale: 1/4" = 1'-0"

www.homedepot.com 105

Irondale — Elevations

Scale: 1/4" = 1'-0"

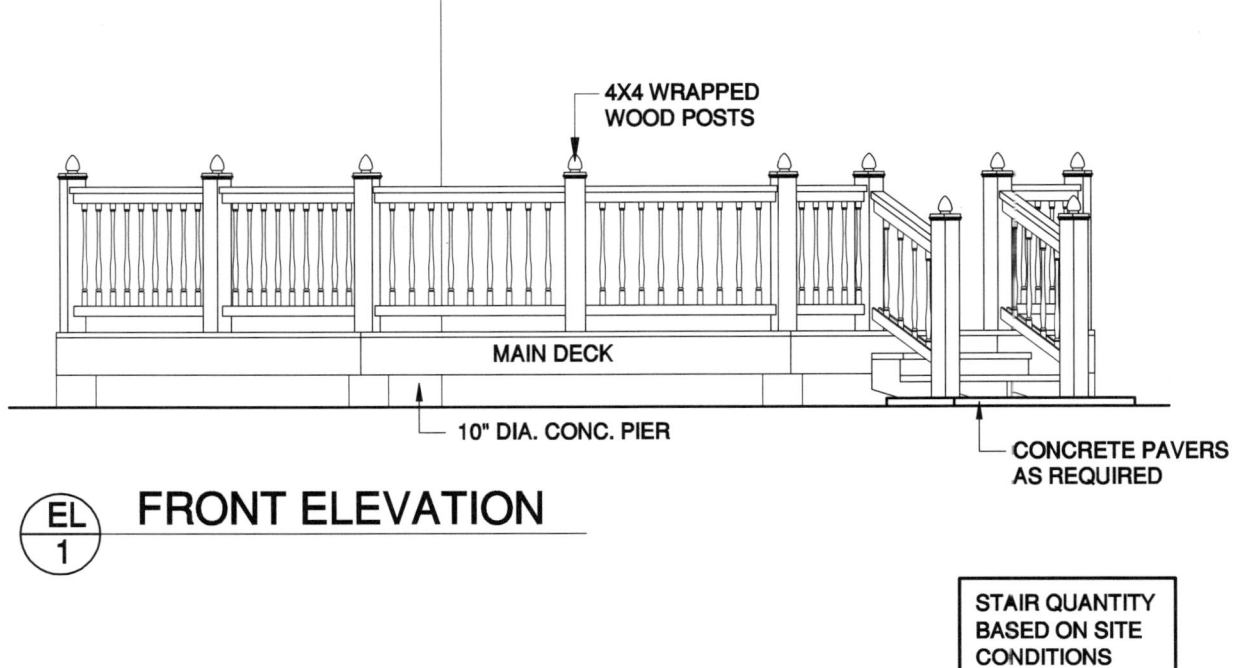

FRONT ELEVATION — EL/1

- 4X4 WRAPPED WOOD POSTS
- MAIN DECK
- 10" DIA. CONC. PIER
- CONCRETE PAVERS AS REQUIRED

STAIR QUANTITY BASED ON SITE CONDITIONS

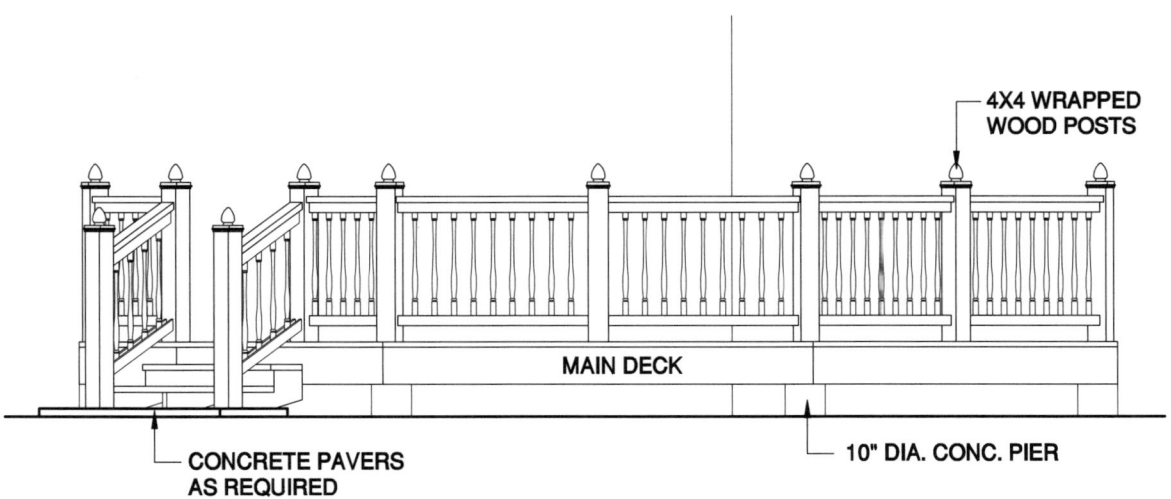

RIGHT ELEVATION — EL/2

- 4X4 WRAPPED WOOD POSTS
- MAIN DECK
- CONCRETE PAVERS AS REQUIRED
- 10" DIA. CONC. PIER

IRONDALE — Elevations

Scale: 1/4" = 1'-0"

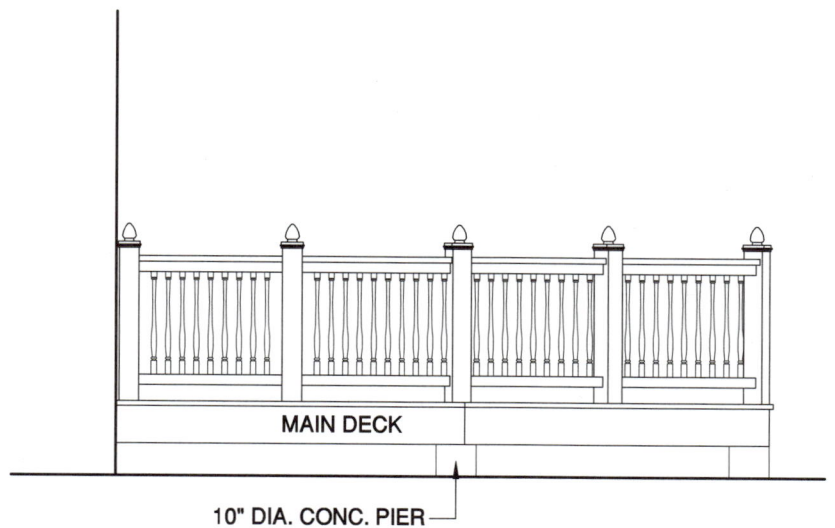

LEFT ELEVATION (EL/3)

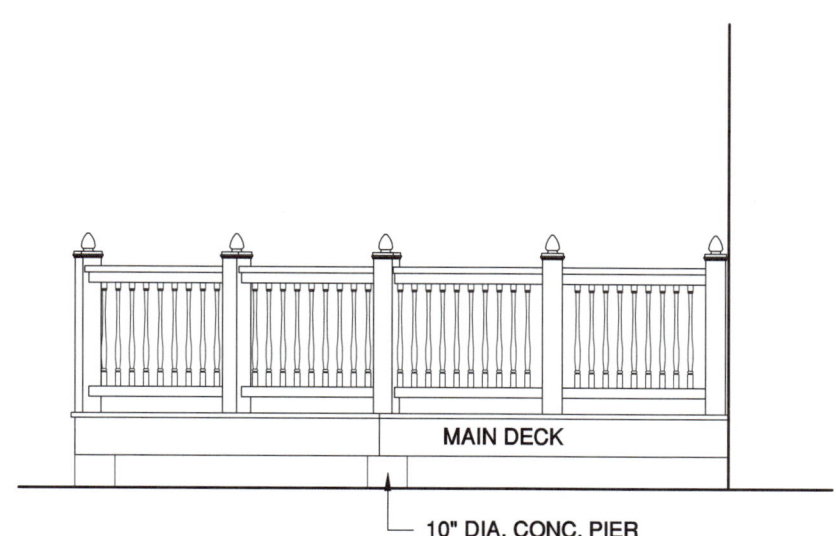

REAR ELEVATION (EL/4)

www.homedepot.com   107

IRONDALE Details

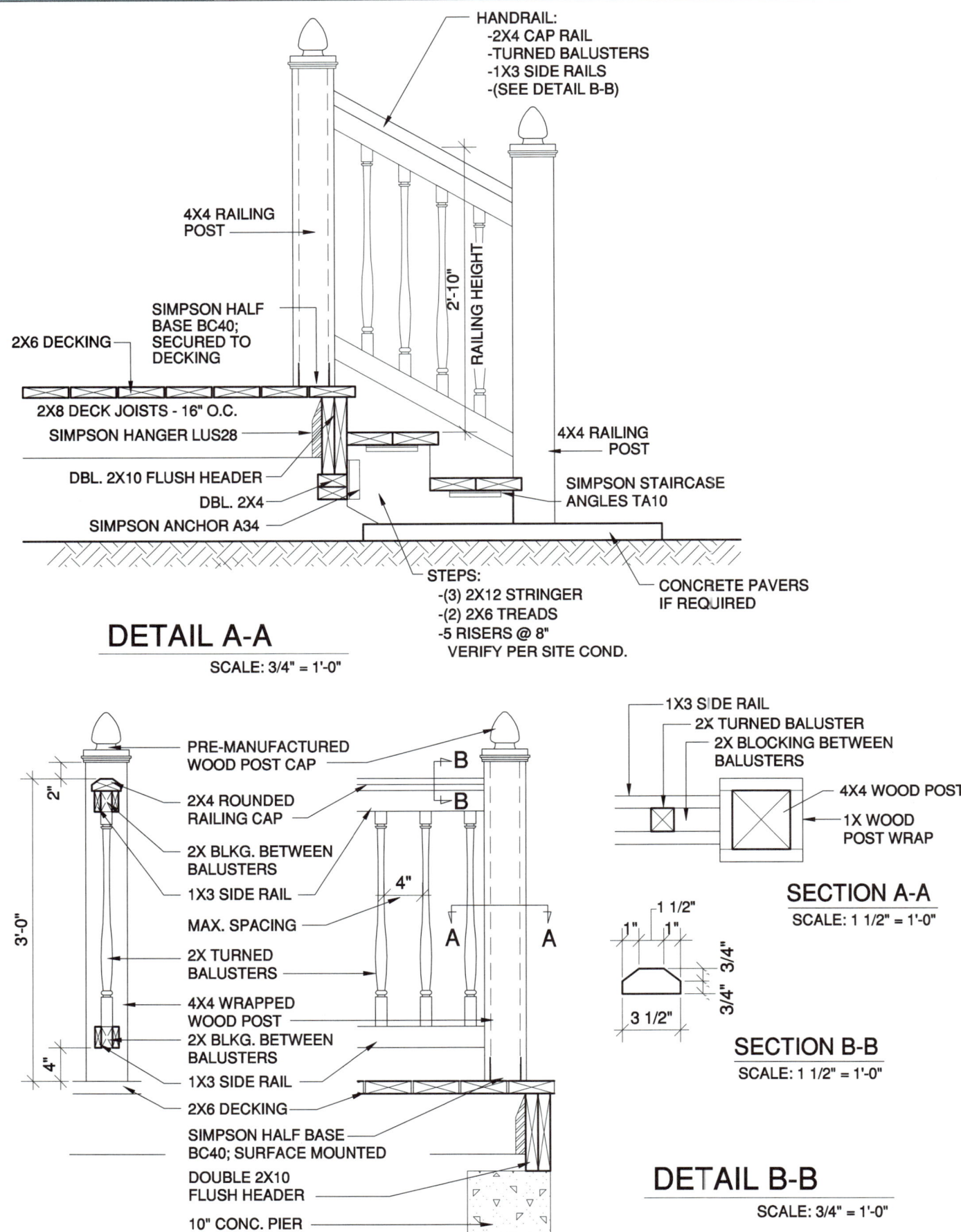

Irondale — Details

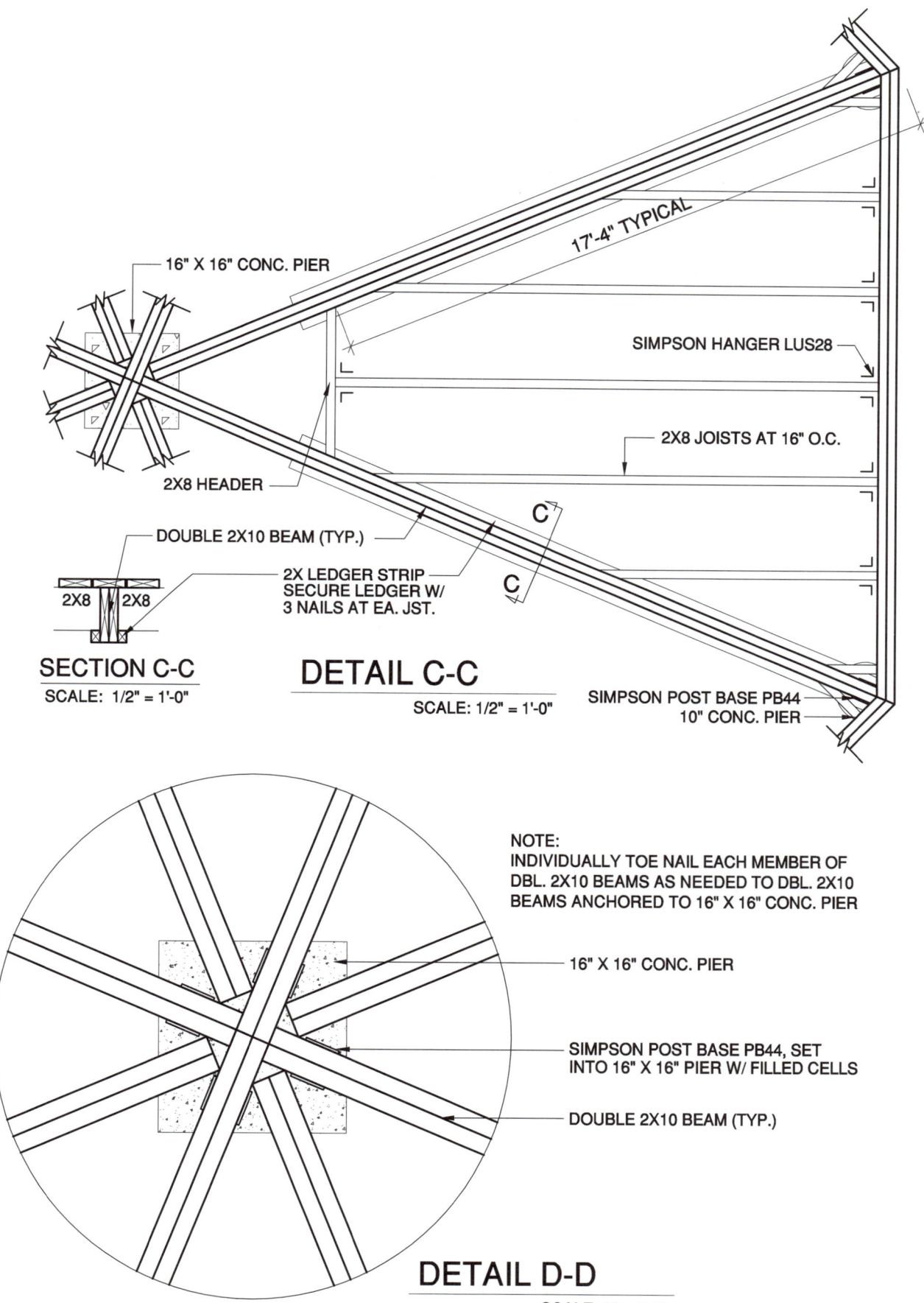

IRONDALE — Material List

FOUNDATION

Item	Location	Qty	UM
60# Concrete Mix	Pier	42	BG
10"x48" Fiber Tube	Pier	6	EA
2x4 - 10' Std. & Btr.	Batterboard	8	EA
2x12 - 10' Treated	Nailer	2	EA
2x2 - 10' Treated	Nailer	2	EA
Post Base (PB44)	Pier	10	EA
Crushed Gravel	Pier	16	BG
1x5 - 10' Zee Bar	Ledger	2	EA
5# 16d Galv. Nails	General Framing	1	EA
3/8"x4" Lag Screws	Ledger	24	EA
3/8"x1-1/2" Washer	Ledger	24	EA
10 oz. - Paintable Caulk	Ledger/Bolt	3	TB

FRAMING

Item	Location	Qty	UM
2x12 - 24' Treated	Beam	2	EA
2x10 - 8' Treated	Beam/Flush Hdr.	8	EA
2x10 - 12' Treated	Beam	8	EA
2x10 - 10' Treated	Flush Header	10	EA
2x2 - 8' Treated	Beam Ledger	4	EA
2x2 - 10' Treated	Beam Ledger	12	EA
2x8 - 8' Treated	Joist	28	EA
2x8 - 10' Treated	Joist	3	EA
2x4 - 10' Treated	Stair Nailer	2	EA
5# 16d Galv. Nails	General Framing	3	EA
2x8 Jst. Hanger (LUS28)	Ledger Joist	42	EA
Framing Anchor (A34)	End/Header Joist	2	EA
1# 8d 1-1/2" Hanger Nails	Connector	3	EA
5# 8d Zinc Ctd. Box Nails	General Framing	1	EA

FINISH/RAILING/SKIRTING

Item	Location	Qty	UM
4x4 - 8' Treated	Post	9	EA
Post Cap (BC40)	Post	16	EA
2x6 - 12' Treated	Decking/Stair Trd.	38	EA
2x6 - 16' Treated	Decking/Stair Trd.	28	EA
1# 2-1/2" Ctd. Screws	Decking/Railing	10	EA
2x12 - 16' Treated	Stringer	1	EA
3x5 Heavy Angle (HL35)	Stringer	6	EA
5/16"x1-1/2" Lag Screws	Heavy Angle	24	EA
2x4 - 8' Treated	Cap Rail	8	EA
1-3/8"x1-3/8" - 3' Trnd. Blstr.	Baluster	134	EA
1x3 - 8' Treated	Side Rail	32	EA
2x3 - 8' Treated	Railing	16	EA
5# 16d Galv. Nails	General Framing	2	EA
5# 8d Ctd. Box Nails	General Framing	1	EA
Post Cap	Post	18	EA
1x4 - 8' Treated	Post Wrap	18	EA
1x6 - 8' Treated	Post Wrap	18	EA

CHAPTER 5

THE PLYMOUTH

HPM-1111

This spacious deck is anchored by a lovely planter in each corner. The built-in bench adds additional seating beyond traditional patio furniture and accessories. Turned posts and spindles give the deck a country feel and create a unique and warm final touch.

Dimensions for this deck are 16' X 14'.

PLYMOUTH — Plan View

Scale: 1/4" = 1'-0"

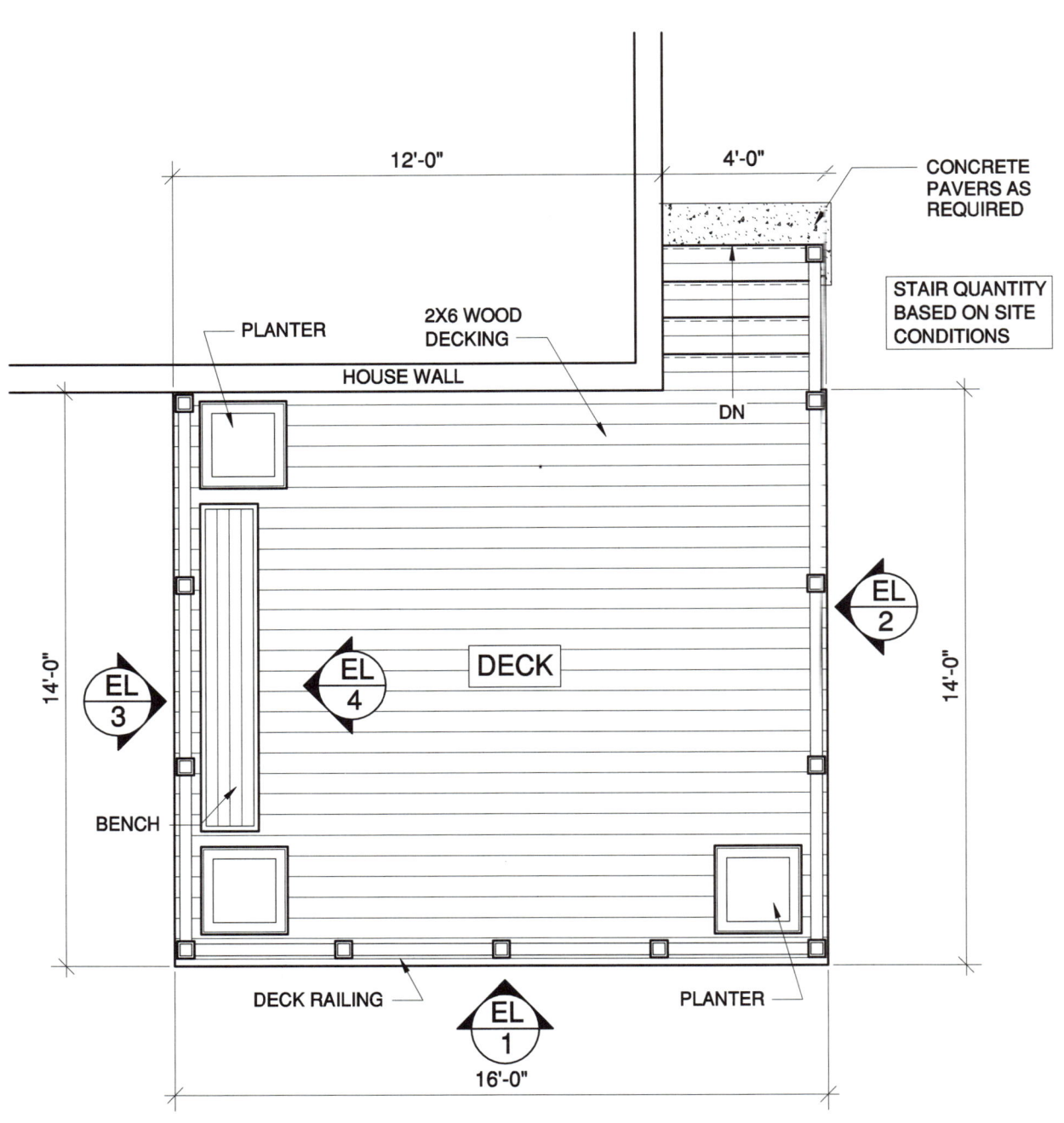

PLYMOUTH — Pier Layout

Scale: 1/4" = 1'-0"

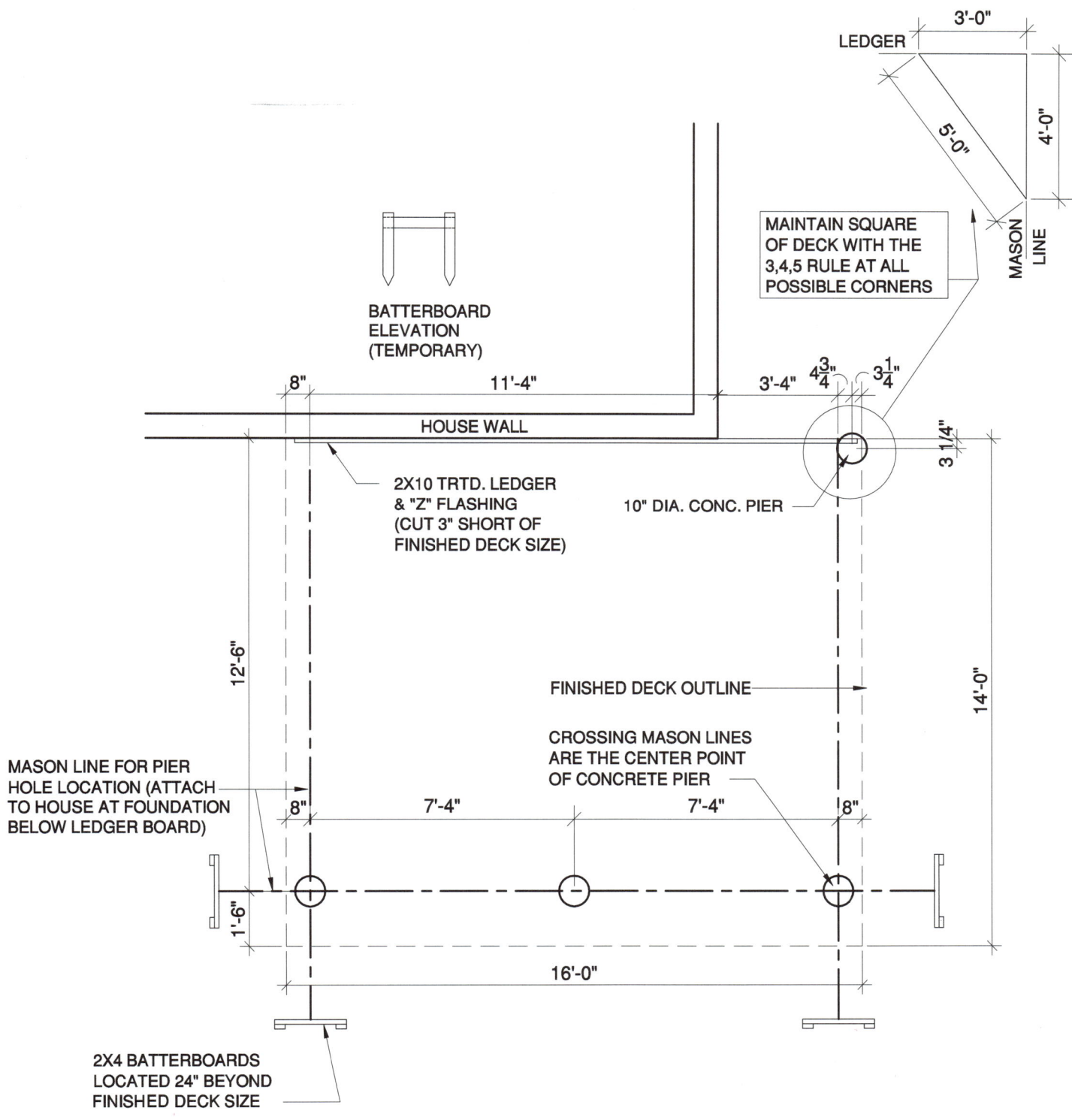

www.homedepot.com 113

Plymouth — Framing Plan

Scale: 1/4" = 1'-0"

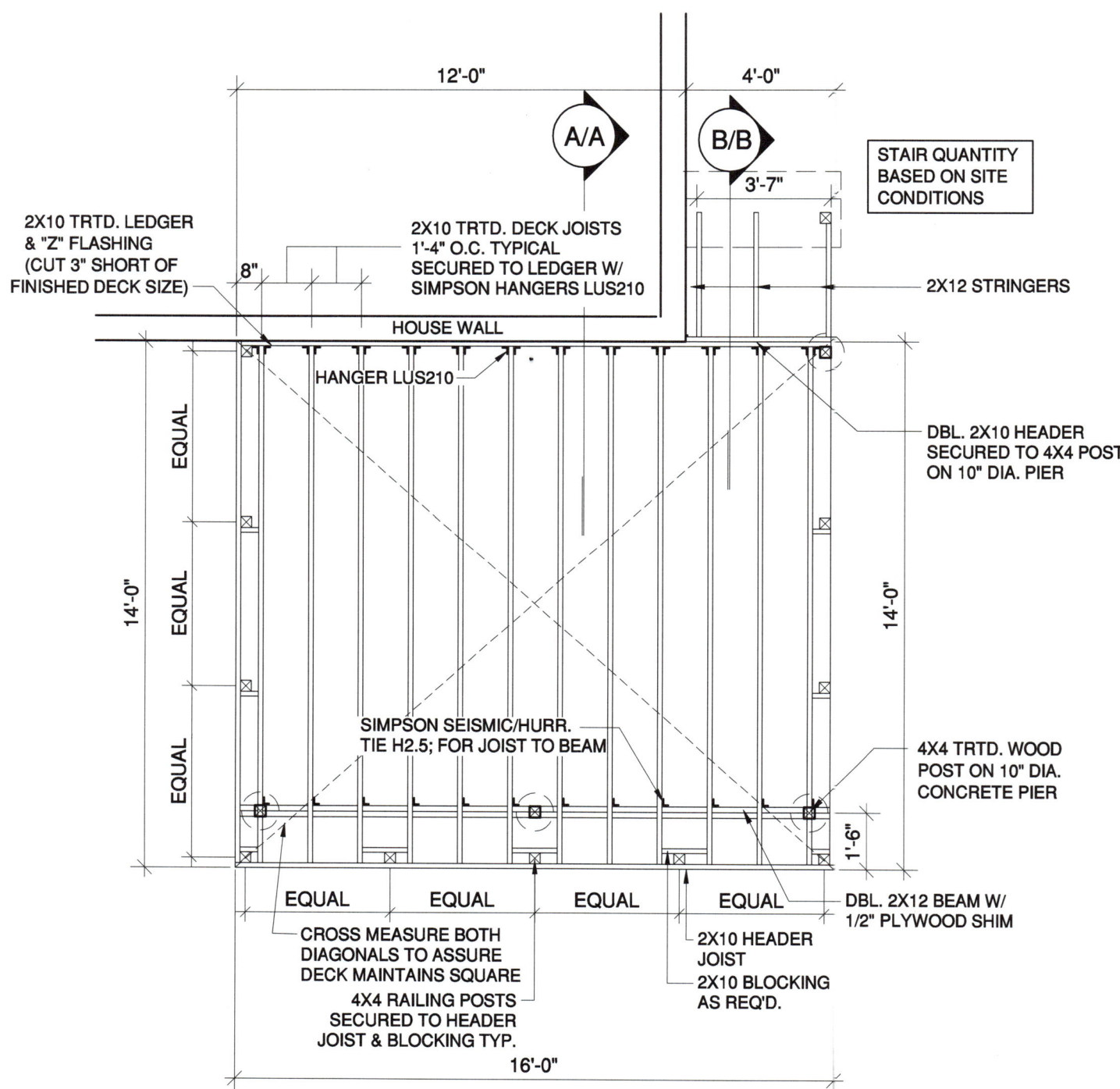

PLYMOUTH — Elevations

Scale: 1/4" = 1'-0"

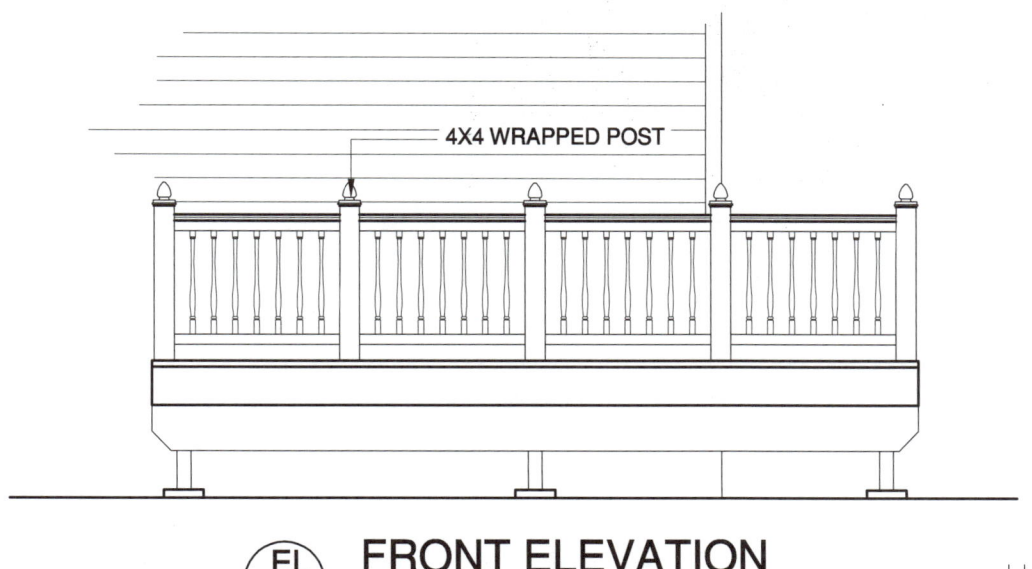

FRONT ELEVATION
EL/1

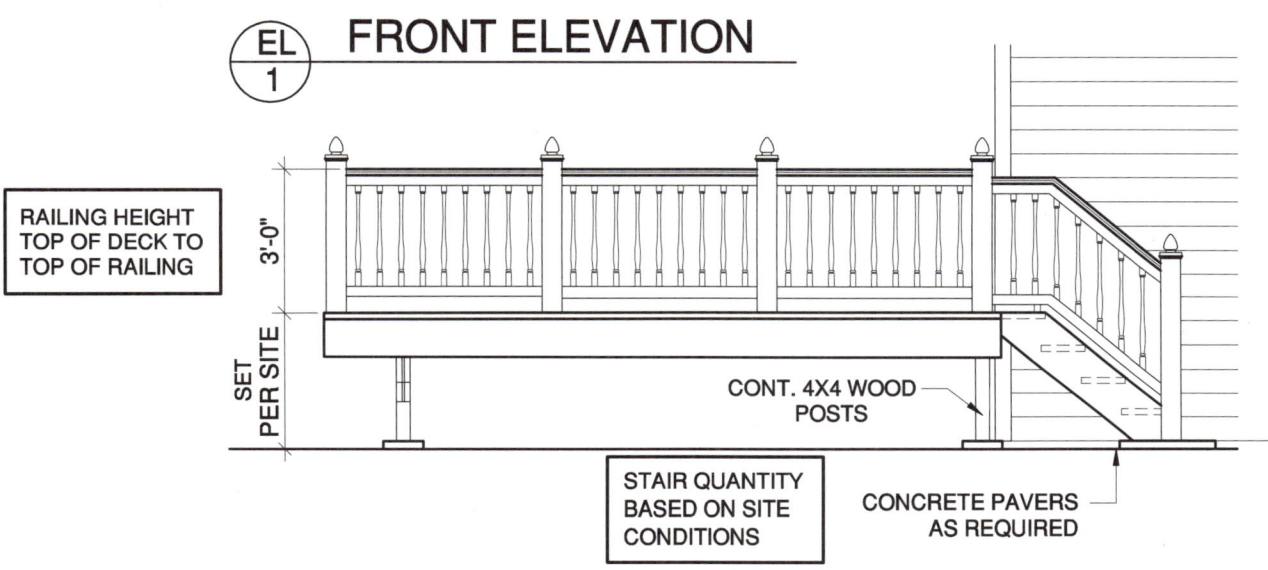

RAILING HEIGHT TOP OF DECK TO TOP OF RAILING

3'-0"

SET PER SITE

CONT. 4X4 WOOD POSTS

STAIR QUANTITY BASED ON SITE CONDITIONS

CONCRETE PAVERS AS REQUIRED

RIGHT ELEVATION
EL/2

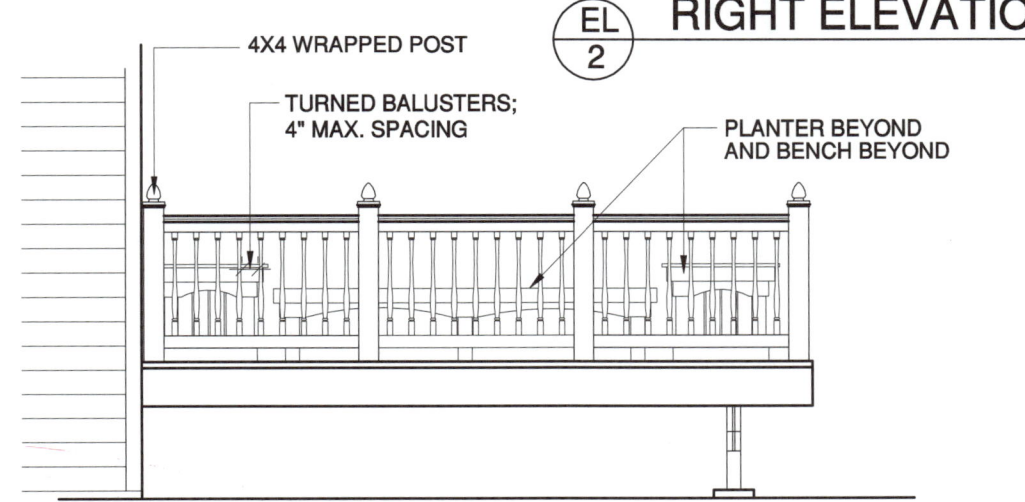

4X4 WRAPPED POST

TURNED BALUSTERS; 4" MAX. SPACING

PLANTER BEYOND AND BENCH BEYOND

LEFT ELEVATION
EL/3

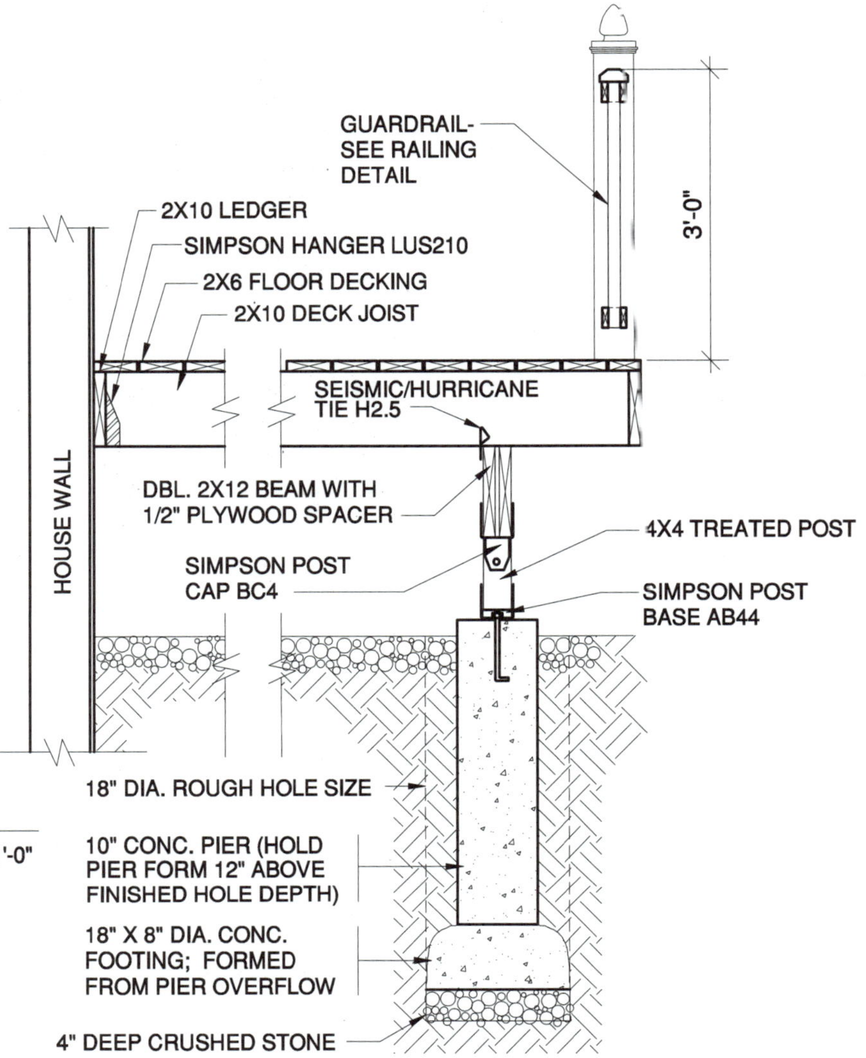

PLYMOUTH — Details

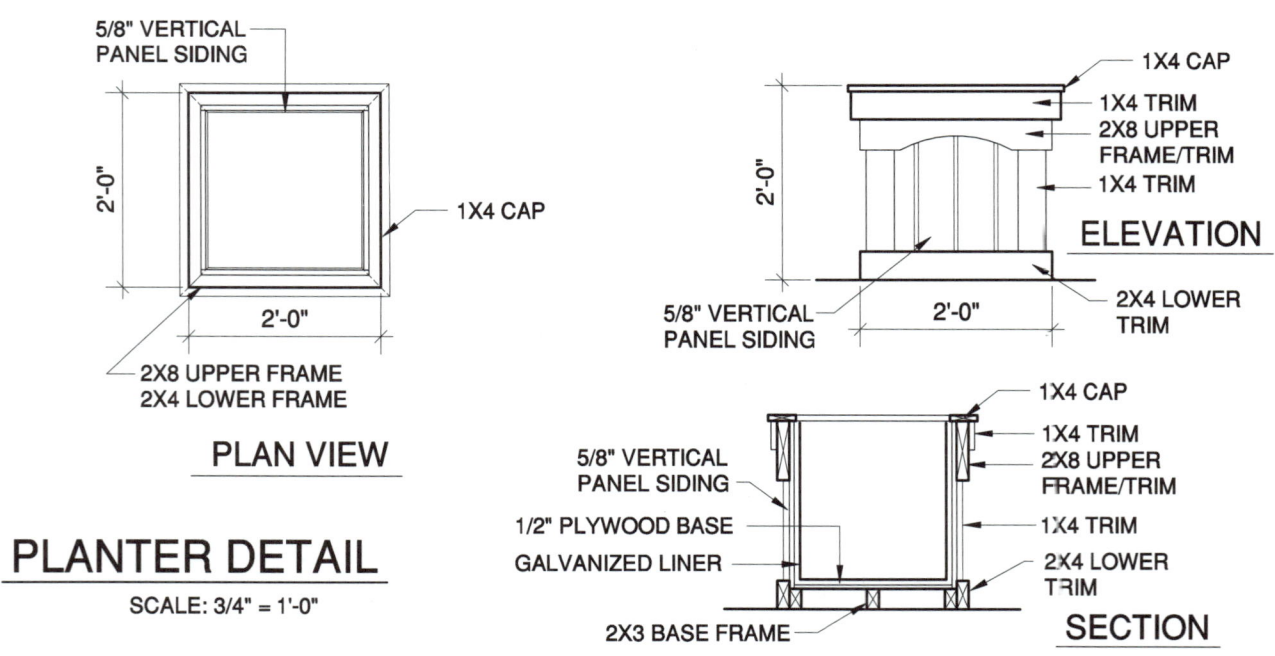

DETAIL A-A
SCALE: 1/2" = 1'-0"

- GUARDRAIL- SEE RAILING DETAIL
- 2X10 LEDGER
- SIMPSON HANGER LUS210
- 2X6 FLOOR DECKING
- 2X10 DECK JOIST
- SEISMIC/HURRICANE TIE H2.5
- DBL. 2X12 BEAM WITH 1/2" PLYWOOD SPACER
- 4X4 TREATED POST
- SIMPSON POST CAP BC4
- SIMPSON POST BASE AB44
- HOUSE WALL
- 3'-0"
- 18" DIA. ROUGH HOLE SIZE
- 10" CONC. PIER (HOLD PIER FORM 12" ABOVE FINISHED HOLE DEPTH)
- 18" X 8" DIA. CONC. FOOTING; FORMED FROM PIER OVERFLOW
- 4" DEEP CRUSHED STONE

PLANTER DETAIL
SCALE: 3/4" = 1'-0"

PLAN VIEW
- 5/8" VERTICAL PANEL SIDING
- 1X4 CAP
- 2X8 UPPER FRAME
- 2X4 LOWER FRAME
- 2'-0" x 2'-0"

ELEVATION
- 1X4 CAP
- 1X4 TRIM
- 2X8 UPPER FRAME/TRIM
- 1X4 TRIM
- 5/8" VERTICAL PANEL SIDING
- 2X4 LOWER TRIM
- 2'-0"

SECTION
- 1X4 CAP
- 1X4 TRIM
- 2X8 UPPER FRAME/TRIM
- 1X4 TRIM
- 2X4 LOWER TRIM
- 5/8" VERTICAL PANEL SIDING
- 1/2" PLYWOOD BASE
- GALVANIZED LINER
- 2X3 BASE FRAME

PLYMOUTH — Details

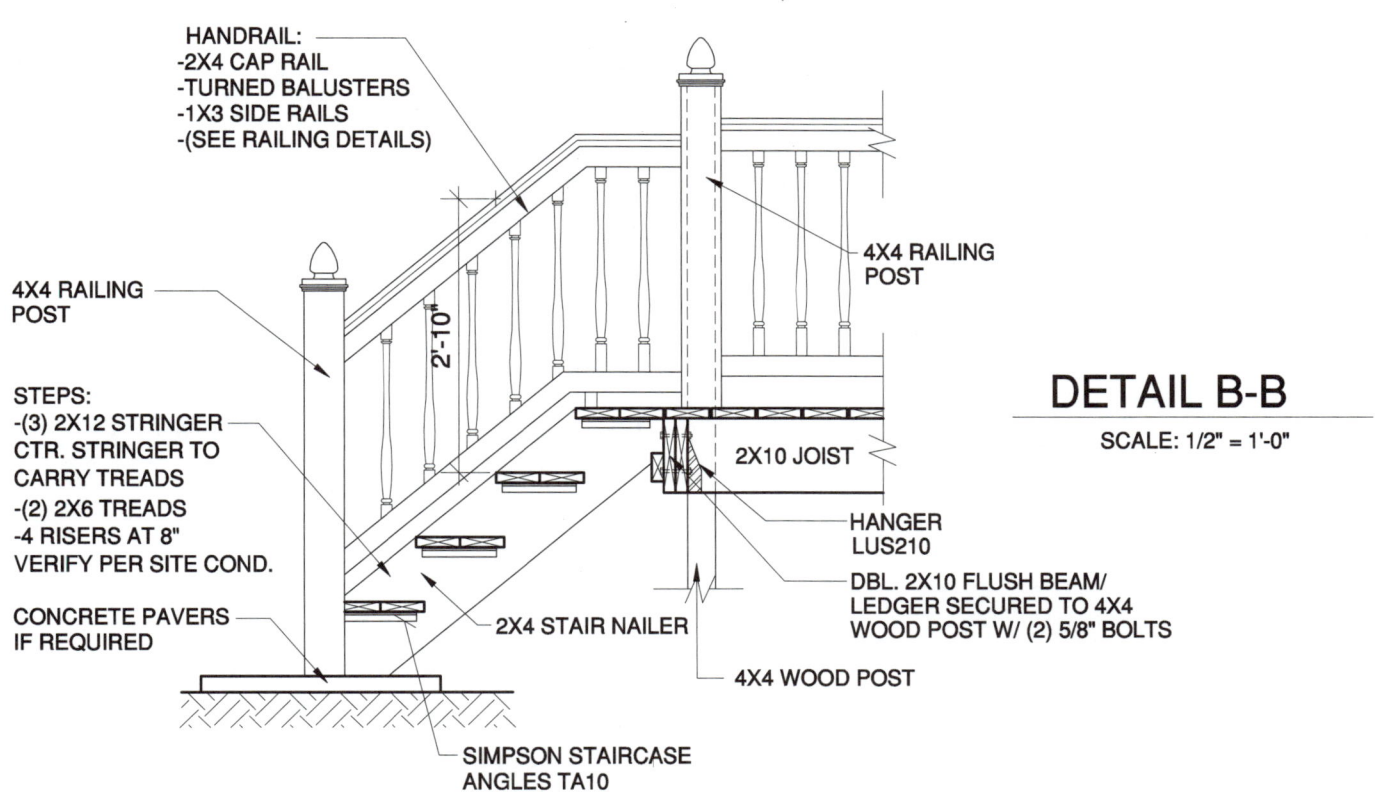

DETAIL B-B
SCALE: 1/2" = 1'-0"

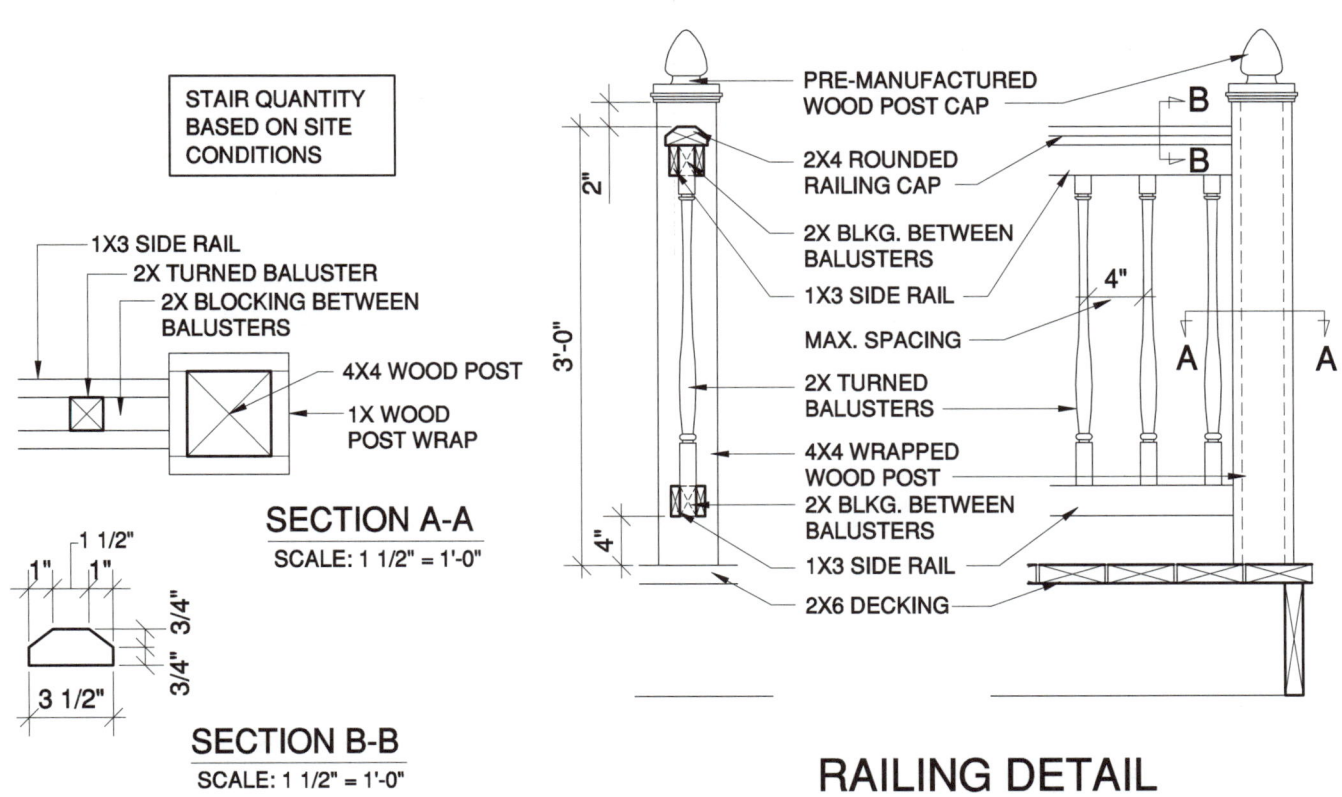

SECTION A-A
SCALE: 1 1/2" = 1'-0"

SECTION B-B
SCALE: 1 1/2" = 1'-0"

RAILING DETAIL
SCALE: 3/4" = 1'-0"

PLYMOUTH — Material List

FOUNDATION

Item	Location	Qty	UM
60# Concrete Mix	Pier	20	BG
10"x48" Fiber Tube	Pier	4	EA
2x4 - 10' Std. & Btr.	Batterboard	3	EA
1/2"x6" Anchor Bolt/Nut/Wash.	Pier	4	EA
Post Base (ABA44)	Pier	4	EA
Crushed Gravel	Pier	8	BG
2x10 - 16' Treated	Ledger	1	EA
1x5 - 10' Zee Bar	Ledger	2	EA
5# 6d Galv. Nails	General Framing	1	EA
3/8"x4" Lag Screws	Ledger	18	EA
3/8" x 1-1/2" Washer	Ledger	18	EA
10 oz. - Paintable Caulk	Ledger/Bolt	3	TB

FRAMING

Item	Location	Qty	UM
2x12 - 16' Treated	Beam	2	EA
2x10 - 14' Treated	Joist	14	EA
2x10 - 16' Treated	Joist/Blocking	3	EA
1/2" CDX - 5 Ply Plywd.	Beam	1	EA
4x4 - 8' Timber Post	Post	1	EA
Post Cap (PC44-16)	Post/Beam	3	EA
5# 16d Galv. Nails	General Framing	3	EA
2x10 Jst. Hngr. (LUS210)	Ledger Joist	12	EA
Hurricane Tie (H2.5)	Joist/Beam	12	EA
Framing Anchor (A34)	End/Header Joist	6	EA
1# 8d 1-1/2" Hanger Nails	Connector	3	EA
5# 8d Ctd. Box Nails	General Framing	1	EA

FINISH/RAILING/SKIRTING

Item	Location	Qty	UM
4x4 - 10' Treated	Post	6	EA
3/8"x4" Lag Screws	Post	24	EA
3/8"x1-1/2" Washer	Post	24	EA
2x6 - 16' Treated	Decking/Stair Trd.	31	EA
1# 2-1/2" Ctd. Screws	Decking/Railing	10	EA
2x12 - 16' Treated	Stringer	1	EA
3x5 Heavy Angle (HL35)	Stringer	5	EA
5/16"x1-1/2" Lag Screws	Heavy Angle	20	EA
2x4 - 10' Treated	Cap Rail	6	EA
1x3 - 10' Treated	Side Rail	24	EA
2x3 - 10' Treated	Blstr. Blocking	12	EA
1-3/8"x1-3/8" - 3' Trnd. Blstr.	Baluster	94	EA
Post Cap	Post	12	EA
1x4 - 10' Treated	Post Wrap	12	EA
1x6 - 10' Treated	Post Wrap	12	EA
2x4 - 8' Treated	Bench	7	EA
2x6 - 8' Treated	Bench	2	EA
4x4 - 8' Treated	Bench	1	EA
1x4 - 8' Treated	Planter	13	EA
2x8 - 8' Treated	Planter	3	EA
2x4 - 8' Treated	Planter	3	EA
2x3 - 10' Treated	Planter	3	EA
1/2" CDX - 5 Ply Plywd.	Planter	2	EA
5/8" T1-11 Siding	Planter	3	EA
5# 16d Galv. Nails	General Framing	2	EA
5# 8d Ctd. Box Nails	General Framing	1	EA

HIGHBRIDGE Plan View

Scale: 1/4" = 1'-0"

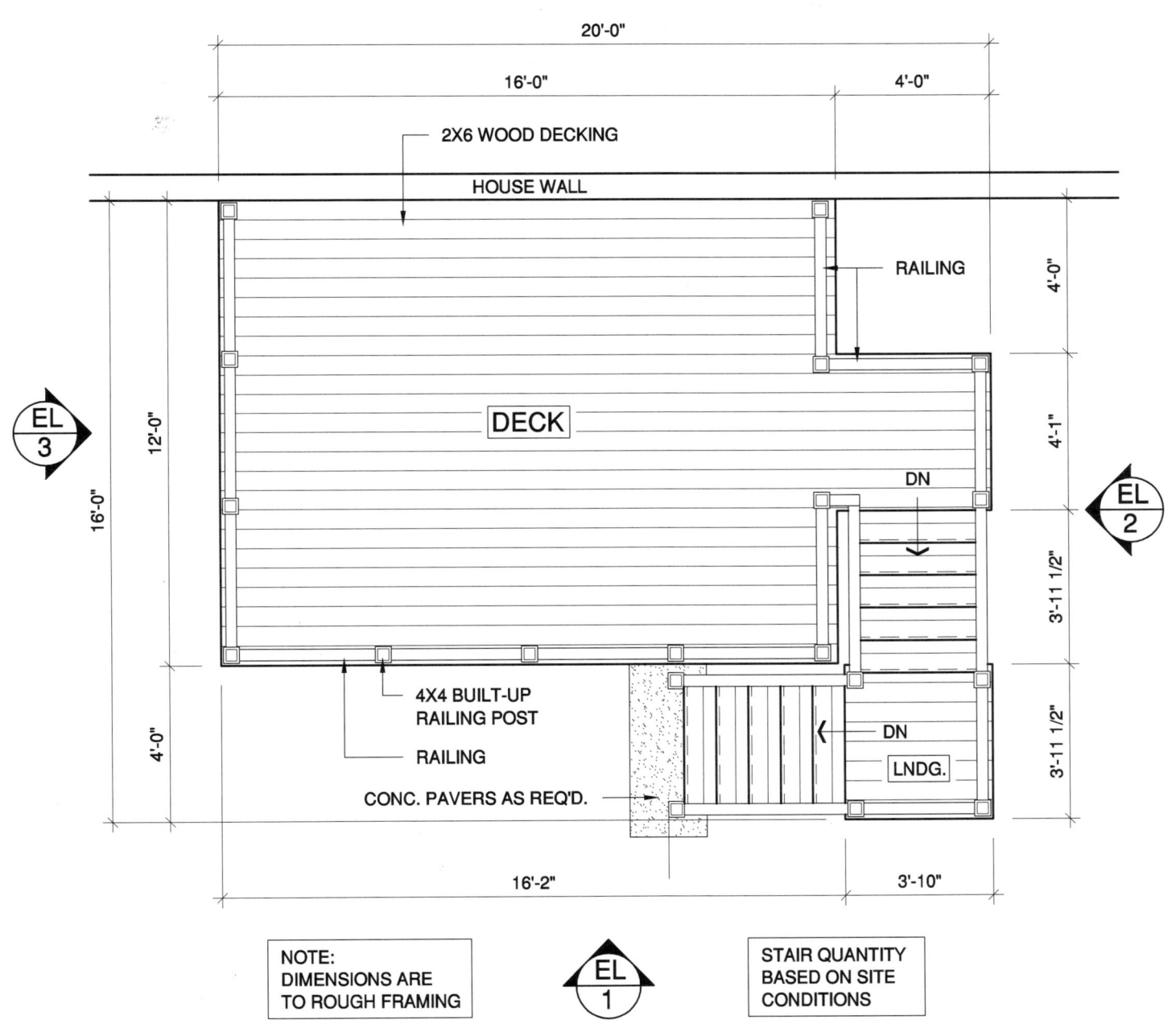

www.homedepot.com

HIGHBRIDGE — Pier Layout

Scale: 1/4" = 1'-0"

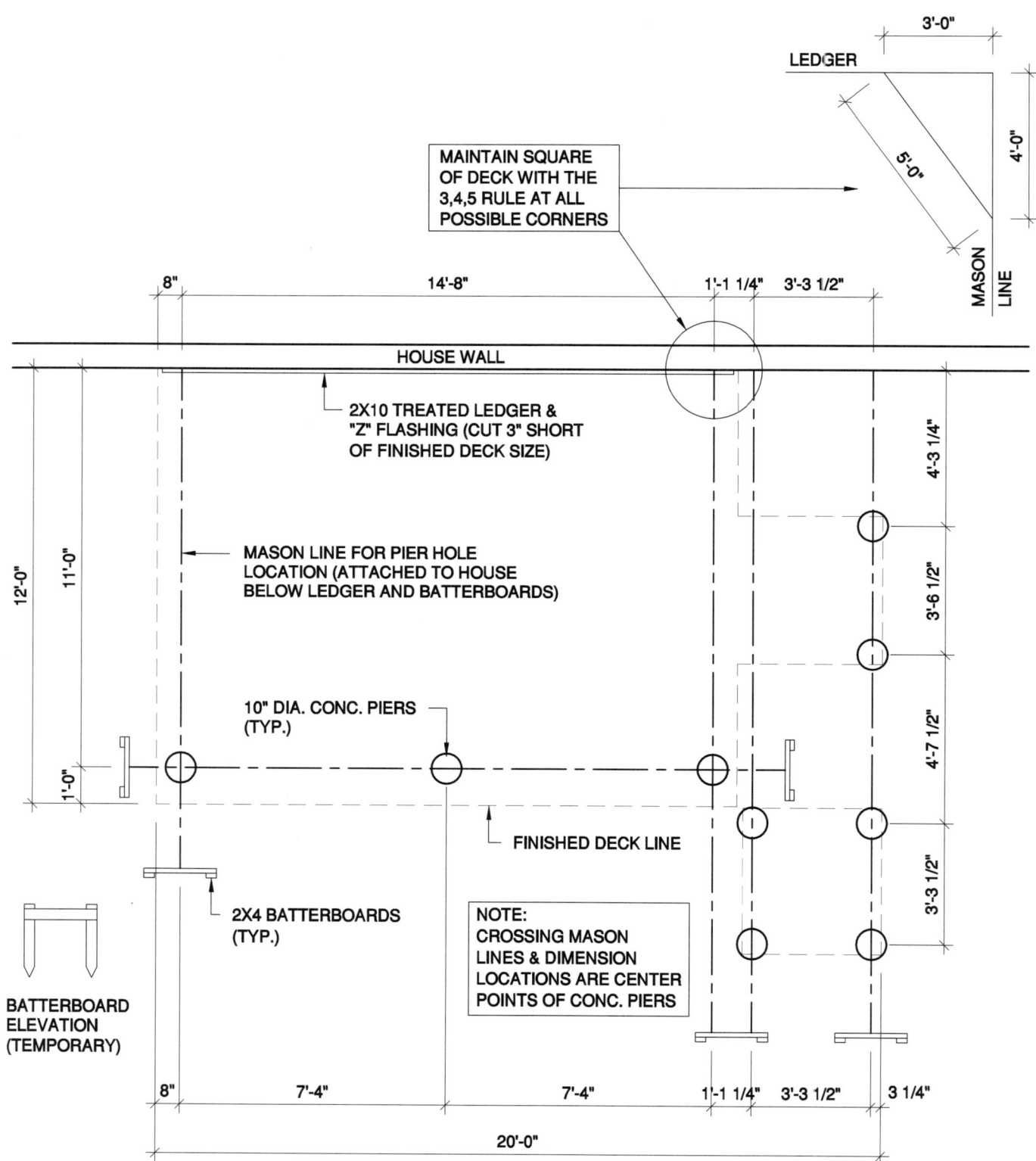

HIGHBRIDGE — Framing Plan

Scale: 1/4" = 1'-0"

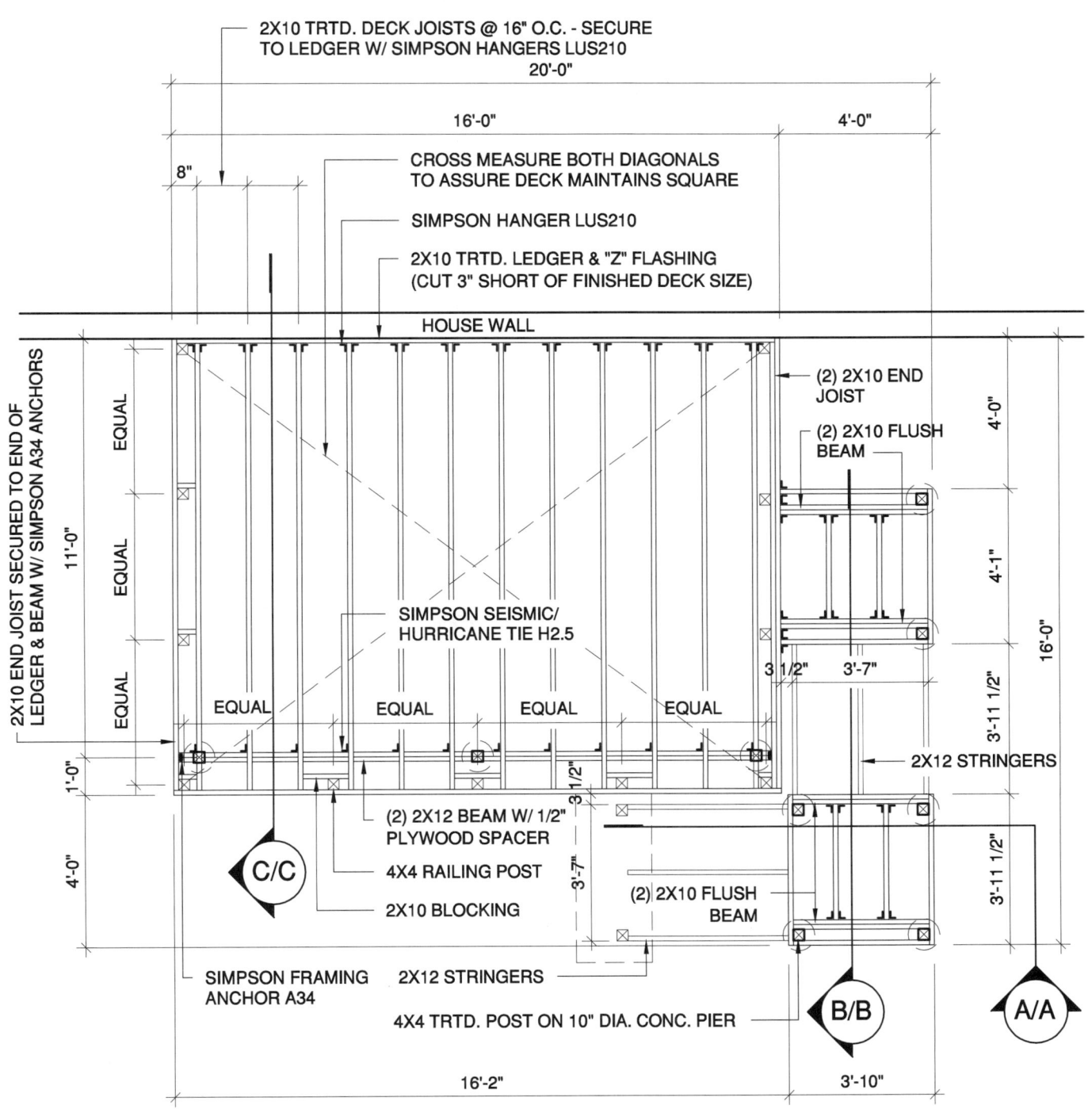

www.homedepot.com 123

HIGHBRIDGE — Elevations

Scale: 1/4" = 1'-0"

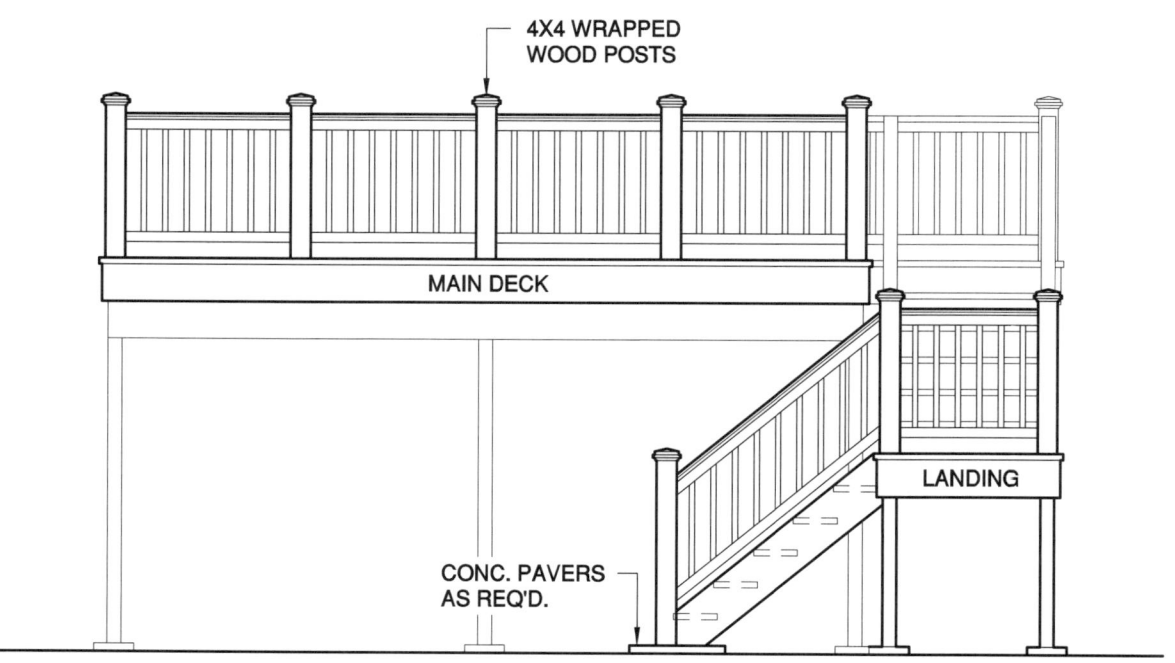

EL/1 **FRONT ELEVATION**

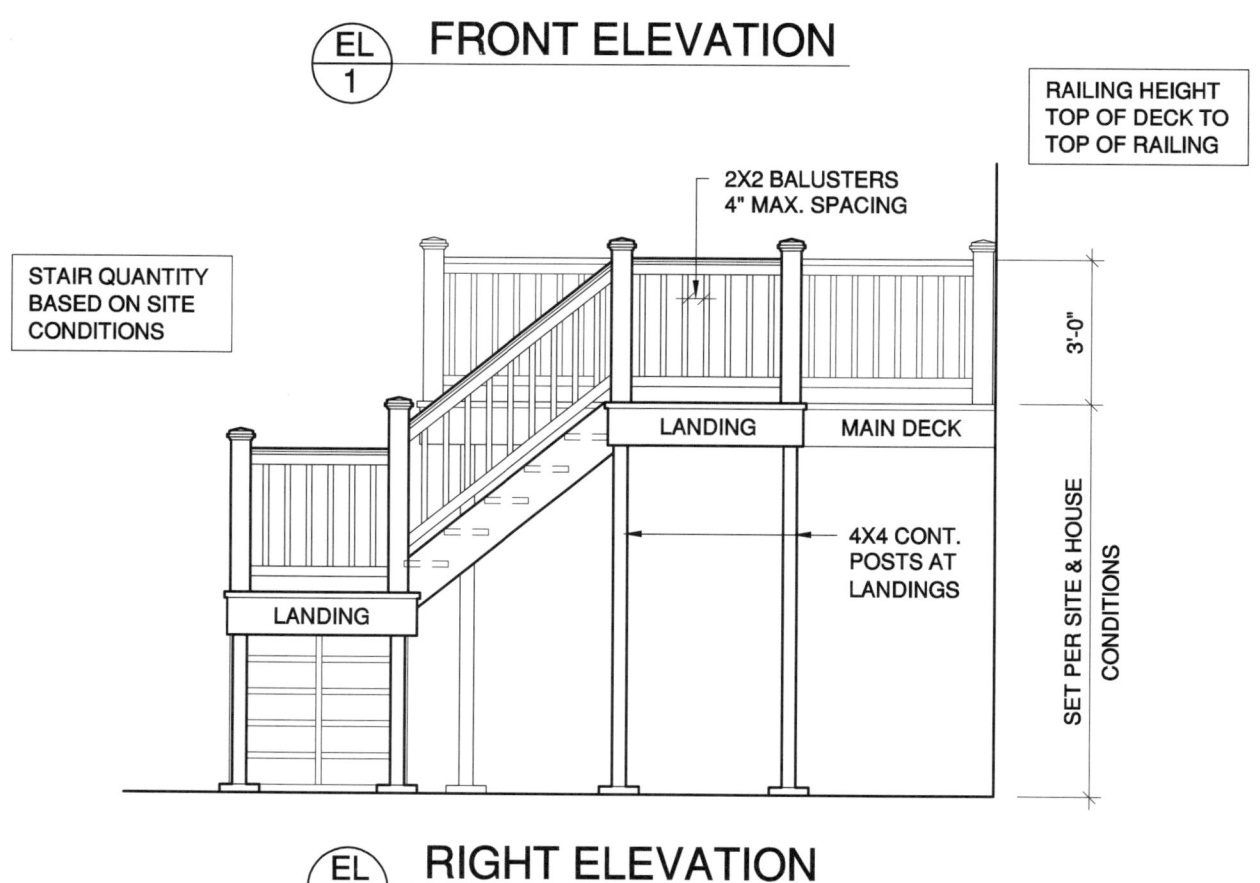

EL/2 **RIGHT ELEVATION**

HIGHBRIDGE — Elevation and Details

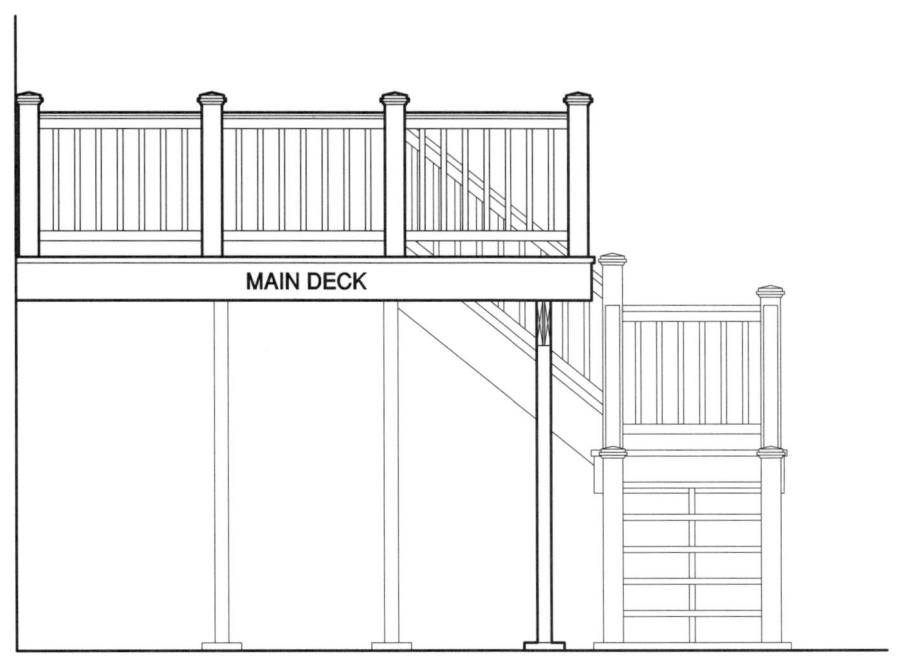

LEFT ELEVATION
SCALE: 1/4" = 1'-0"
EL/3

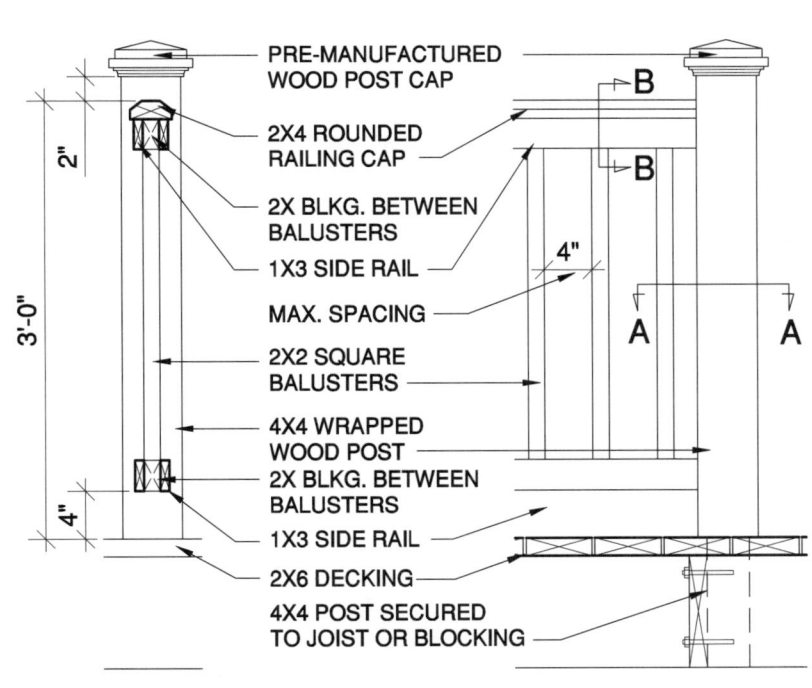

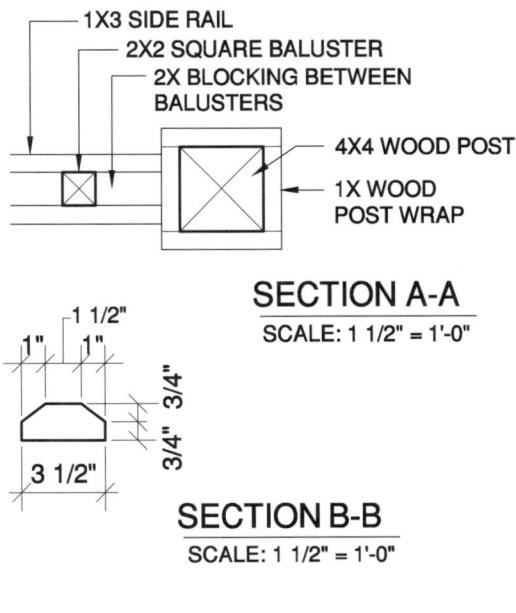

SECTION A-A
SCALE: 1 1/2" = 1'-0"

SECTION B-B
SCALE: 1 1/2" = 1'-0"

RAILING DETAILS
SCALE: 3/4" = 1'-0"

www.homedepot.com — 125

HIGHBRIDGE Sections

Scale: 3/8" = 1'-0"

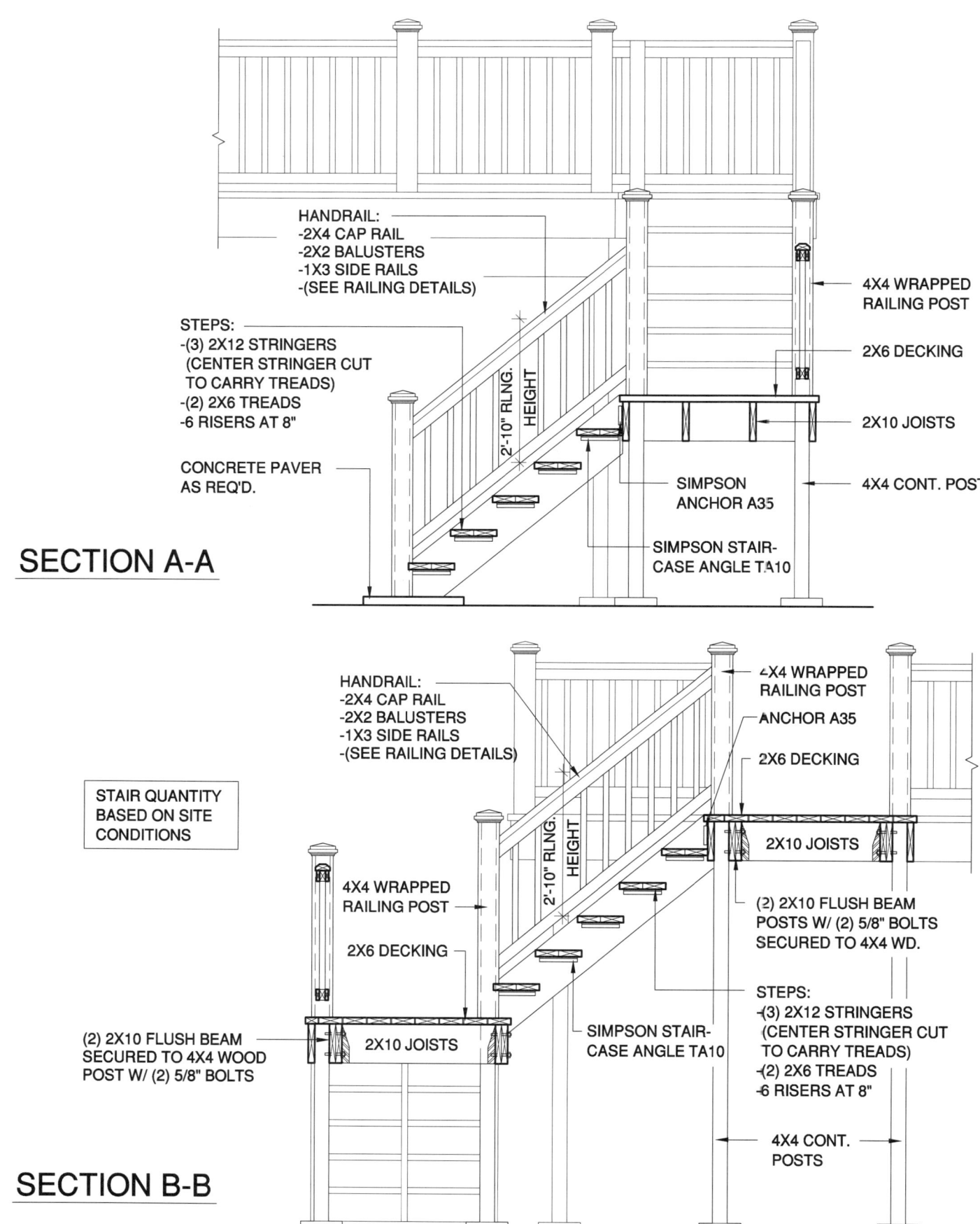

SECTION A-A

SECTION B-B

HIGHBRIDGE — Section

Scale: 1/2" = 1'-0"

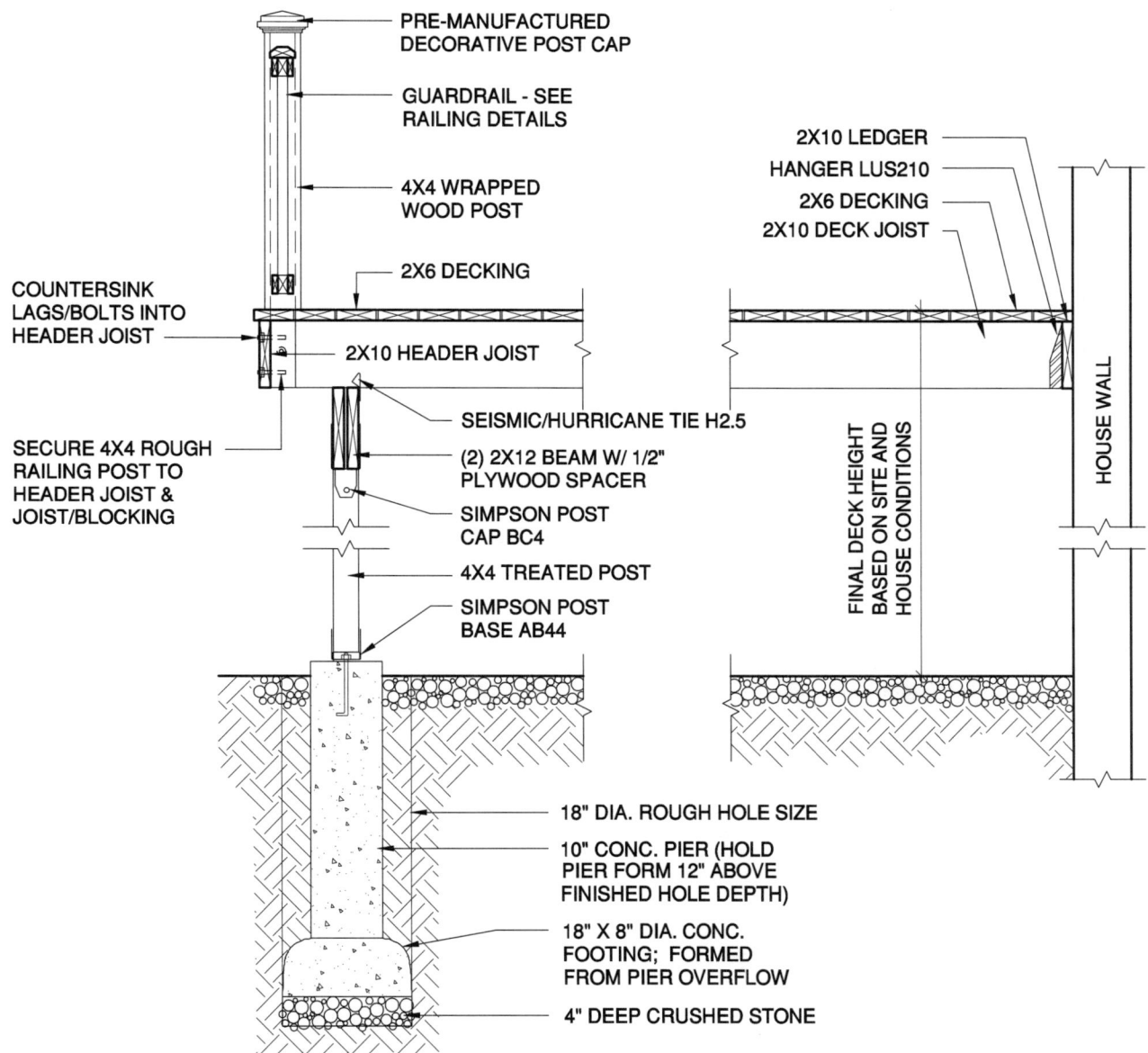

SECTION C-C

HIGHBRIDGE Material List

FOUNDATION

Item	Location	Qty	UM
60# Concrete Mix	Pier	45	BG
10"x48" Fiber Tube	Pier	9	EA
2x4 - 10' Std. & Btr.	Batterboard	3	EA
1/2"x6" Anchor Bolt/Nut/Wash.	Pier	9	EA
Post Base (ABA44)	Pier	9	EA
Crushed Gravel	Pier	18	BG
2x10 - 16' Treated	Ledger	1	EA
1x5 - 10' Zee Bar	Ledger	2	EA
5# 16d Galv. Nails	General Framing	1	EA
3/8"x4" Lag Screws	Ledger	24	EA
3/8"x1-1/2" Washer	Ledger	24	EA
10 oz. - Paintable Caulk	Ledger/Bolt	3	TB

FRAMING

Item	Location	Qty	UM
2x12 - 16' Treated	Beam	2	EA
2x10 - 16' Treated	Joist/Flush Beam	1	EA
2x10 - 12' Treated	Header Joist	21	EA
1/2" CDX - 5 Ply Plywd.	Beam/Spacer	1	EA
4x4 - 8' Treated	Post	5	EA
4x4 - 10' Treated	Post	2	EA
4x4 - 12' Treated	Post	2	EA
Post Cap (PC44-16)	Post/Beam	3	EA
5# 16d Galv. Nails	General Framing	3	EA
2x10 Jst. Hngr. (LUS210)	Ledger Joist	22	EA
2x10 Jst. Hngr. (LUS210-2)	Ledger Joist	2	EA
Hurricane Tie (H2.5)	Joist/Beam	12	EA
Framing Anchor (A34)	End/Header Joist	6	EA
1# 8d 1-1/2" Hanger Nails	Connector	3	EA
5# 8d Ctd. Box Nails	General Framing	5	EA

FINISH/RAILING/SKIRTING

Item	Location	Qty	UM
4x4 - 8' Treated	Post	7	EA
3/8"x4" Lag Screws	Post	28	EA
3/8"x1-1/2" Washer	Post	28	EA
2x6 - 12' Treated	Decking/Stair Trd.	24	EA
2x6 - 16' Treated	Decking/Stair Trd.	18	EA
1# 2-1/2" Ctd. Screws	Decking/Railing	10	EA
2x12 - 16' Treated	Stringer	3	EA
3x5 Heavy Angle (HL35)	Stringer	12	EA
5/16"x1-1/2" Lag Screws	Heavy Angle	36	EA
Framing Angle (A34)	Tread	20	EA
2x4 - 8' Treated	Cap Rail	12	EA
1-3/8"x1-3/8" - 3' Sq. Cut Blstr.	Baluster	136	EA
5# 16d Galv. Nails	General Framing	2	EA
5# 8d Ctd. Box Nails	General Framing	1	EA
1x3 - 8' Treated	Side Rail	36	EA
2x3 - 8' Treated	Rail Blocking	24	EA
1x4 - 8' Treated	Post Wrap	20	EA
1x6 - 8' Treated	Post Wrap	20	EA
Wood Post Cap	Post	20	EA

CHAPTER 5

THE LONGVIEW

HPM-1107

Want privacy from a busy street, close neighbors or unwanted noise? This deck's lattice wall performs double duty as a privacy fence and a source for shade. Grow vines on the lattice for a natural touch. This durable deck will be enjoyed for years to come.

Dimensions for this deck are 16' X 14'.

Longview

Plan View

Scale: 1/4" = 1'-0"

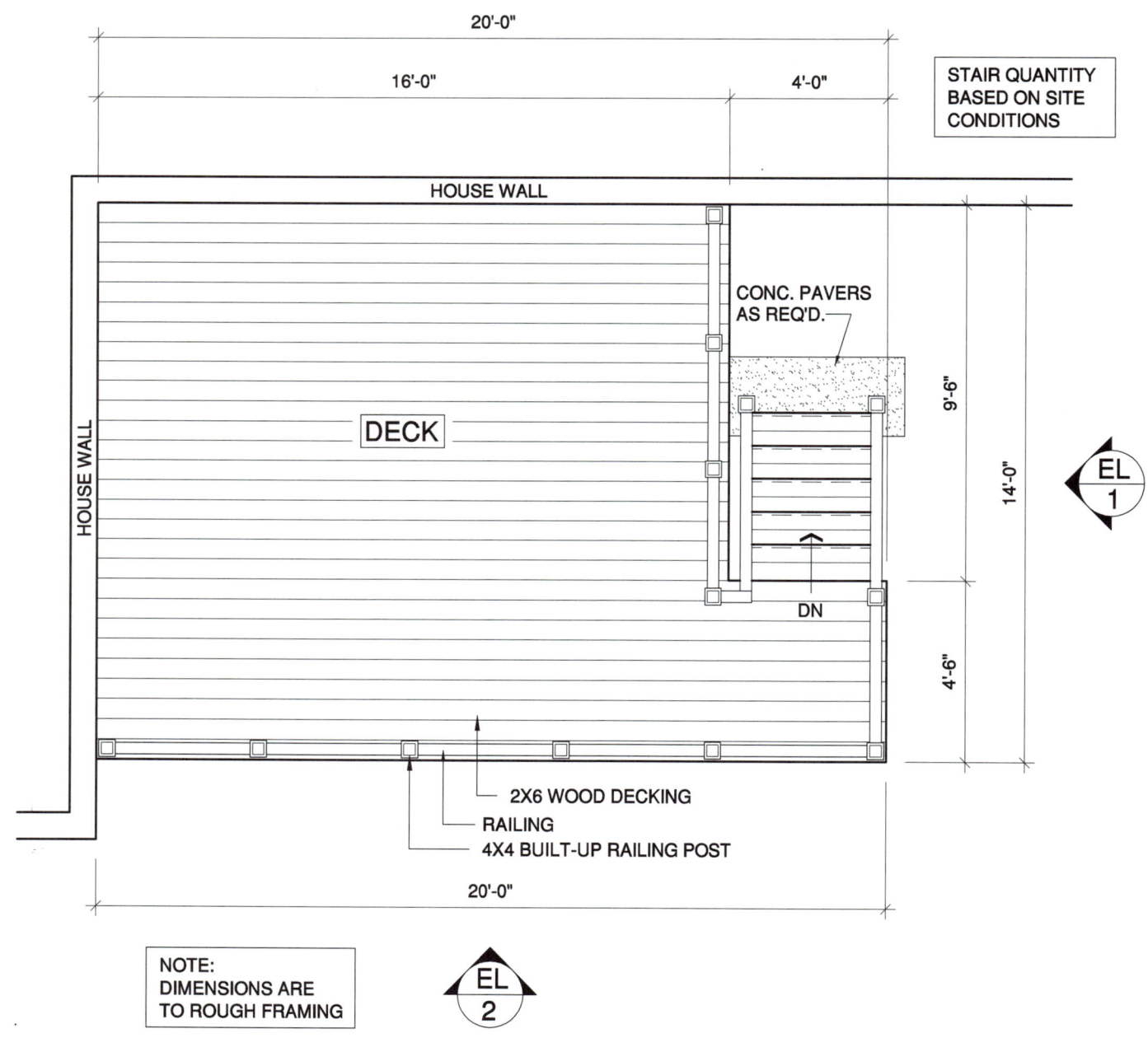

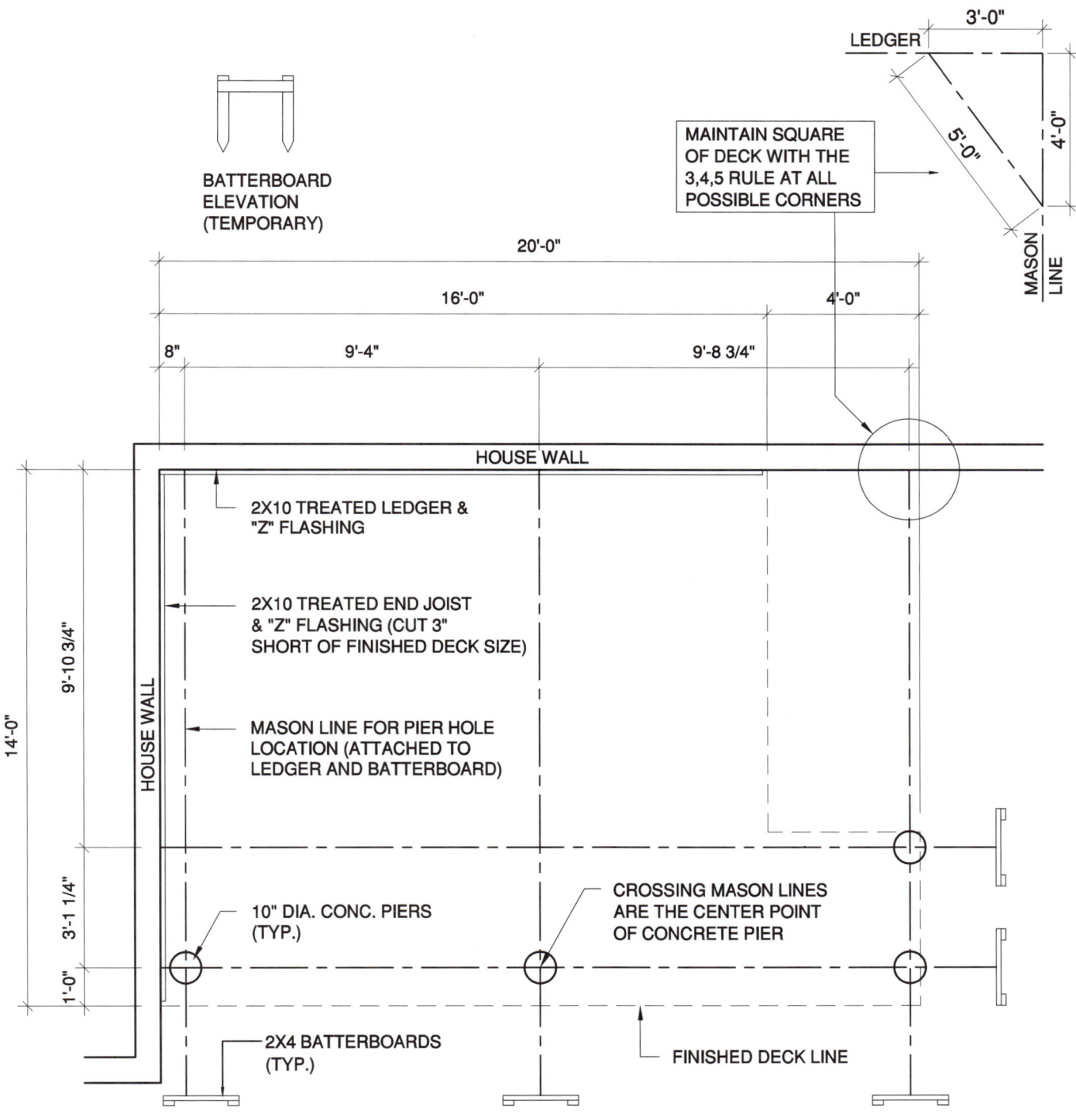

LONGVIEW — Framing Plan

Scale: 1/4" = 1'-0"

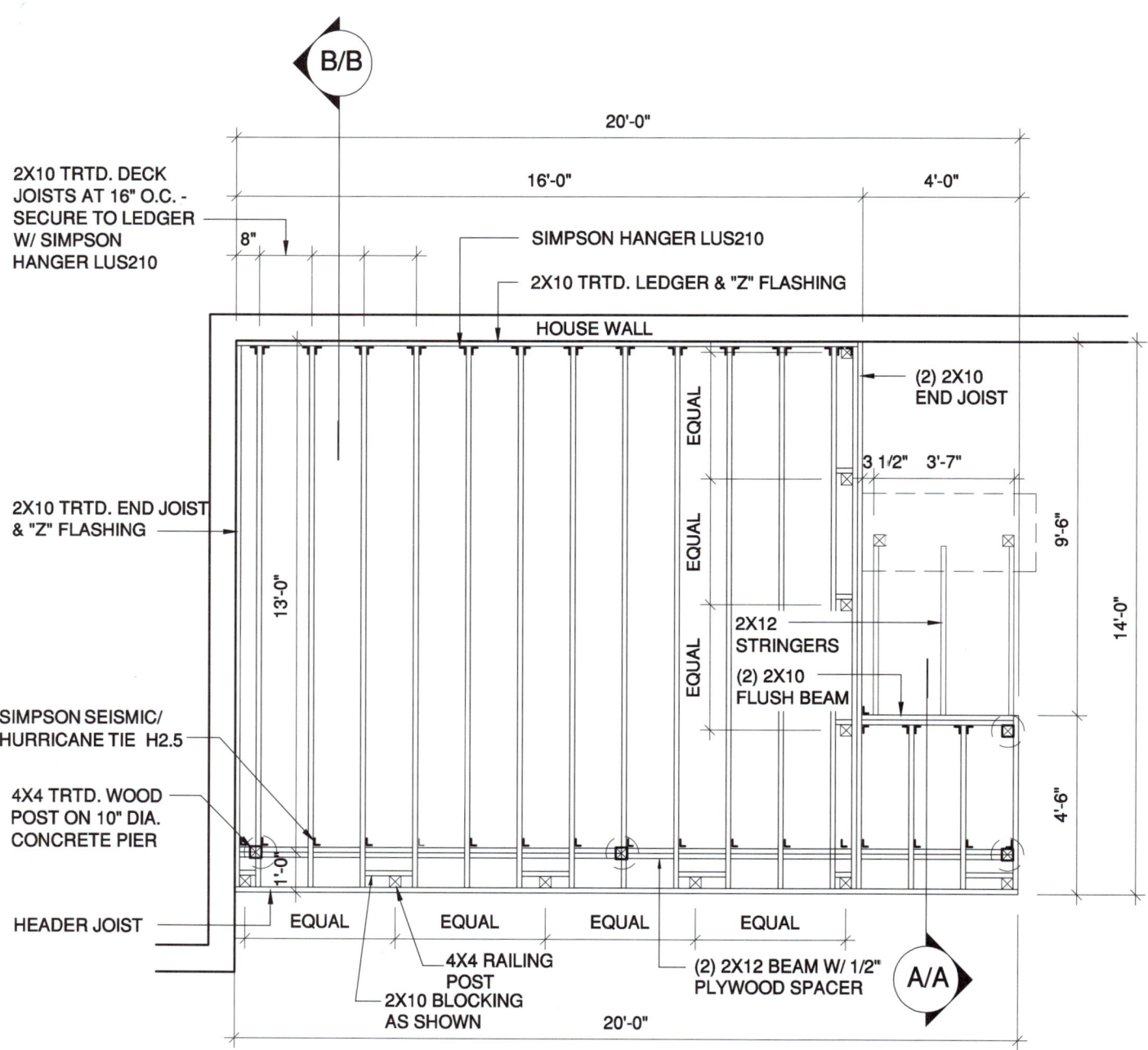

132   www.DreamIt-BuildIt.com

Longview — Elevations

Scale: 1/4" = 1'-0"

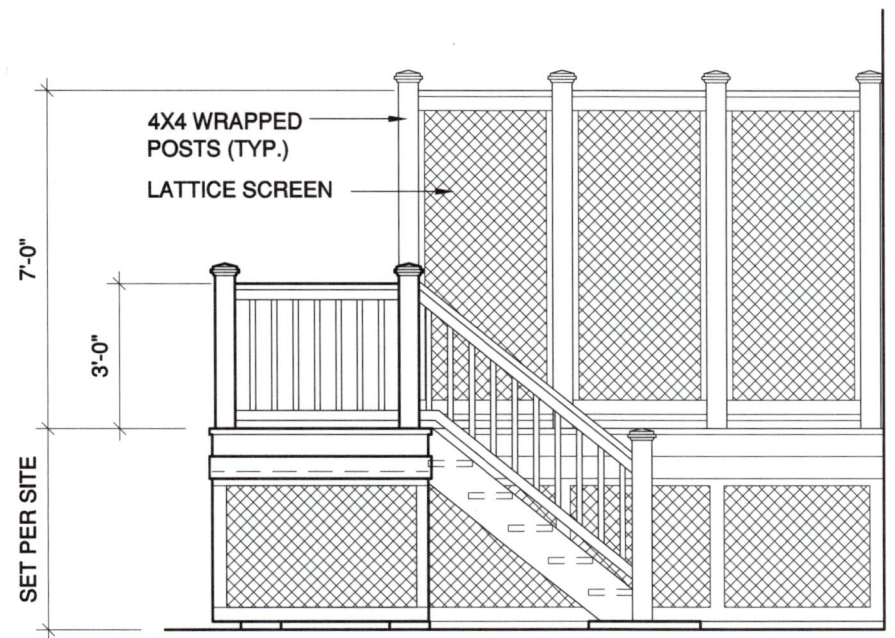

RIGHT ELEVATION — EL/1

STAIR QUANTITY BASED ON SITE CONDITIONS

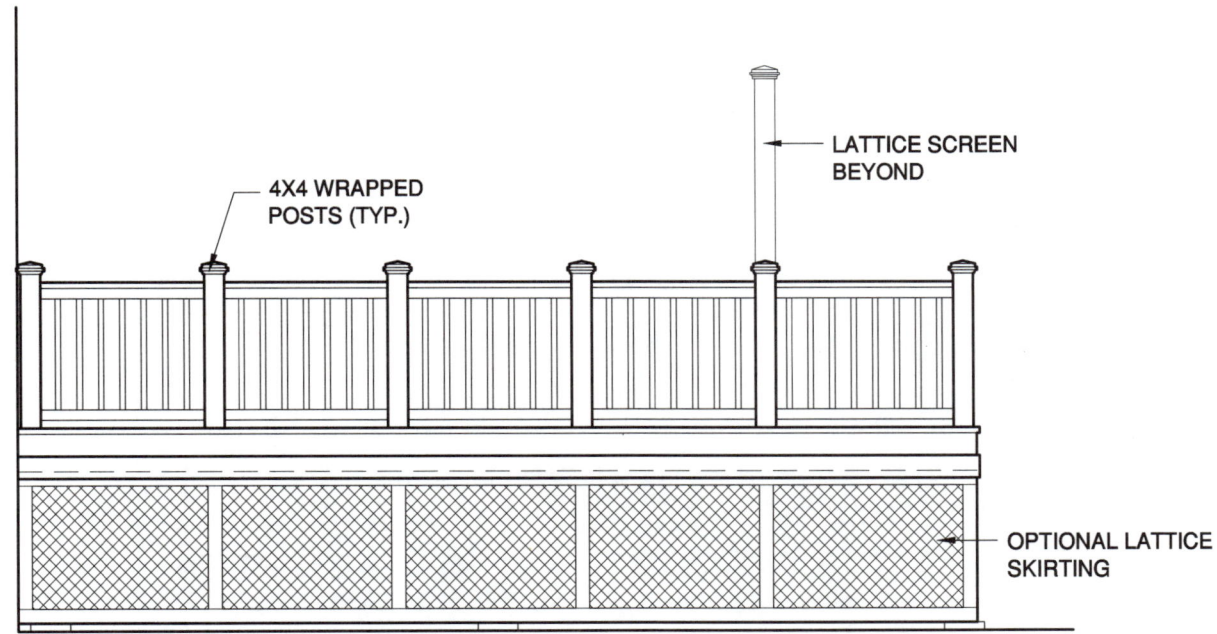

FRONT ELEVATION — EL/2

www.homedepot.com

LONGVIEW — Sections

Scale: 3/8" = 1'-0"

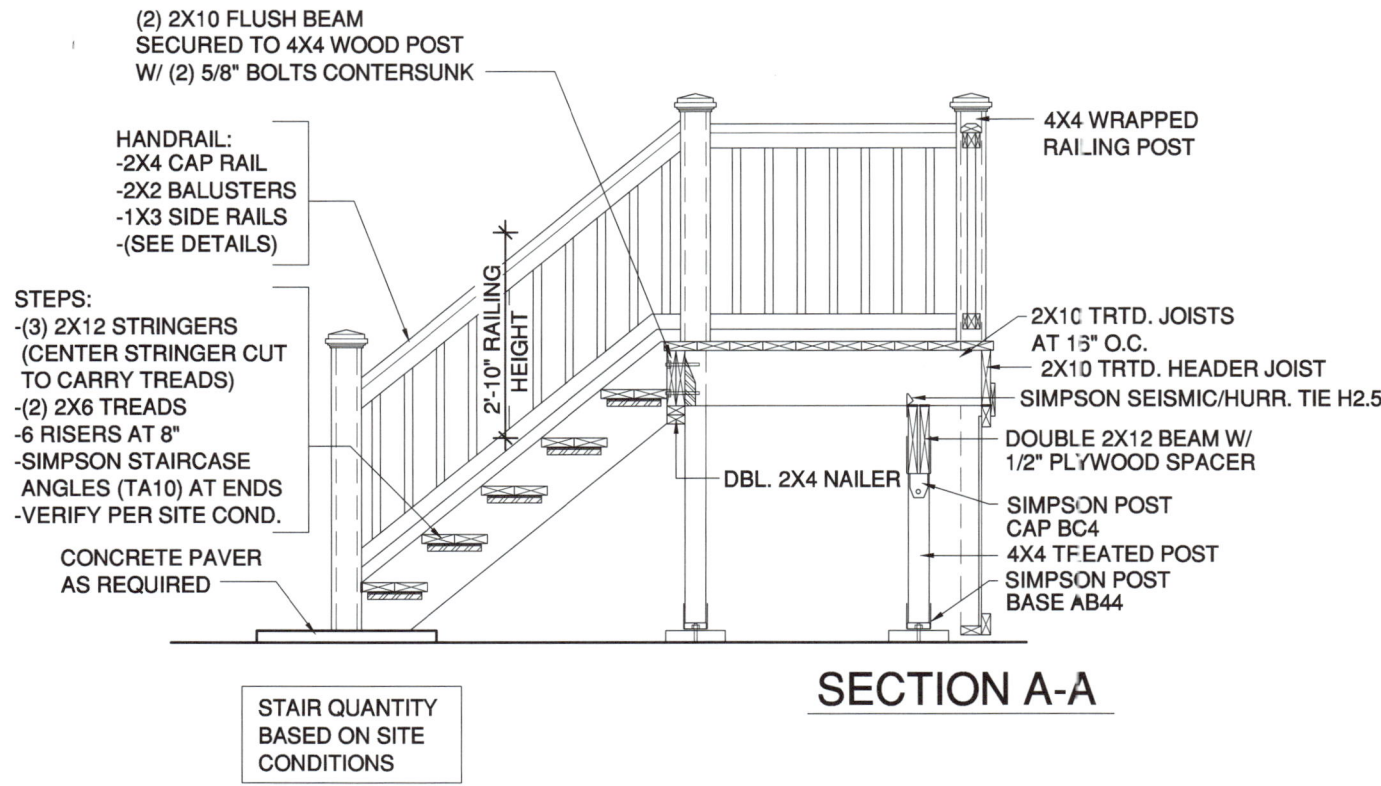

SECTION A-A

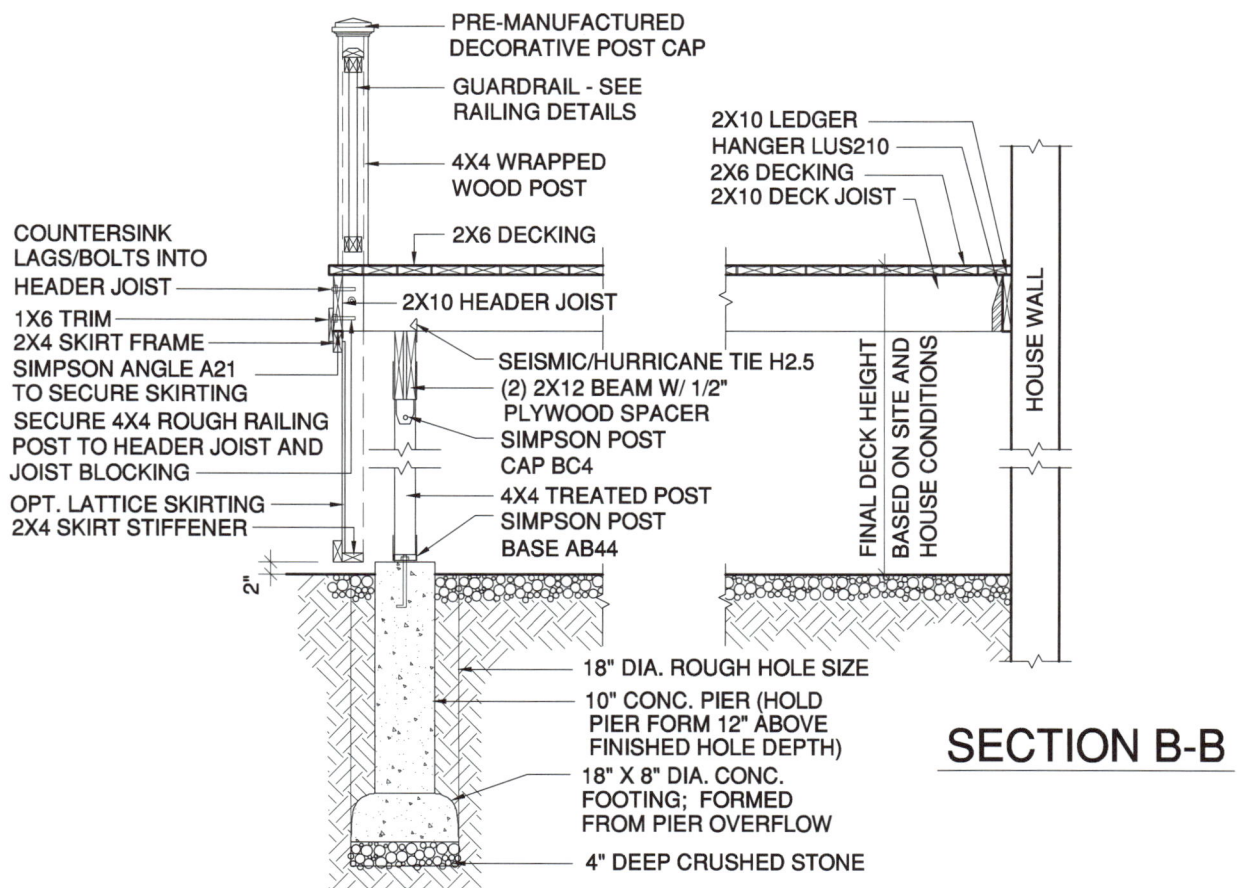

SECTION B-B

LONGVIEW — Details

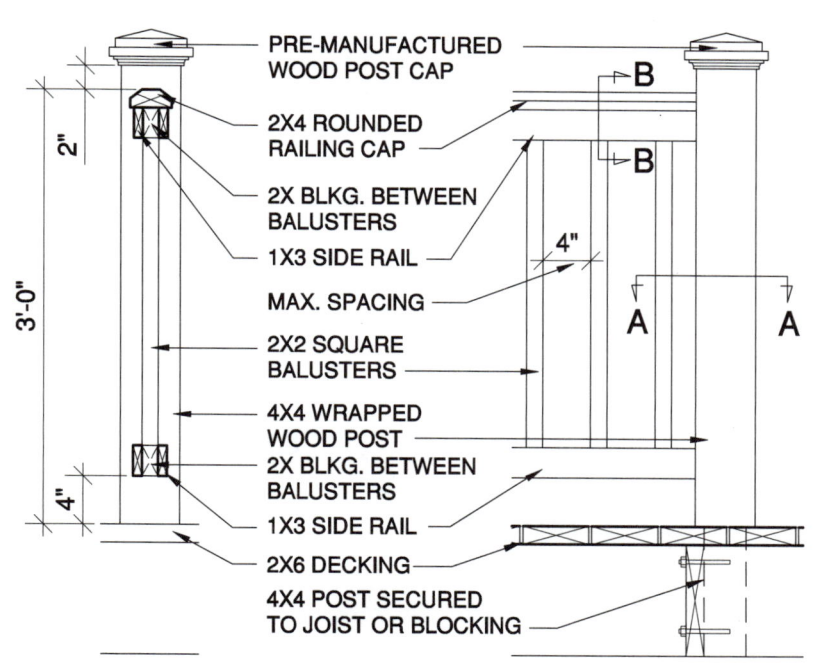
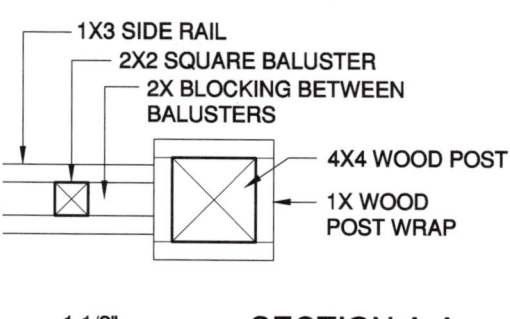
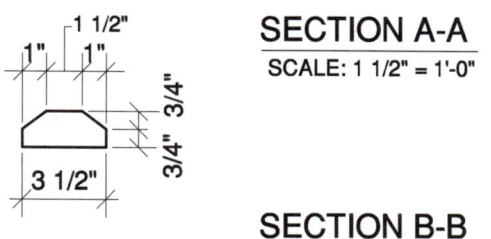

RAILING DETAILS
SCALE: 3/4" = 1'-0"

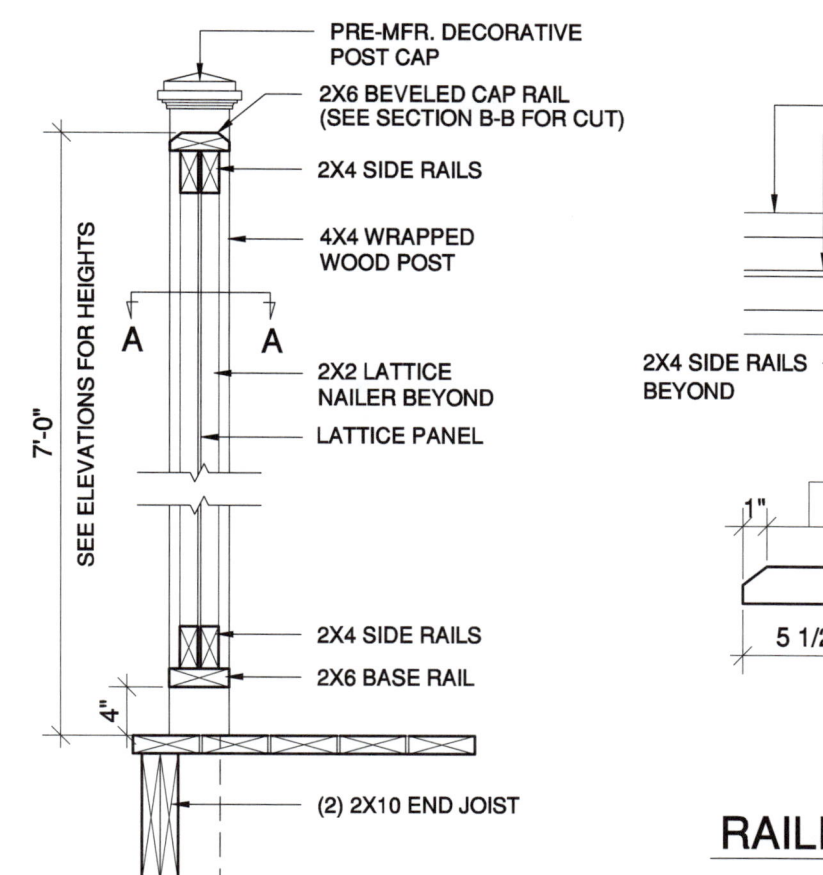
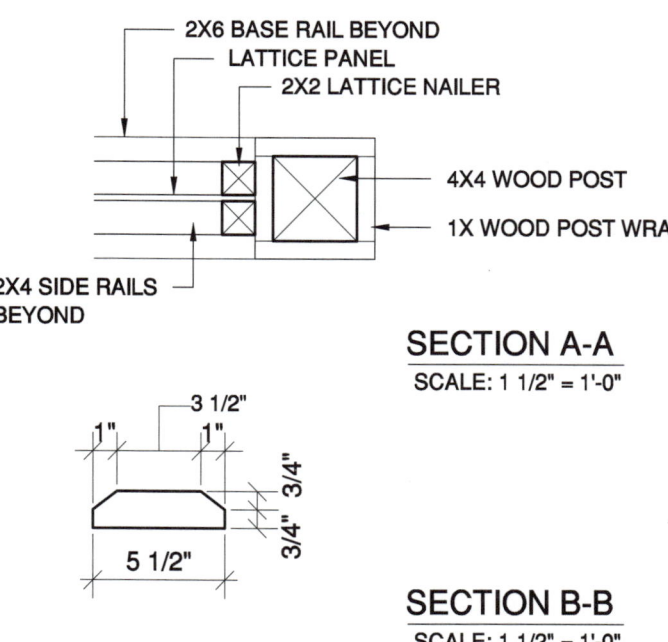

RAILING/SCREEN DETAILS
SCALE: 3/4" = 1'-0"

LONGVIEW — Material List

FOUNDATION

Item	Location	Qty	UM
60# Concrete Mix	Pier	20	BG
10"x48" Fiber Tube	Pier	4	EA
2x4 - 10' Std. & Btr.	Batterboard	3	EA
1/2"x6" Anchor Bolt/Nut/Wash.	Pier	4	EA
Post Base (ABA44)	Pier	4	EA
Crushed Gravel	Pier	8	BG
2x10 - 14' Treated	End Joist	1	EA
2x10 - 16' Treated	Ledger	1	EA
1x5 - 10' Zee Bar	Ledger	3	EA
5# 16d Galv. Nails	General Framing	1	EA
3/8"x4" Lag Screws	Ledger	38	EA
3/8"x1-1/2" Washer	Ledger	38	EA
10 oz. - Paintable Caulk	Ledger/Bolt	3	TB

FRAMING

Item	Location	Qty	UM
2x12 - 20' Treated	Beam	2	EA
2x10 - 8' Treated	Beam	1	EA
2x10 - 14' Treated	Joist/Blocking	16	EA
2x10 - 20' Treated	Joist	1	EA
1/2" CDX - 5 Ply Plywd.	Beam	1	EA
4x4 - 8' Treated	Post	1	EA
4x4 - 10' Treated	Post	1	EA
Post Cap (PC44-16)	Post/Beam	3	EA
5# 6d Galv. Nails	General Framing	3	EA
2x10 Jst. Hngr. (LUS210)	Ledger Joist	14	EA
2x10 Jst. Hngr. (LUS210-2)	Ledger Joist	1	EA
Hurricane Tie (H2.5)	Joist/Beam	17	EA
Framing Anchor (A34)	End/Header Joist	5	EA
1# 8d 1-1/2" Hanger Nails	Connector	3	EA
5# 8d Ctd. Box Nails	General Framing	1	EA

FINISH/RAILING/SKIRTING

Item	Location	Qty	UM
4x4 - 8' Treated	Post	9	EA
3/8"x4" Lag Screws	Post	26	EA
3/8"x1-1/2" Washer	Post	26	EA
2x6 - 12' Treated	Decking/Stair Trd.	24	EA
2x6 - 16' Treated	Decking/Stair Trd.	18	EA
1# 2-1/2" Ctd. Screws	Decking/Railing	10	EA
2x12 - 8' Treated	Stringer	3	EA
3x5 Heavy Angle (HL35)	Stringer	9	EA
5/16"x1-1/2" Lag Screws	Heavy Angle	36	EA
2x4 - 8' Treated	Cap Rail	5	EA
1x3 - 8' Treated	Side Rail	20	EA
2x3 - 8' Treated	Baluster Blocking	10	EA
1-3/8"x1-3/8" - 3' Sq. Cut Blstr.	Baluster	66	EA
2x6 - 10' Treated	Cap/Base Rail	2	EA
2x4 - 10' Treated	Side Rail	4	EA
2x2 - 8' Treated	Lattice Nailer	12	EA
1x4 - 8' Treated	Post Wrap	20	EA
1x6 - 8' Treated	Post Wrap	20	EA
2x4 - 8' Treated	Skirt Stiffener/Nlr.	16	EA
2x4 - 12' Treated	Skirt Stiffener	10	EA
Garden Weave Lattice	Lattice	8	EA
Wood Post Cap	Post	13	EA
5# 16d Galv. Nails	General Framing	2	EA
5# 8d Ctd. Box Nails	General Framing	1	EA

CHAPTER 5

THE ROYALE

HPM-1108

Relax and enjoy the outdoors on this unique freestanding deck. A lattice wall rises at one end, shielding a built-in seating area. Use this highly flexible deck to "get away" and relax, or enjoy your gardening or potting hobbies in or out of the sun.

Dimensions for this deck are 14' X 14'.

ROYALE   Plan View

Scale: 1/4" = 1'-0"

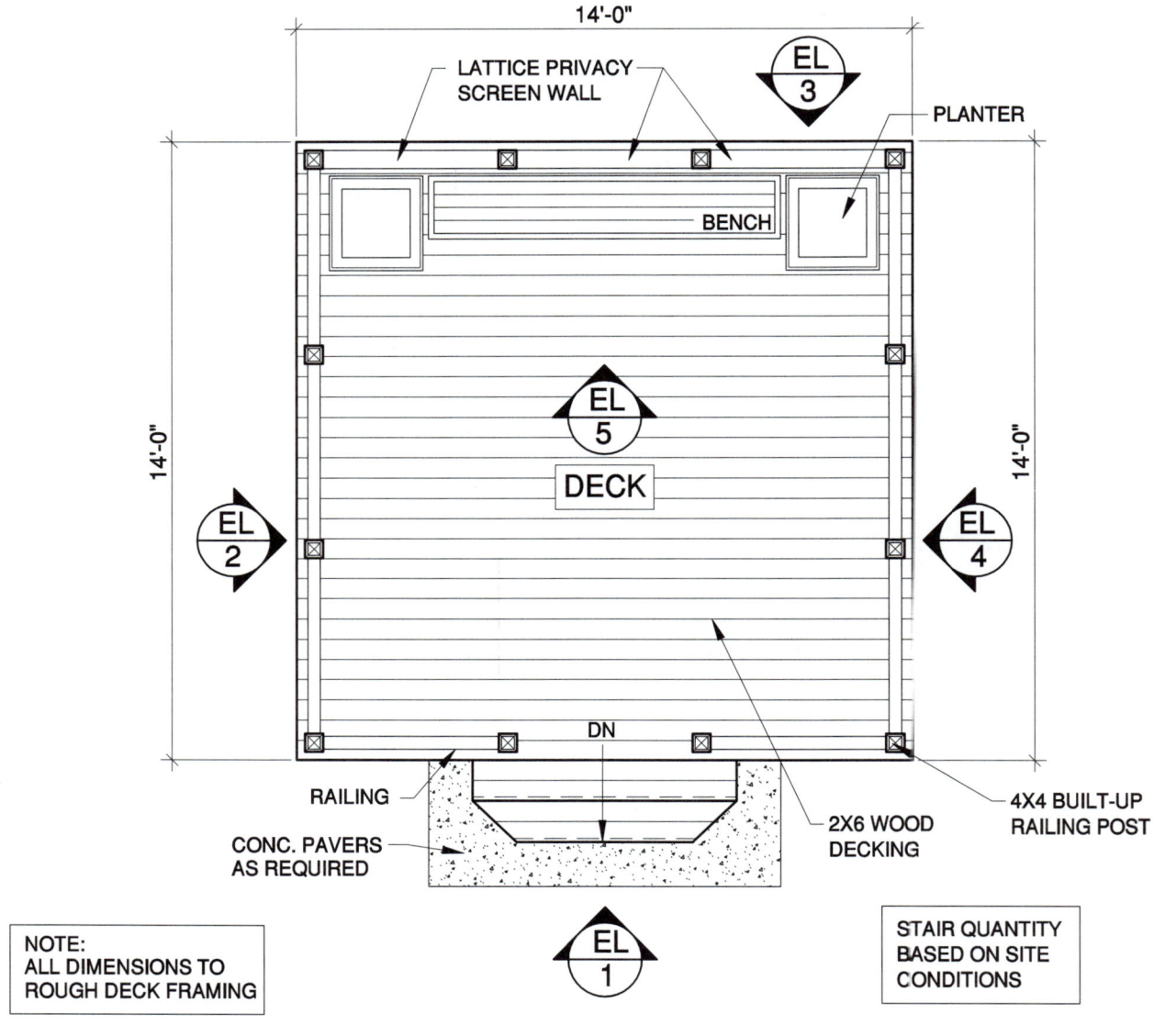

ROYALE — Pier Layout

Scale: 1/4" = 1'-0"

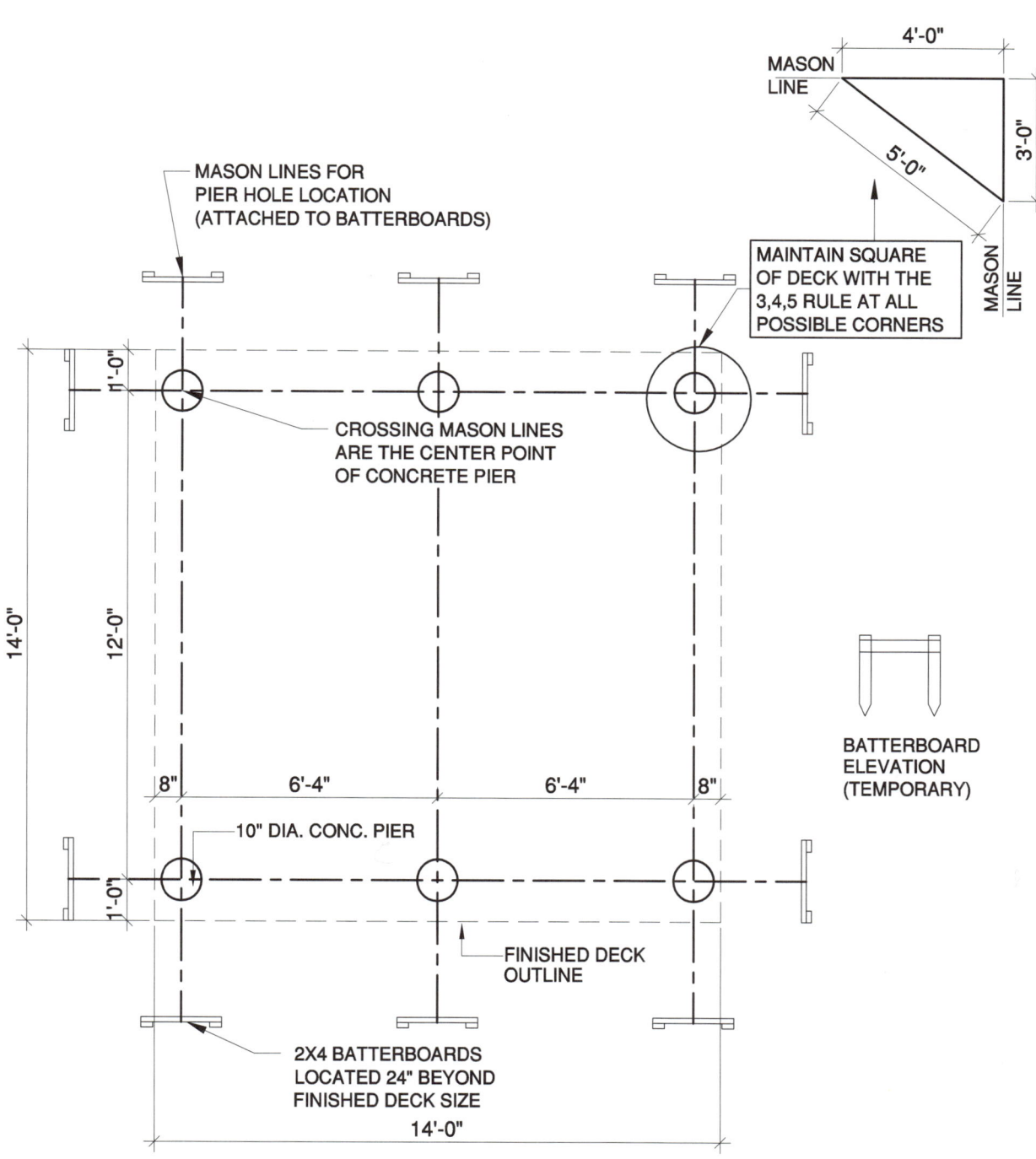

www.homedepot.com 139

ROYALE — Framing Plan

Scale: 1/4" = 1'-0"

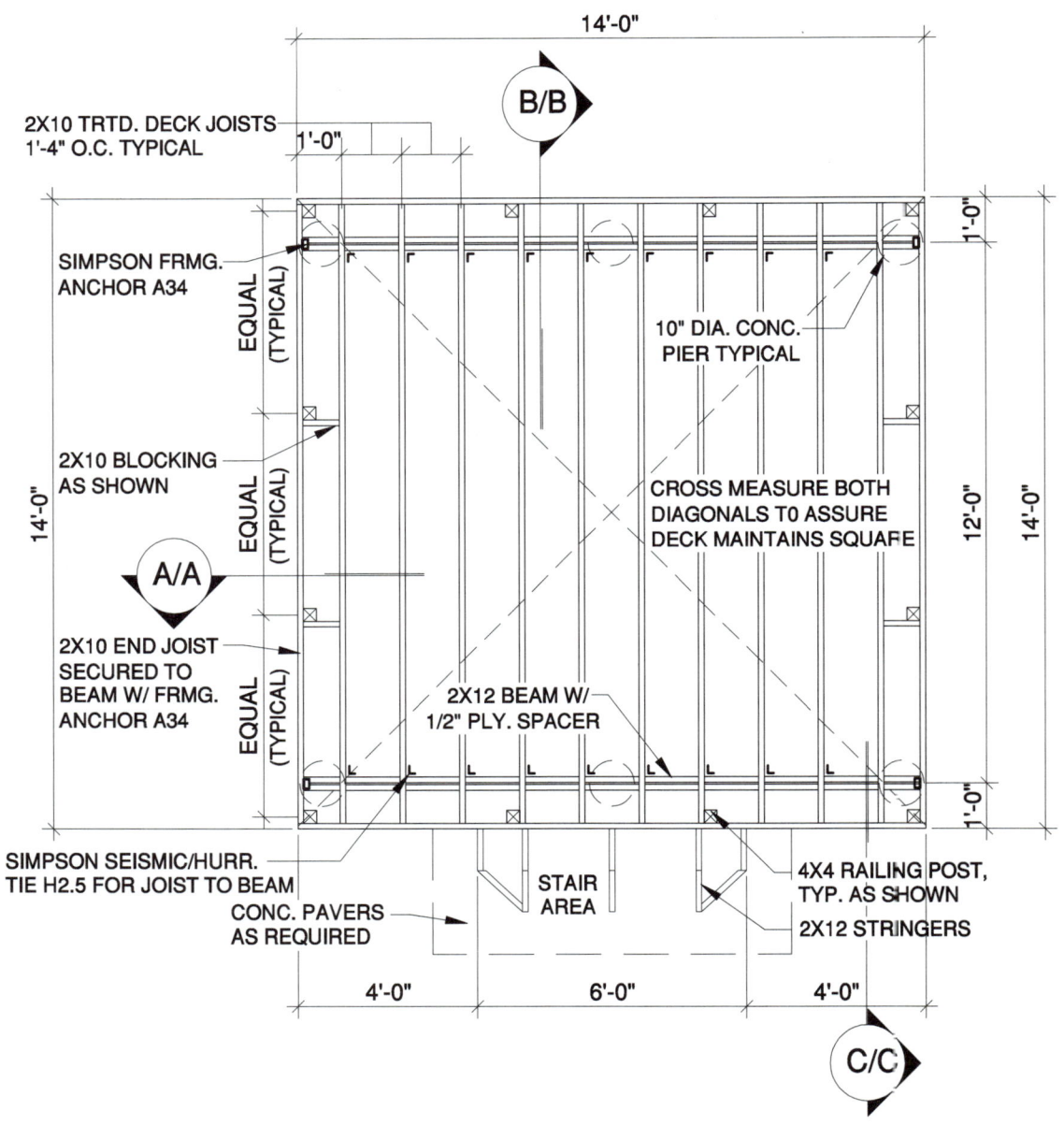

www.DreamIt-BuildIt.com

ROYALE — Elevations

Scale: 1/4" = 1'-0"

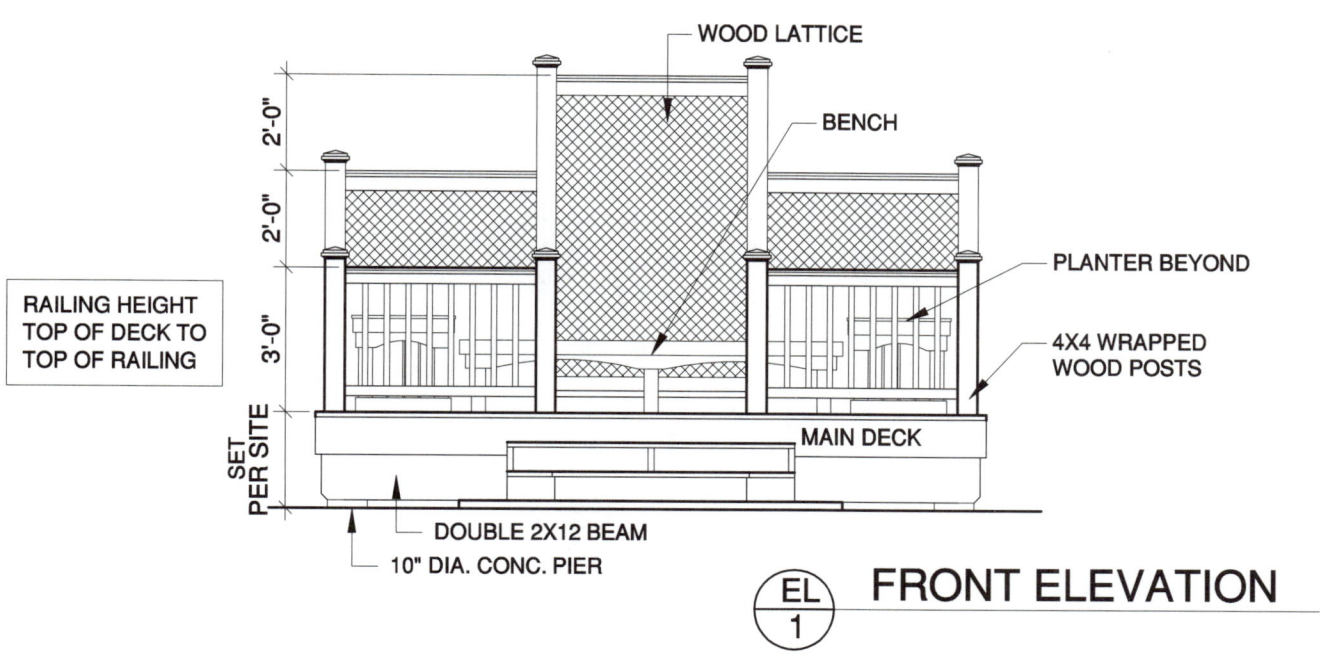

FRONT ELEVATION (EL/1)

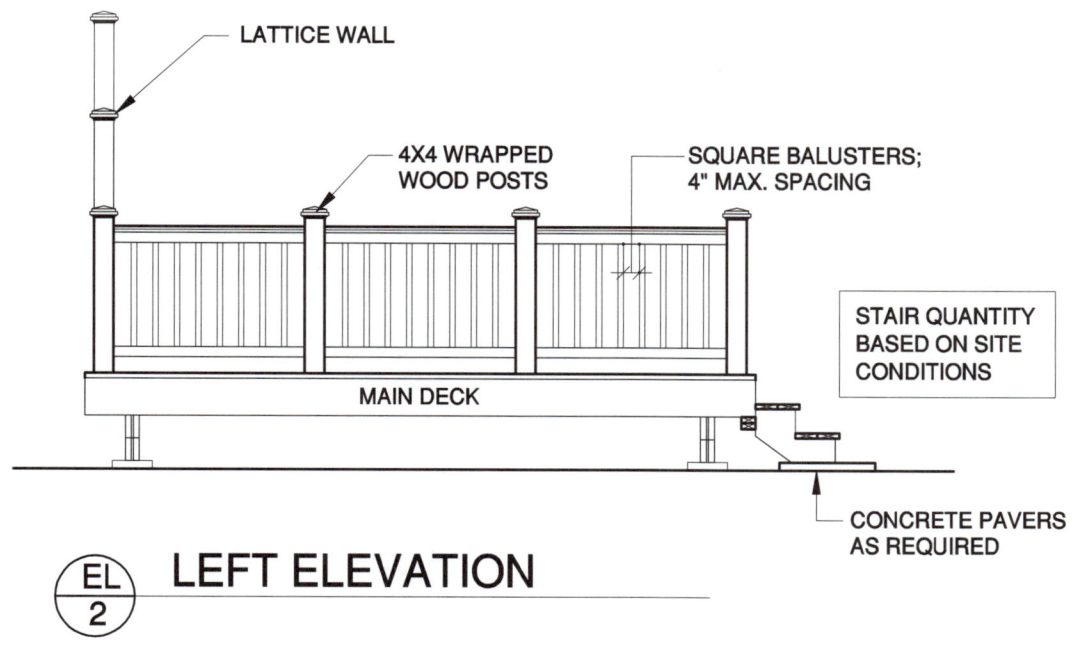

LEFT ELEVATION (EL/2)

ROYALE — Elevations

Scale: 1/4" = 1'-0"

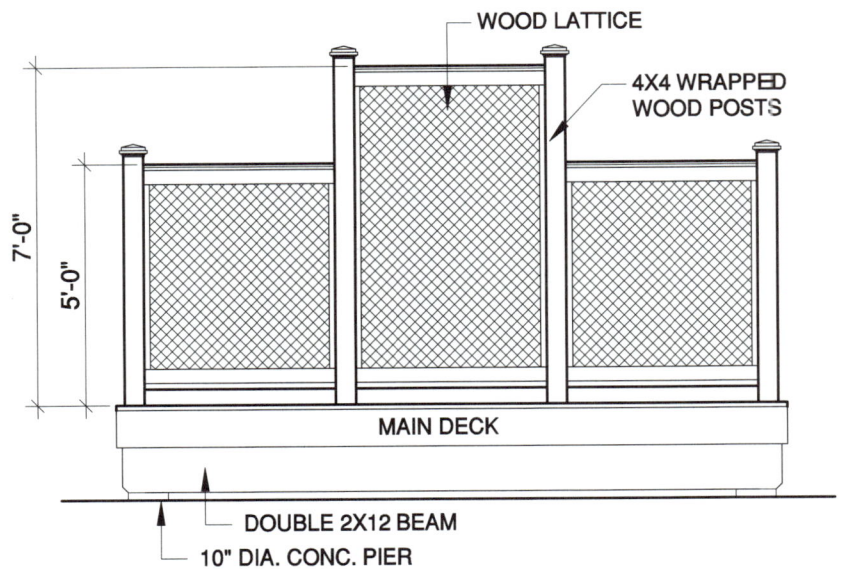

REAR ELEVATION (EL 3)

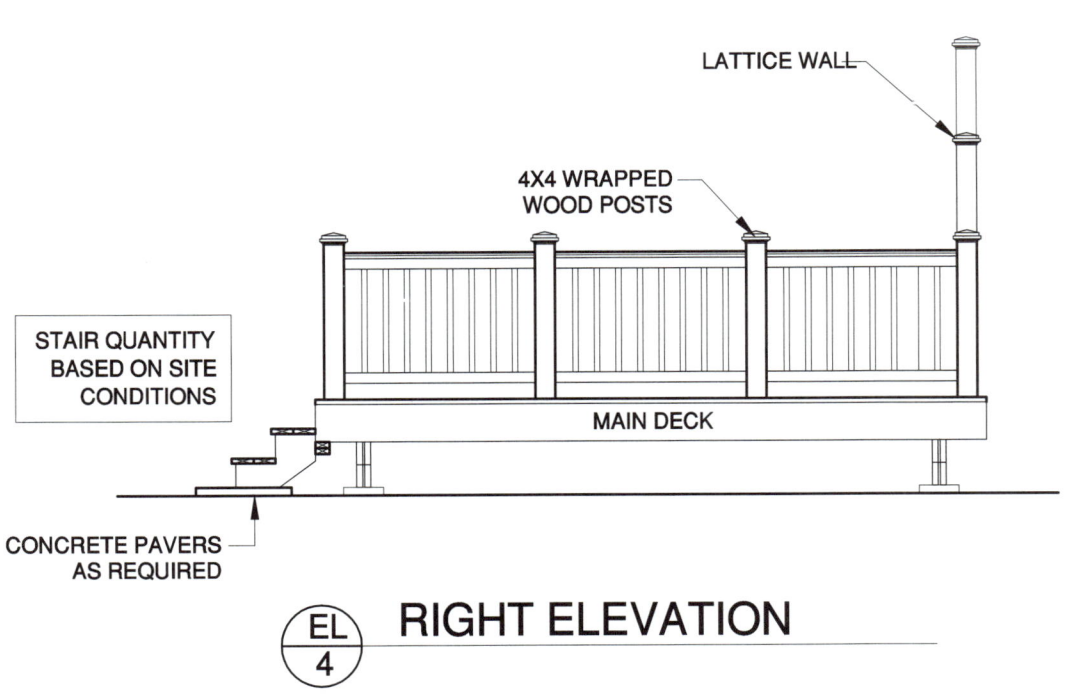

RIGHT ELEVATION (EL 4)

ROYALE Details

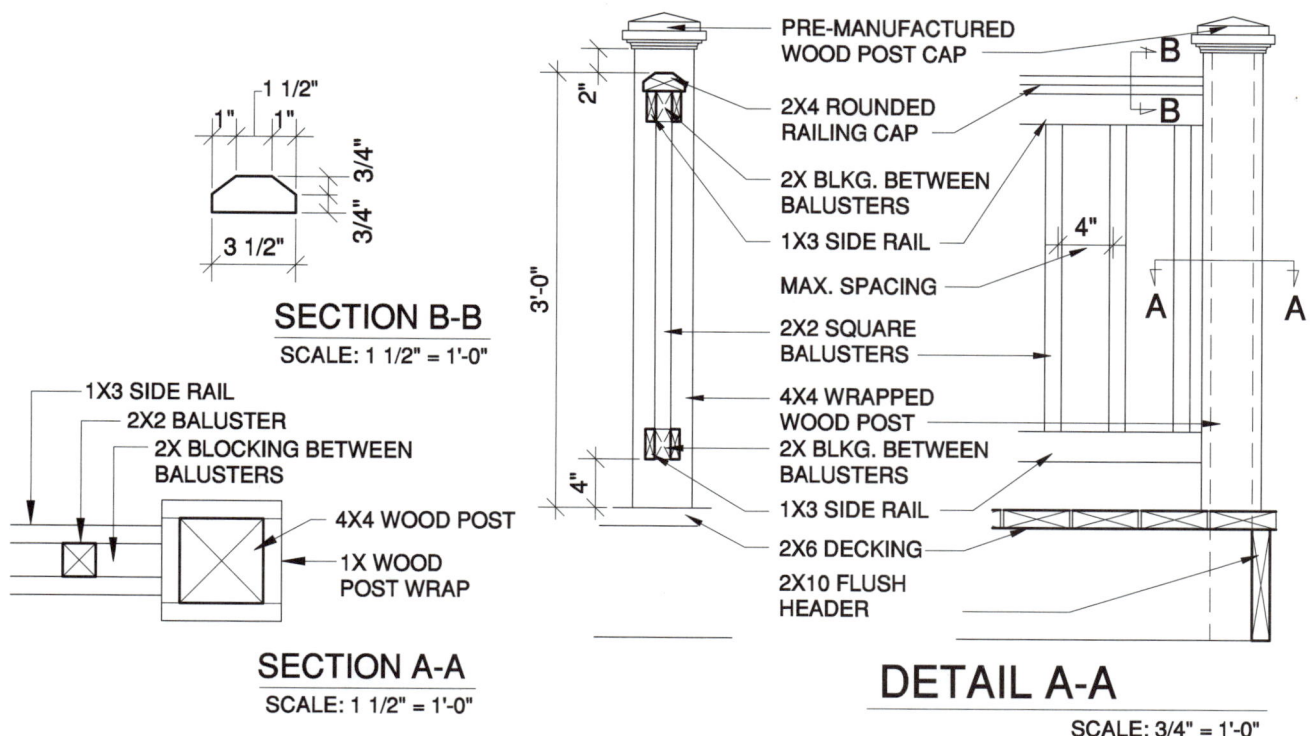

RAILING DETAILS

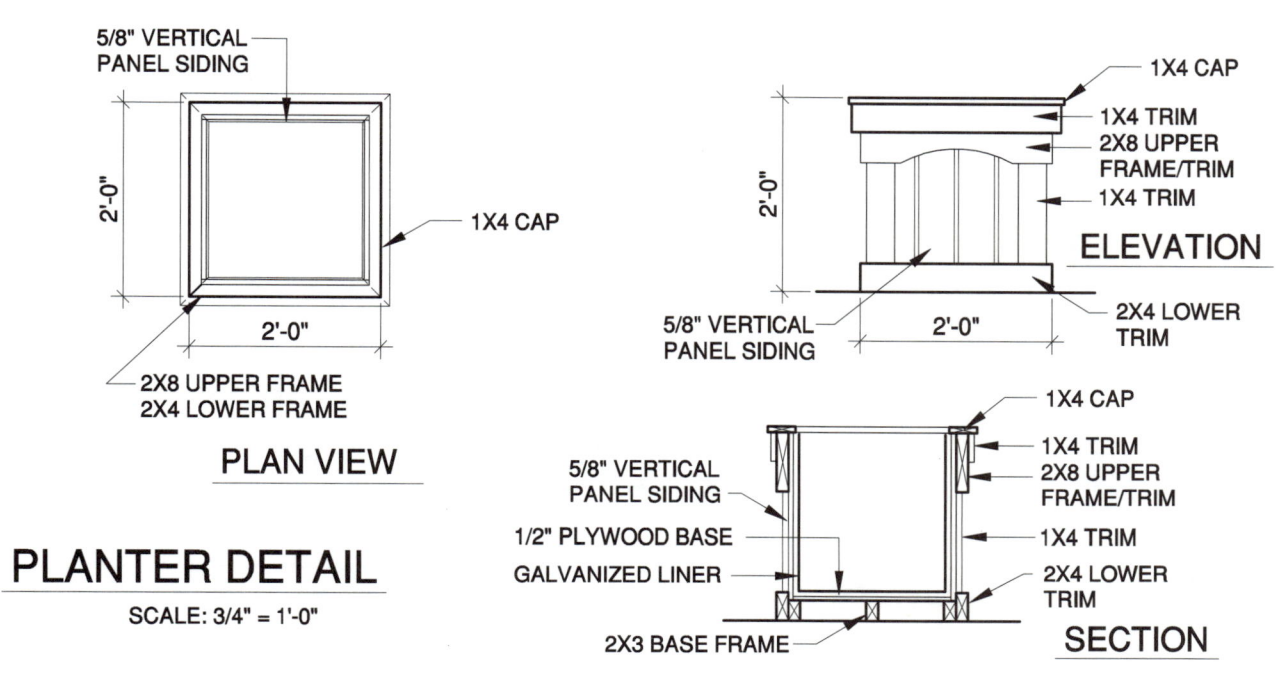

PLANTER DETAIL

ROYALE — Details

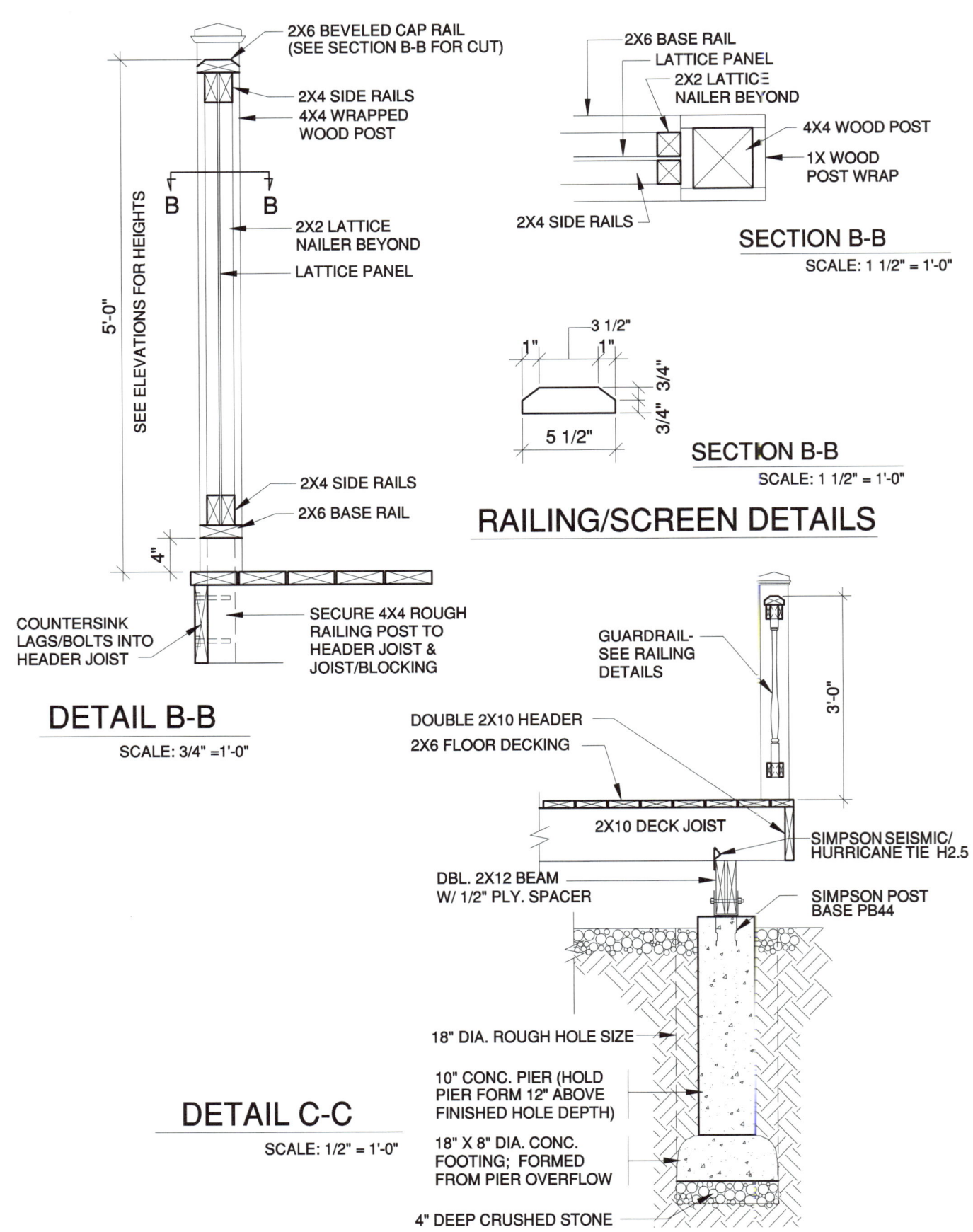

RAILING/SCREEN DETAILS

ROYALE — Elevation and Detail

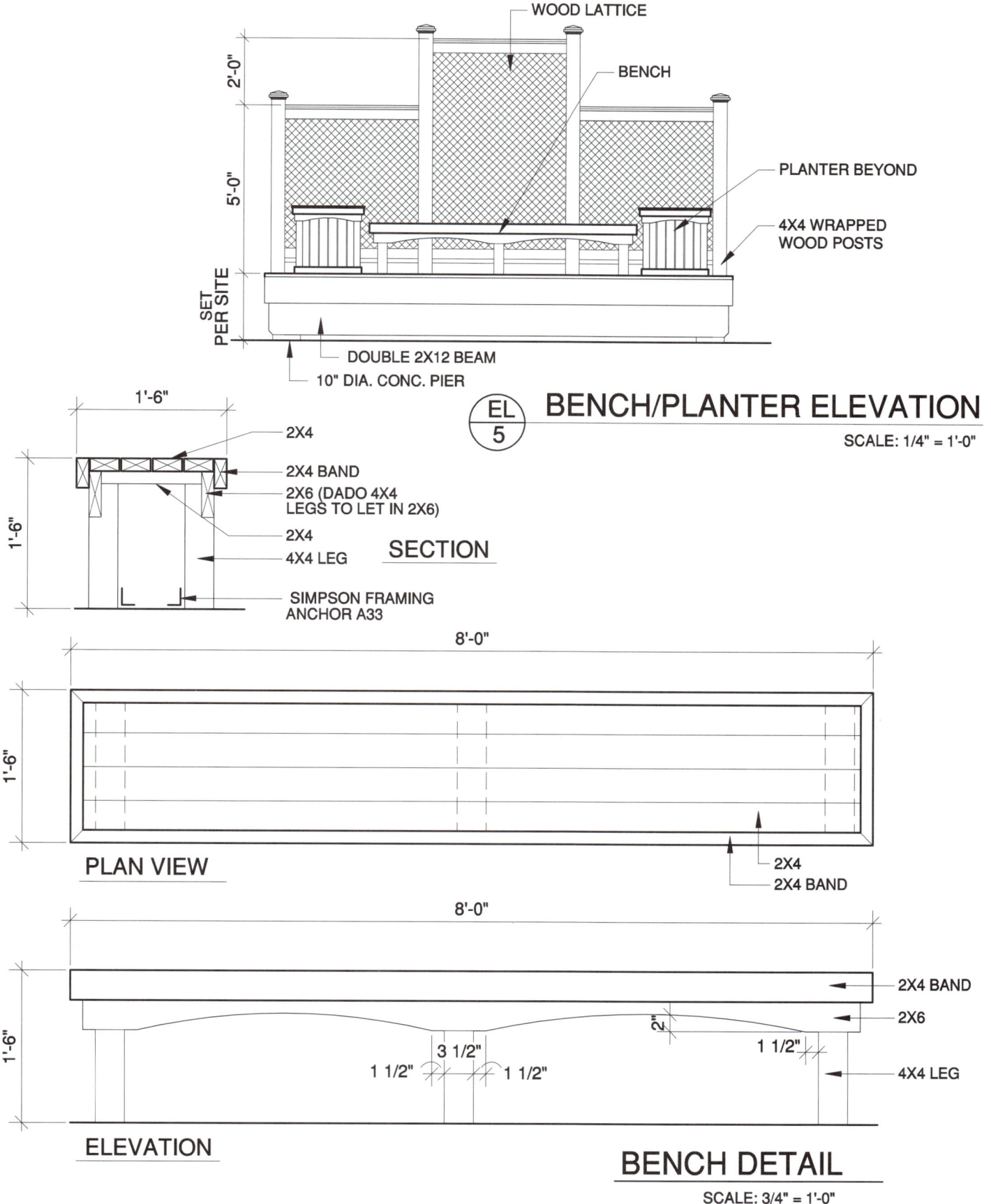

145

ROYALE — Material List

FOUNDATION

Item	Location	Qty	UM
60# Concrete Mix	Pier	30	BG
10"x48" Fiber Tube	Pier	6	EA
2x4 - 10' Std. & Btr.	Batterboard	6	EA
Post Base (PB44)	Pier	6	EA
Crushed Gravel	Pier	12	BG
5# 16d Galv. Nails	General Framing	1	EA

FRAMING

Item	Location	Qty	UM
2x12 - 14' Treated	Beam	4	EA
2x10 - 14' Treated	Joist/Blocking	15	EA
1/2" CDX - 5 Ply Plywd.	Beam Spacer	1	EA
5# 16d Galv. Nails	General Framing	3	EA
Hurricane Tie (H2.5)	Joist/Beam	20	EA
Framing Anchor (A34)	End/Header Joist	4	EA
1# 8d 1-1/2" Hanger Nails	Connector	3	EA
5# 8d Ctd. Box Nails	General Framing	1	EA

FINISH/RAILING/SKIRTING

Item	Location	Qty	UM
4x4 - 8' Treated	Post	6	EA
4x4 - 12' Treated	Post	1	EA
3/8"x4" Lag Screws	Post	24	EA
3/8"x1-1/2" Washer	Post	24	EA
2x6 - 12' Treated	Stair Tread	2	EA
2x6 - 16' Treated	Decking	32	EA
1# 2-1/2" Ctd. Screws	Decking/Railing	10	EA
2x12 - 12' Treated	Stringer	2	EA
3x5 Heavy Angle (HL35)	Stringer	10	EA
5/16"x1-1/2" Lag Screws	Heavy Angle	40	EA
2x4 - 12' Treated	Nailer	1	EA
1-3/8"x1-3/8" - 4' Sq. Cut Blstr.	Side Rail	68	EA
5# 16d Galv. Nails	General Framing	1	EA
5# 8d Ctd. Box Nails	General Framing	1	EA
2x4 - 8' Treated	Cap Rail	4	EA
1x3 - 8' Treated	Side Rail	16	EA
2x3 - 8' Treated	Blstr. Blocking	8	EA
Wood Post Cap	Post	12	EA
2x6 - 8' Treated	Cap/Base Rail	3	EA
2x4 - 8' Treated	Side Rail	6	EA
2x2 - 6' Treated	Lattice Nailer	8	EA
2x2 - 8' Treated	Lattice Nailer	2	EA
Garden Weave Lattice	Lattice	3	EA
1x4 - 8' Treated	Post Wrap	16	EA
1x6 - 8' Treated	Post Wrap	16	EA
2x4 - 8' Treated	Bench	7	EA
2x6 - 8' Treated	Bench	2	EA
4x4 - 8' Treated	Bench	1	EA
1x4 - 8' Treated	Planter	9	EA
2x8 - 8' Treated	Planter	2	EA
2x4 - 8' Treated	Planter	2	EA
2x3 - 10' Treated	Planter	2	EA
1/2" CDX - 5 Ply Plywd.	Planter	1	EA
5/8" T1-11 Siding	Planter	2	EA

CHAPTER 5

THE CLIFTON

HPM-1110

A convenient side-entry stoop with stairway access from the front yard makes this deck ideal for a narrow lot. When no access is possible from the back of the home, this functional deck fits the bill. Enjoy all types of outdoor activities atop the deck; use the space below to shelter oversized outdoor items.

Dimensions for this deck are 16' X 12'.

Clifton — Plan View

Scale: 1/4" = 1'-0"

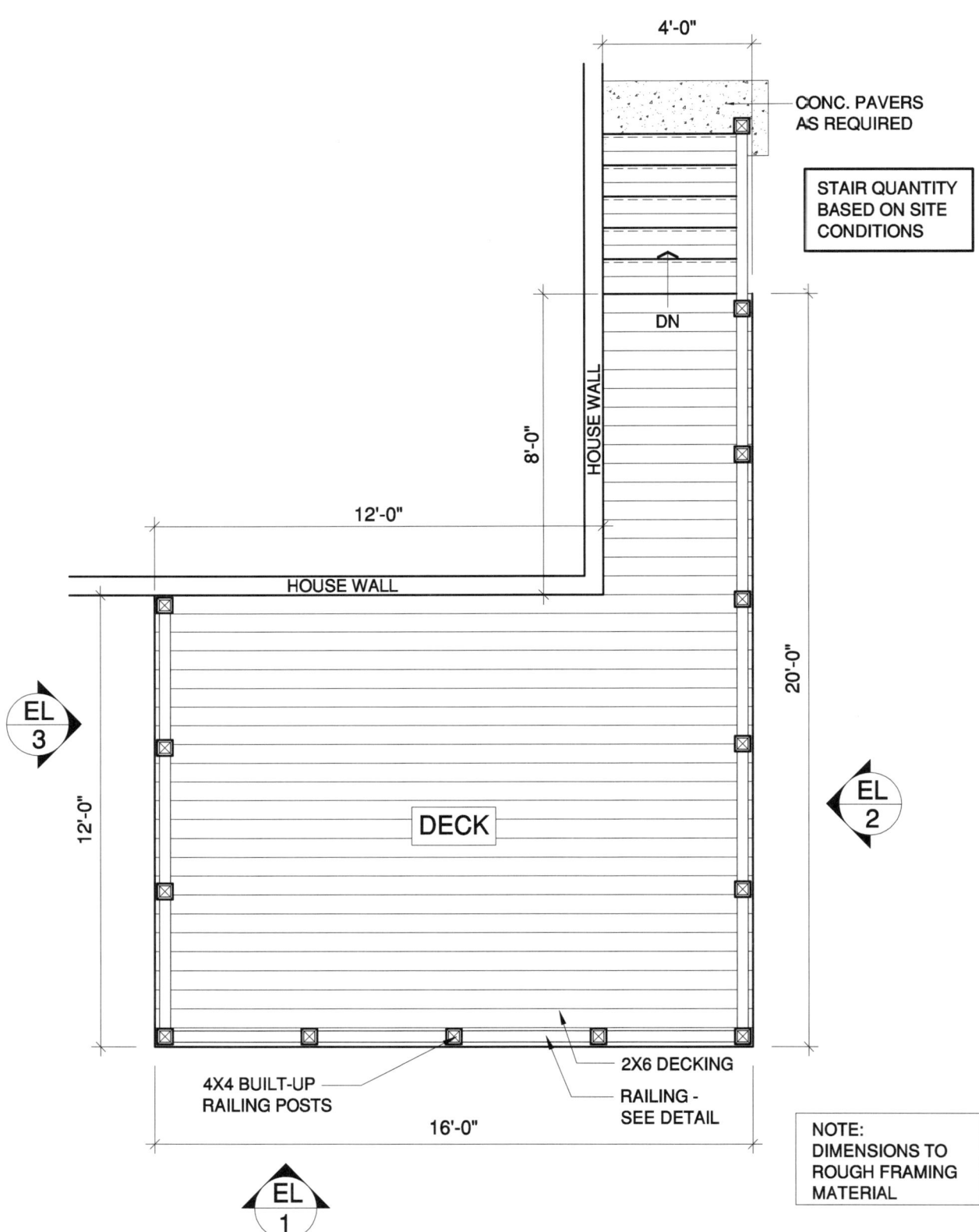

CLIFTON — Pier Layout

Scale: 1/4" = 1'-0"

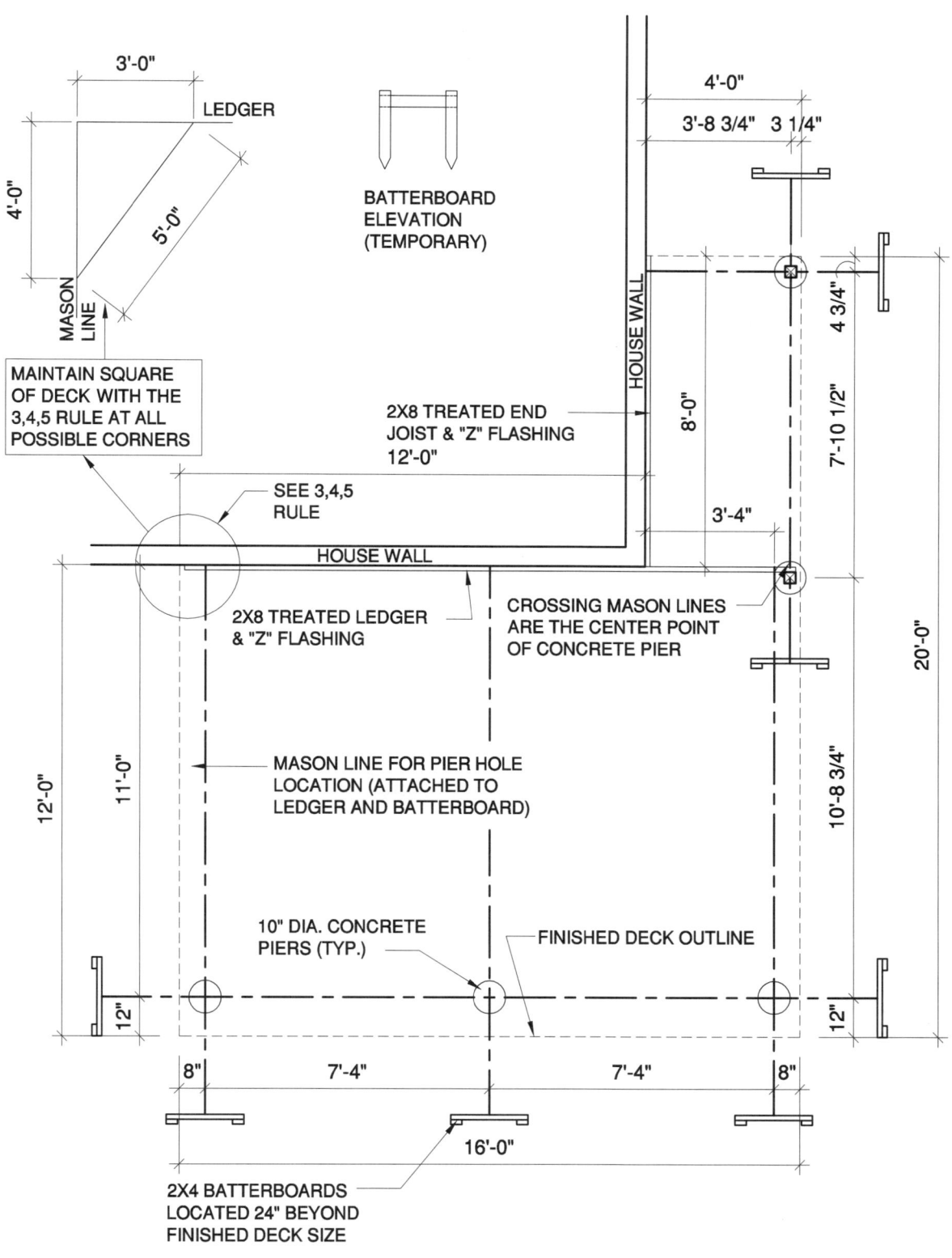

www.homedepot.com 149

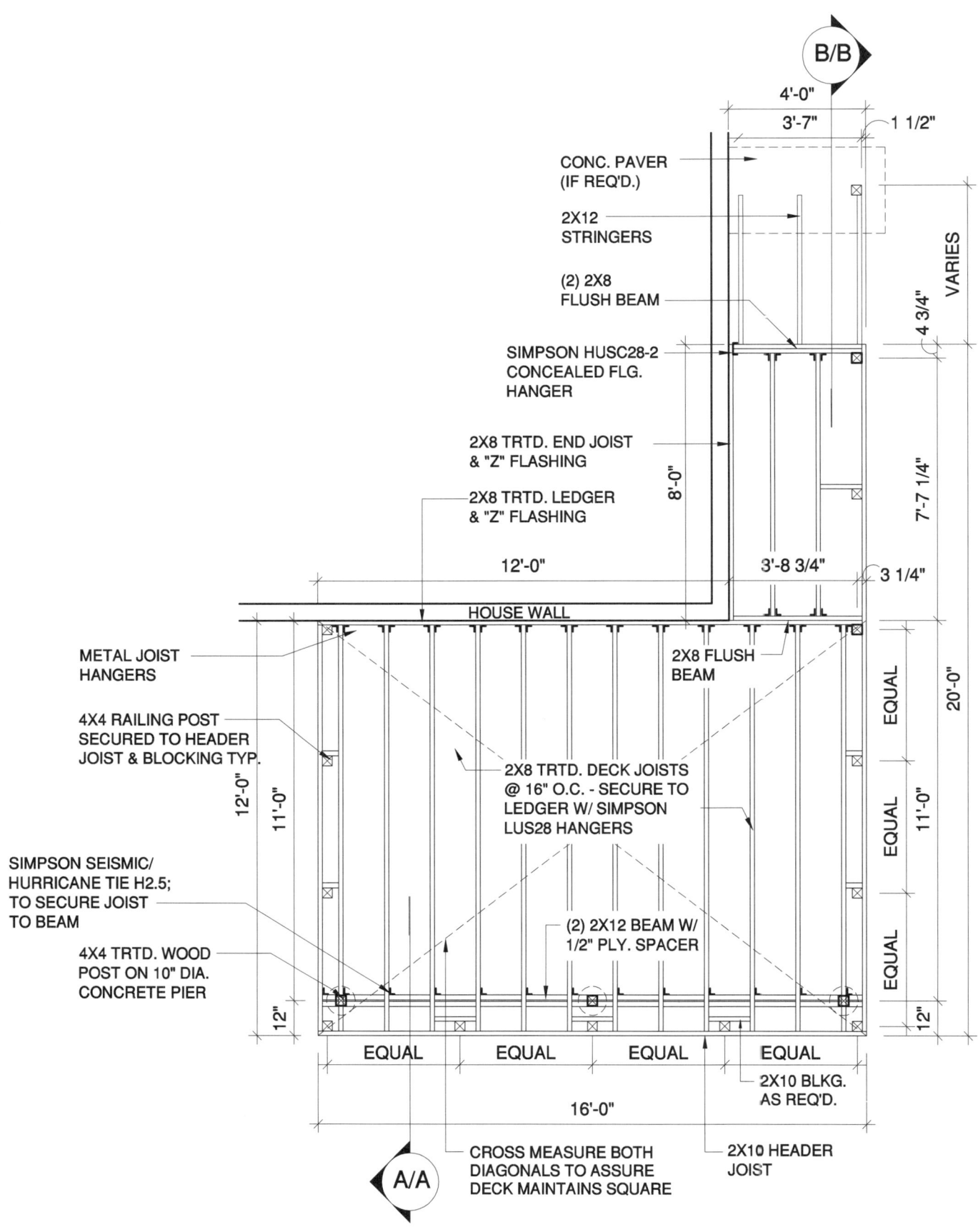

CLIFTON — Elevation and Detail

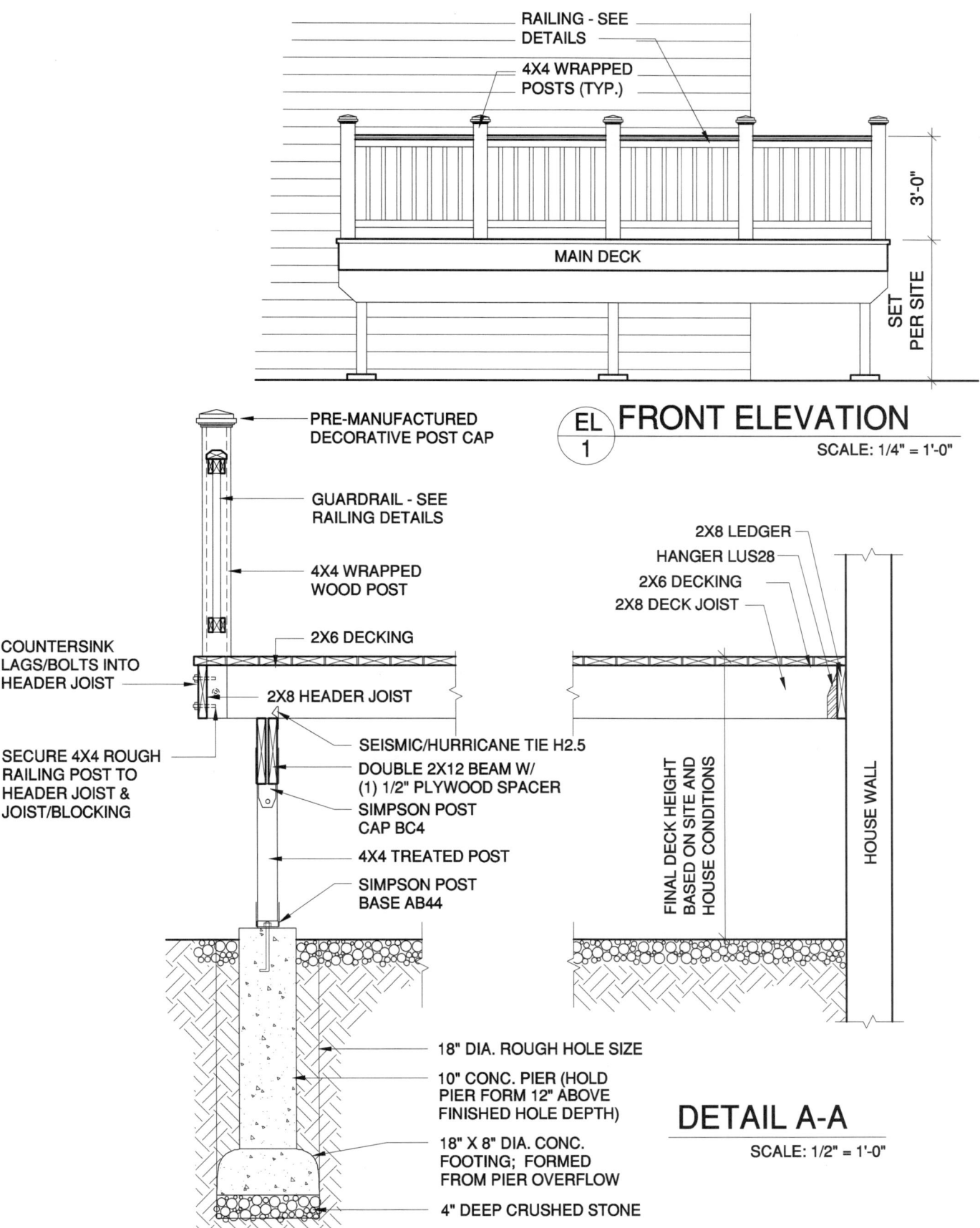

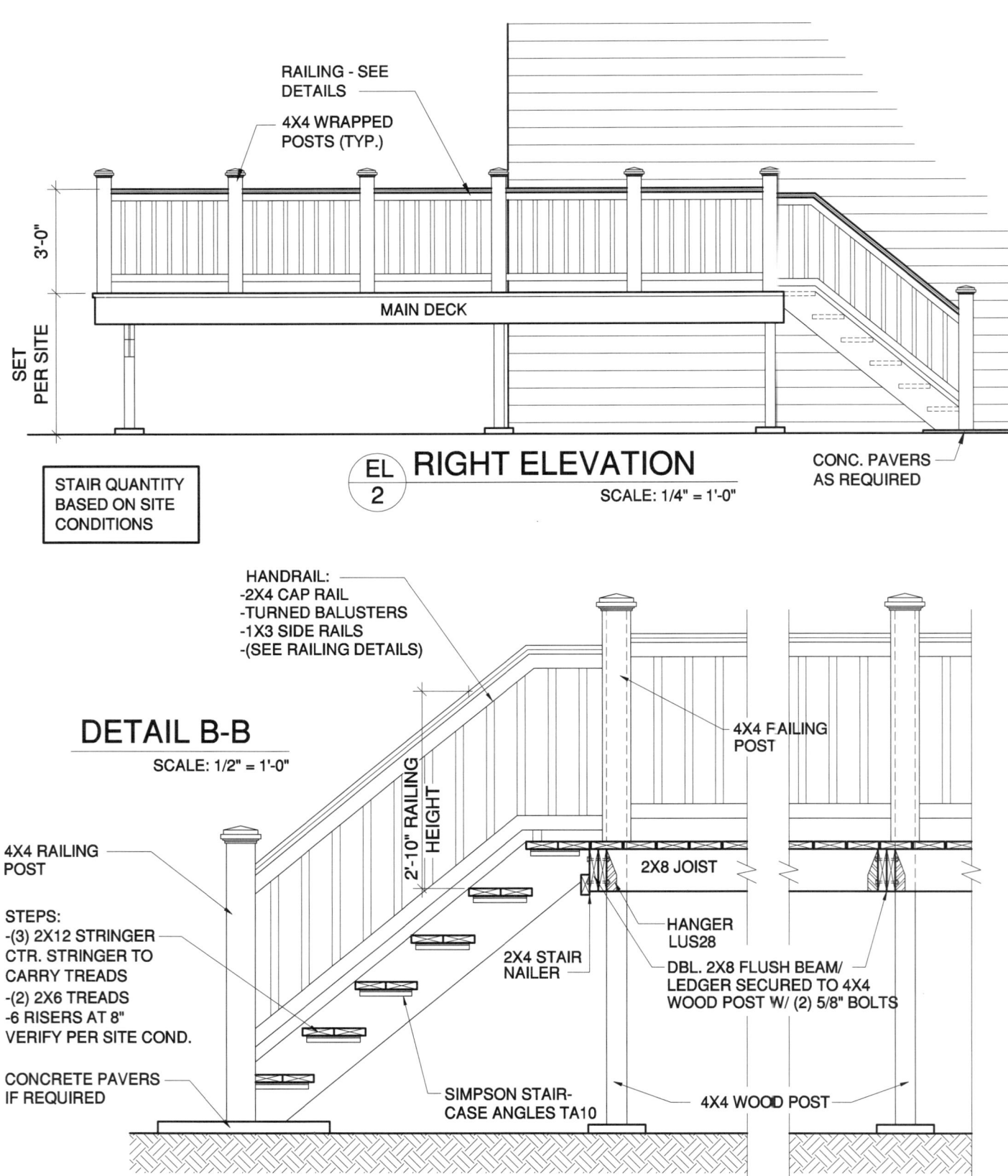

CLIFTON — Elevation and Details

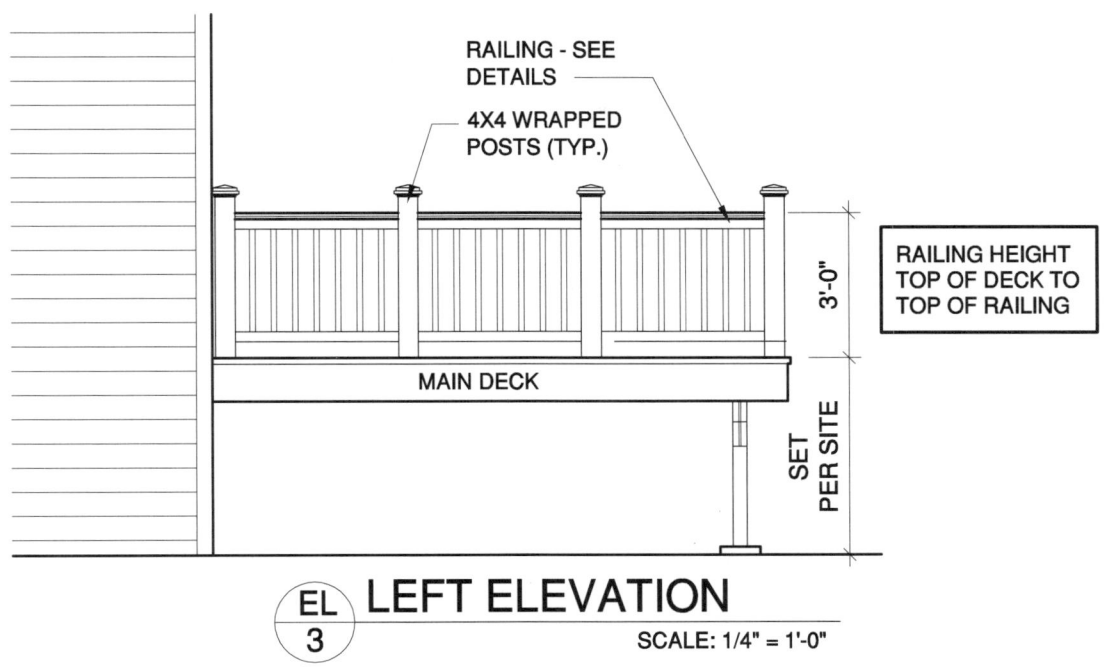

LEFT ELEVATION
SCALE: 1/4" = 1'-0"
EL/3

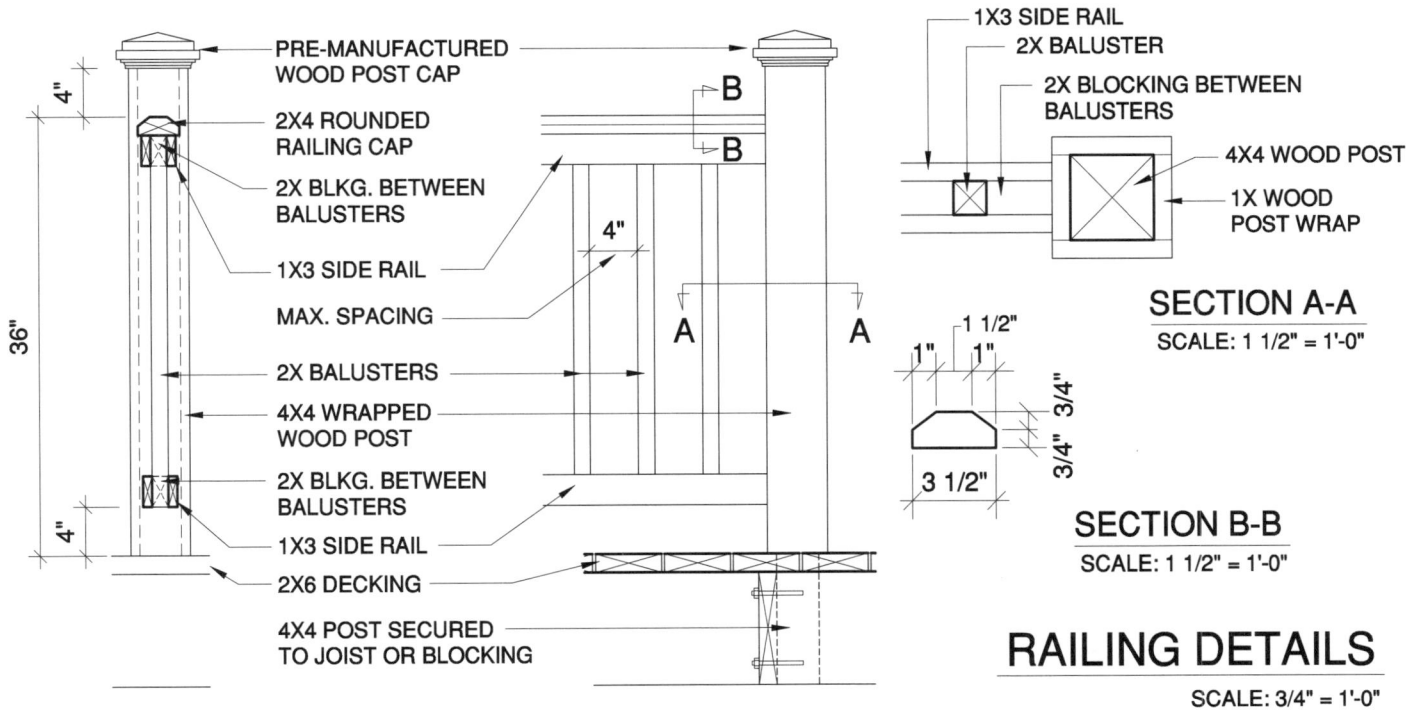

RAILING DETAILS
SCALE: 3/4" = 1'-0"

SECTION A-A
SCALE: 1 1/2" = 1'-0"

SECTION B-B
SCALE: 1 1/2" = 1'-0"

www.homedepot.com

CLIFTON — Material List

FOUNDATION

Item	Location	Qty	UM
60# Concrete Mix	Pier	25	BG
10"x48" Fiber Tube	Pier	5	EA
2x4 - 10' Std. & Btr.	Batterboard	5	EA
1/2"x6" Anchor Bolt/Nut/Wash.	Pier	5	EA
Post Base (ABA44)	Pier	5	EA
Crushed Gravel	Pier	10	BG
2x8 - 8' Treated	Ledger	1	EA
2x8 - 16' Treated	Ledger	1	EA
1x5 - 10' Zee Bar	Ledger	3	EA
5# 16d Galv. Nails	General Framing	1	EA
3/8"x4" Lag Screws	Ledger	30	EA
3/8"x1-1/2" Washer	Ledger	30	EA
10 oz. - Paintable Caulk	Ledger/Bolt	3	TB

FRAMING

Item	Location	Qty	UM
2x12 - 16' Treated	Beam	2	EA
2x8 - 12' Treated	Flush Beam	1	EA
2x8 - 8' Treated	Joist	3	EA
2x8 - 12' Treated	Joist	14	EA
2x8 - 16' Treated	Joist/Blocking	3	EA
1/2" CDX - 5 Ply Plywd.	Beam	1	EA
4x4 - 10' Treated	Post	3	EA
Post Cap (PC44-16)	Post/Beam	3	EA
5# 16d Galv. Nails	General Framing	3	EA
2x10 Jst. Hngr. (LUS210)	Ledger Joist	16	EA
2x10 Jst. Hngr. (LUS210-2)	Ledger Joist	1	EA
Hurricane Tie (H2.5)	Joist/Beam	13	EA
Framing Anchor (A34)	End/Header Joist	7	EA
1# 8d 1-1/2" Hanger Nails	Connector	3	EA
5# 8d Ctd. Box Nails	General Framing	5	LB

FINISH/RAILING/SKIRTING

Item	Location	Qty	UM
4x4 - 8' Treated	Post	6	EA
3/8"x4" Lag Screws	Post	28	EA
3/8"x1-1/2" Washer	Post	28	EA
2x6 - 16' Treated	Decking/Stair Trd.	32	EA
1# 2-1/2" Ctd. Screws	Decking/Railing	10	EA
2x12 - 8' Treated	Stringer	3	EA
3x5 Heavy Angle (HL35)	Stringer	6	EA
5/16"x1-1/2" Lag Screws	Heavy Angle	24	EA
2x4 - 8' Treated	Cap Rail	7	EA
1-3/8"x1-3/8" - 3' Sq. Cut Blstr.	Baluster	100	EA
1x3 - 8' Treated	Side Rail	28	EA
2x3 - 8' Treated	Blstr. Blocking	14	EA
1x4 - 8' Treated	Post Wrap	7	EA
1x6 - 8' Treated	Post Wrap	7	EA
Wood Post Cap	Post	14	EA
5# 16d Galv. Nails	General Framing	2	EA
5# 8d Ctd. Box Nails	General Framing	1	EA

CHAPTER 5

THE GATSBY

HPM-1114

This deck plan is a grand addition to any home. Use the upper level for sunny outdoor meals or sunbathing. The lower level accommodates party overflow and offers some shade and seclusion when quiet relaxation is desired. The overhead beams on the octagonal deck create a stylish gazebo-like structure.

Dimensions for this deck are 22'-7" X 18'-7".

Gatsby — Plan View

Scale: 1/4" = 1'-0"

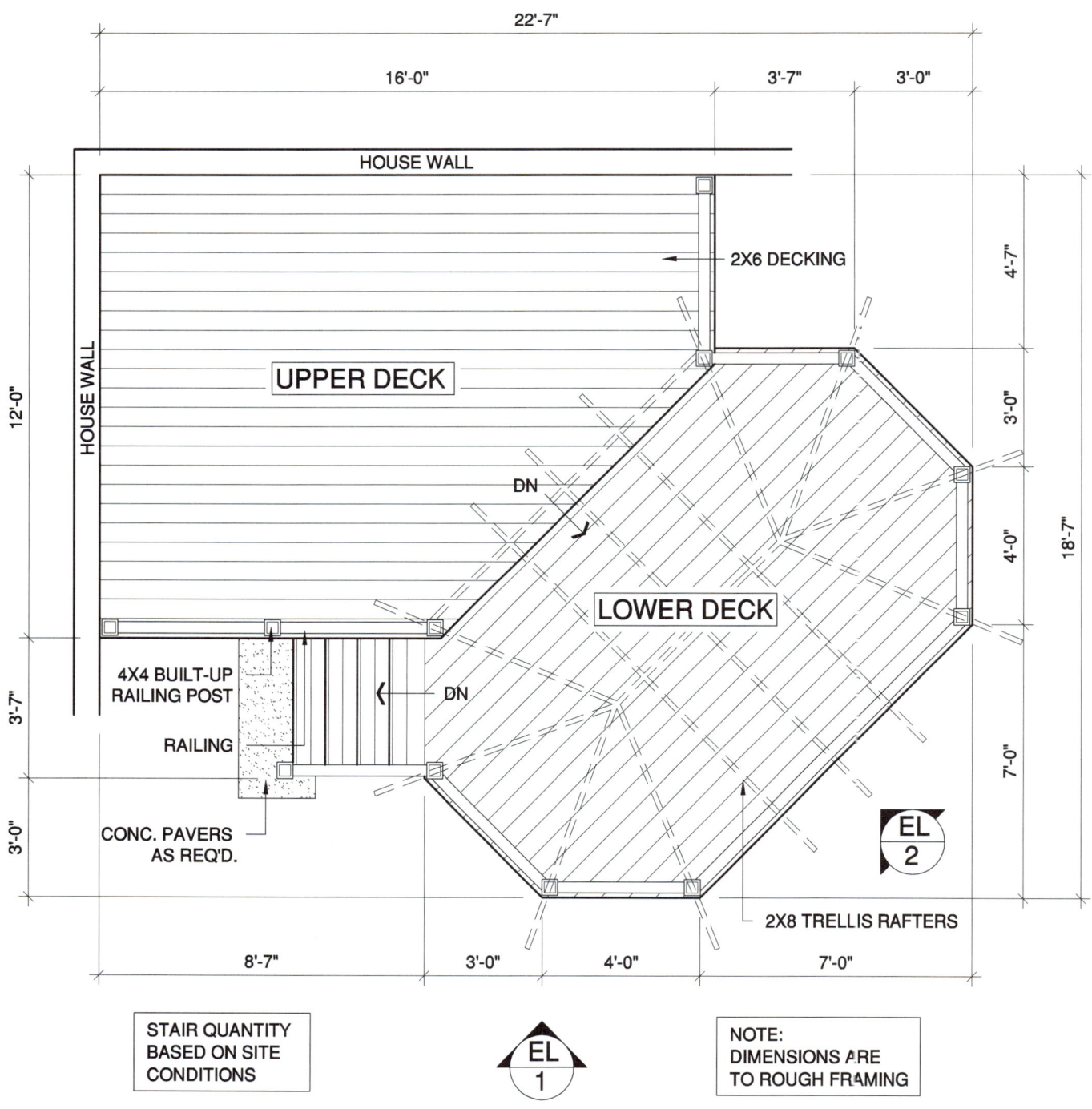

STAIR QUANTITY BASED ON SITE CONDITIONS

NOTE: DIMENSIONS ARE TO ROUGH FRAMING

GATSBY — Pier Layout 1

Scale: 1/4" = 1'-0"

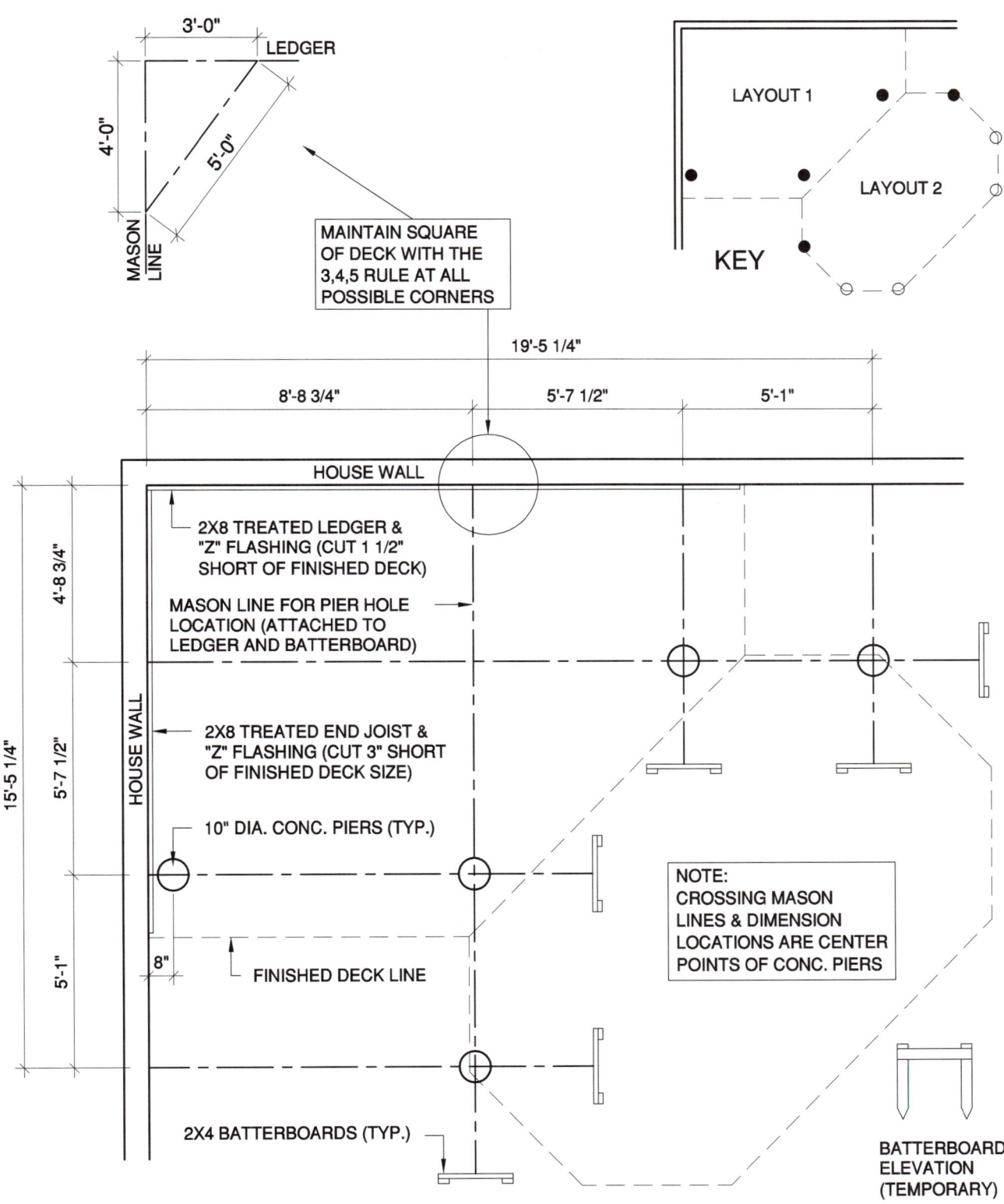

www.homedepot.com 157

Gatsby — Pier Layout 2

Scale: 1/4" = 1'-0"

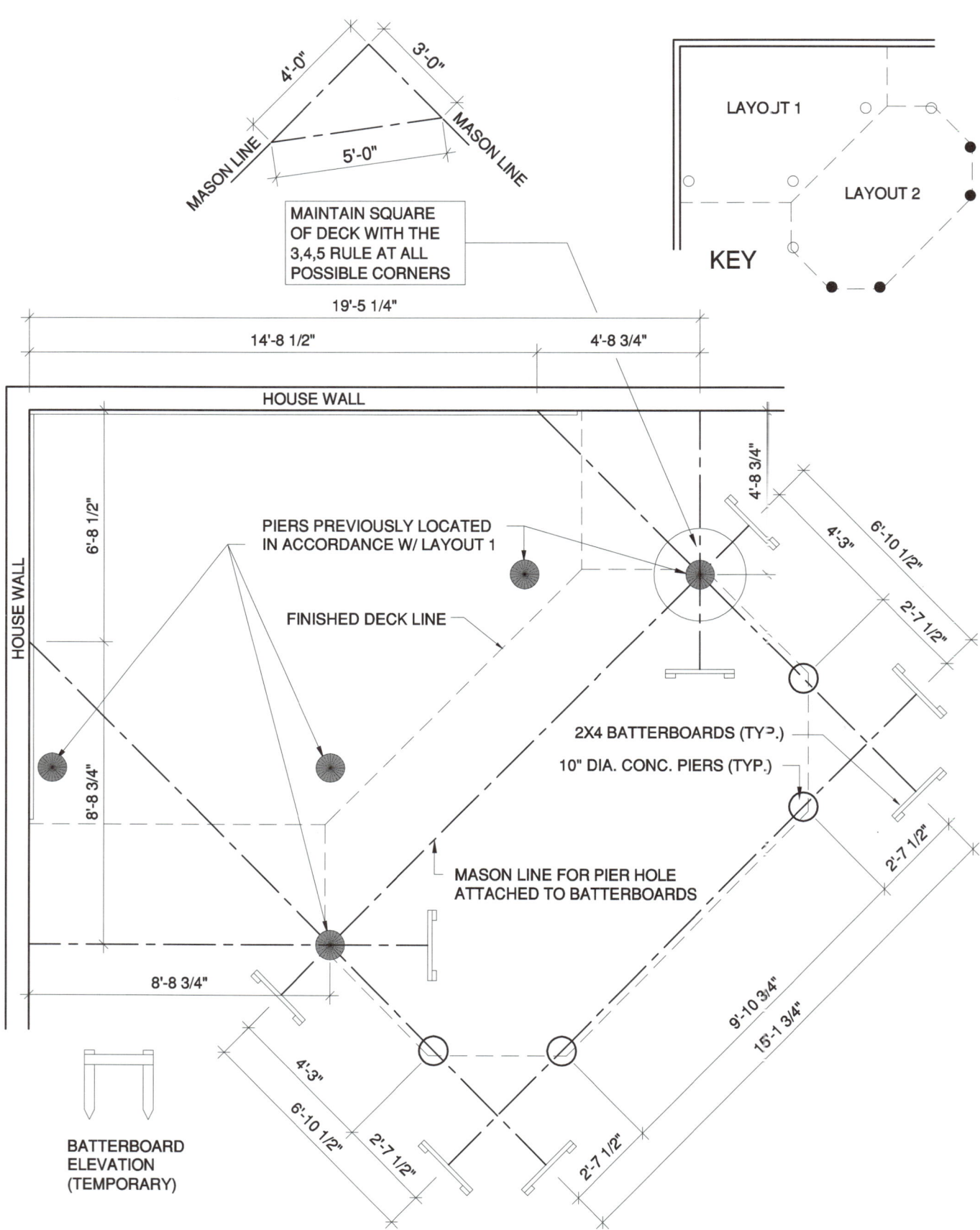

158 www.DreamIt-BuildIt.com

Gatsby — Floor Framing Plan

Scale: 1/4" = 1'-0"

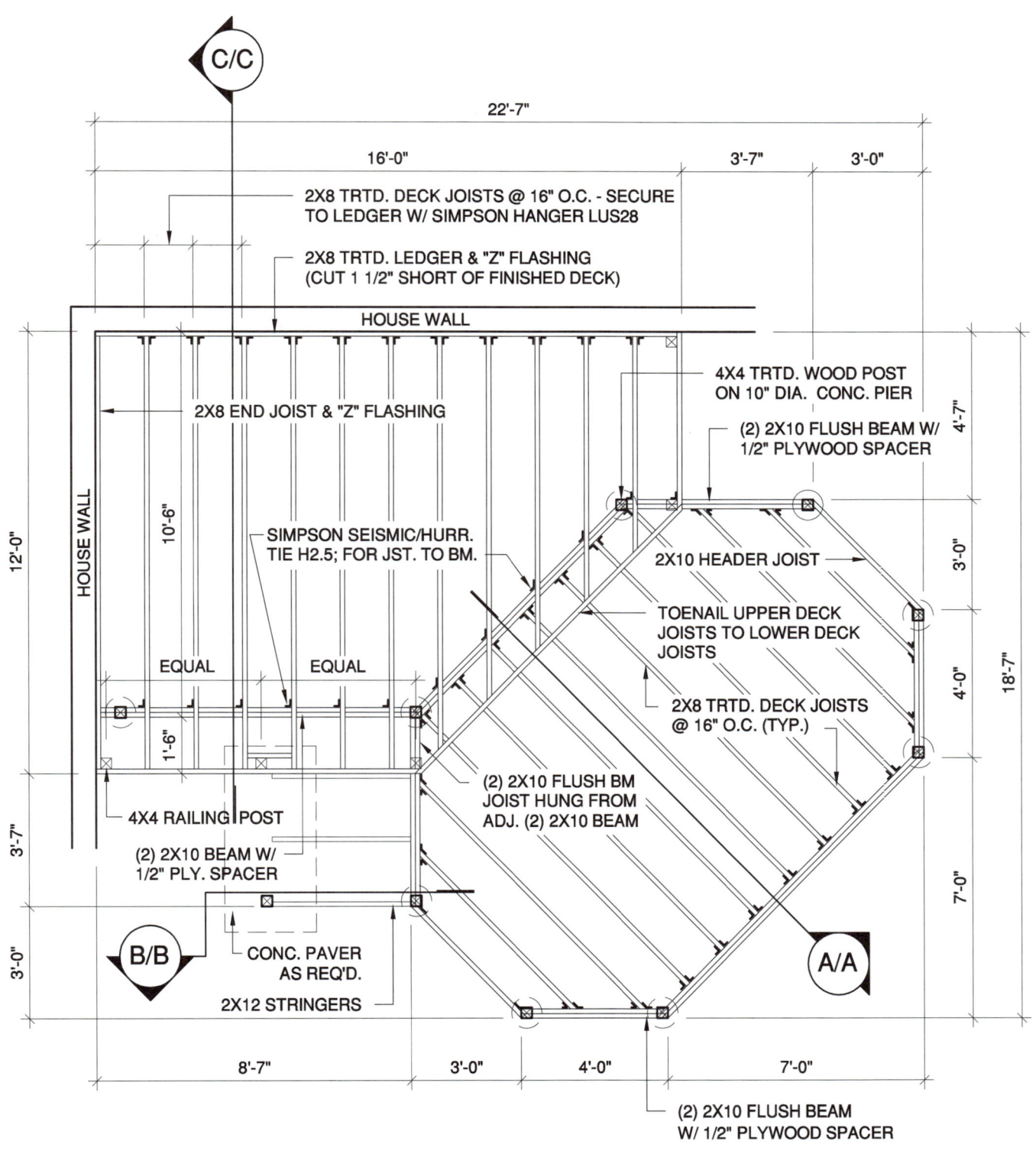

GATSBY — Elevations

Scale: 1/4" = 1'-0"

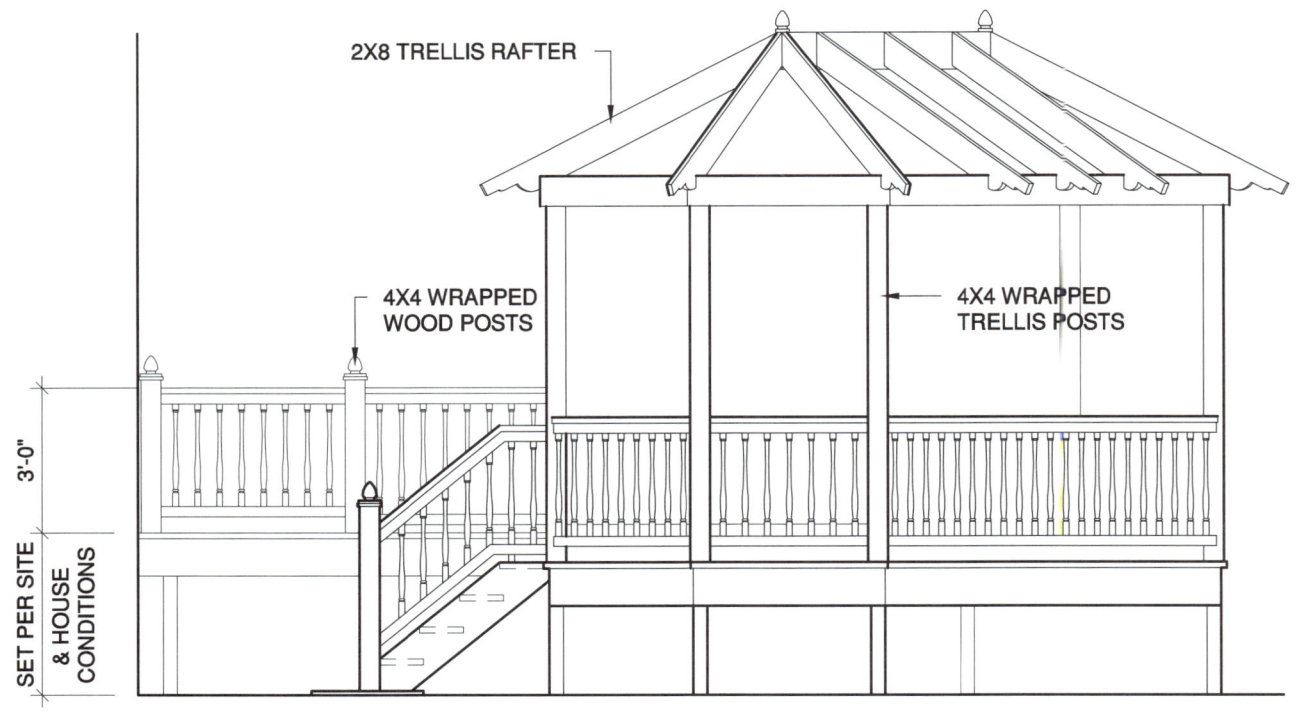

FRONT ELEVATION — EL 1

- 2X8 TRELLIS RAFTER
- 4X4 WRAPPED WOOD POSTS
- 4X4 WRAPPED TRELLIS POSTS
- 3'-0" SET PER SITE & HOUSE CONDITIONS
- RAILING HEIGHT TOP OF DECK TO TOP OF RAILING
- STAIR QUANTITY BASED ON SITE CONDITIONS

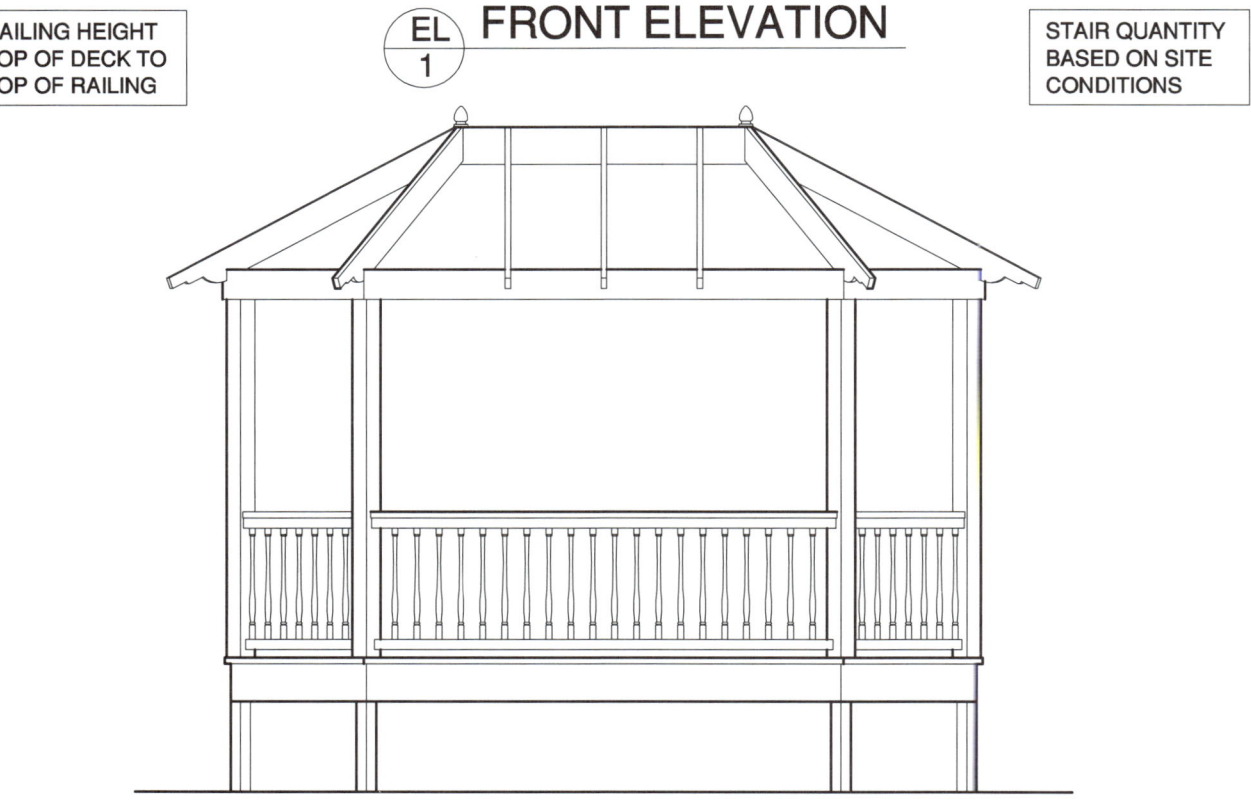

RIGHT ELEVATION — EL 2

Gatsby — Trellis Framing Plan and Detail

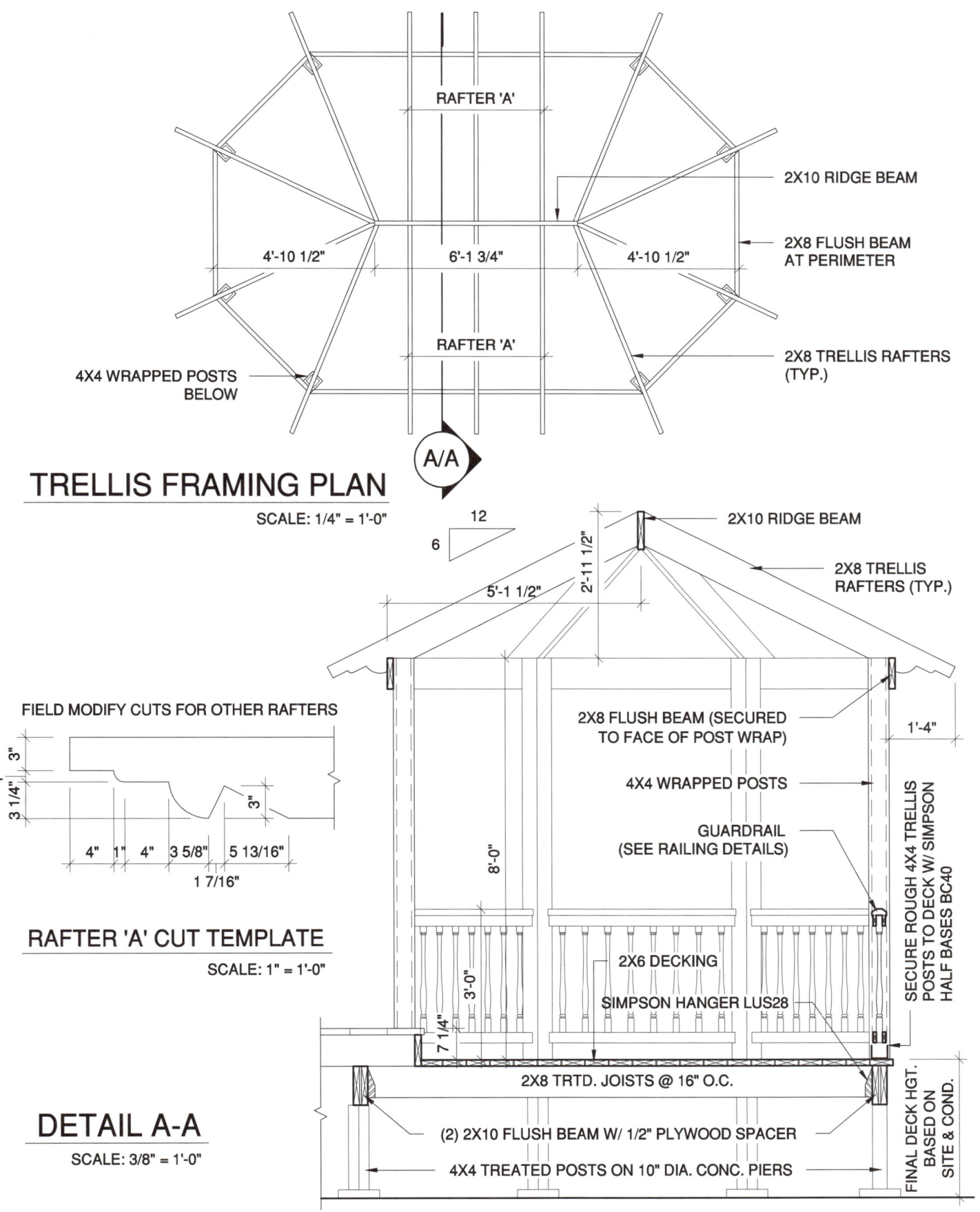

TRELLIS FRAMING PLAN
SCALE: 1/4" = 1'-0"

RAFTER 'A' CUT TEMPLATE
SCALE: 1" = 1'-0"

DETAIL A-A
SCALE: 3/8" = 1'-0"

www.homedepot.com

Gatsby — Details

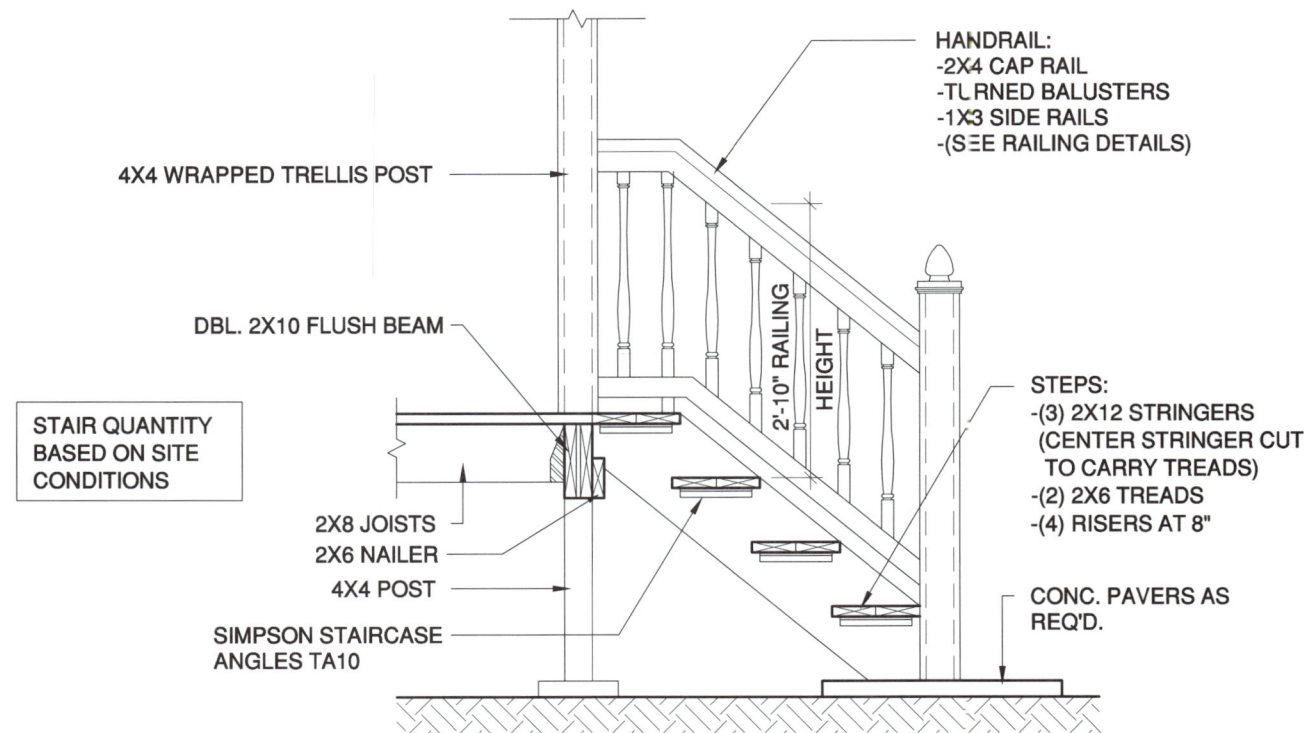

DETAIL B-B
SCALE: 1/2" = 1'-0"

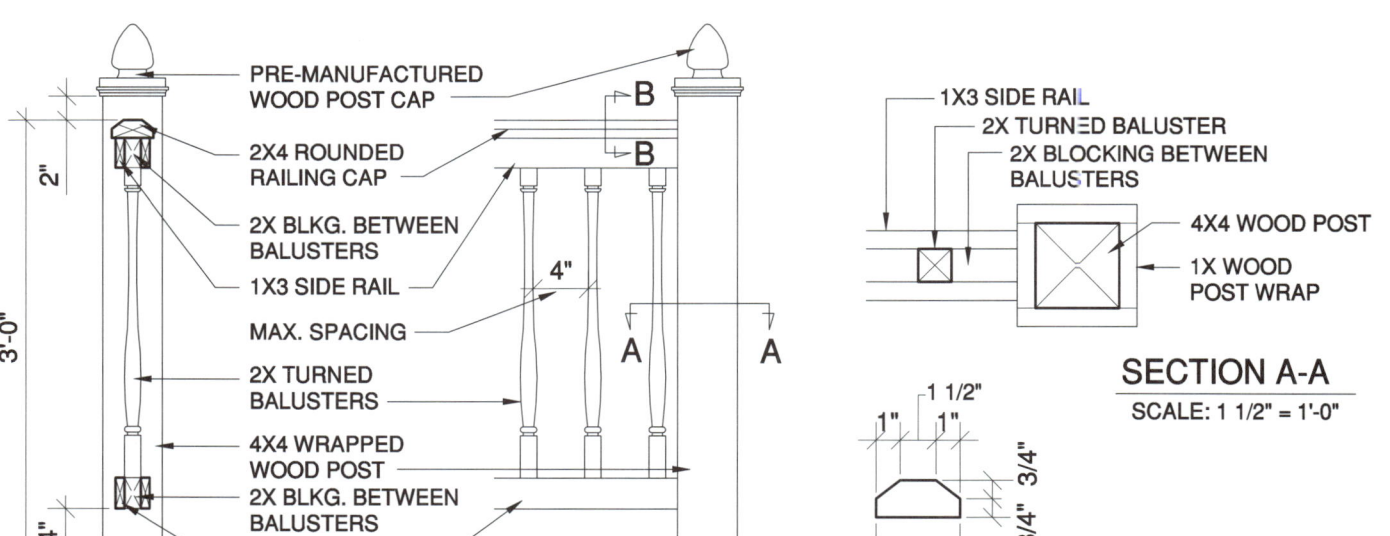

RAILING DETAILS
SCALE: 3/4" = 1'-0"

SECTION A-A
SCALE: 1 1/2" = 1'-0"

SECTION B-B
SCALE: 1 1/2" = 1'-0"

Gatsby — Detail

Scale: 1/2" = 1'-0"

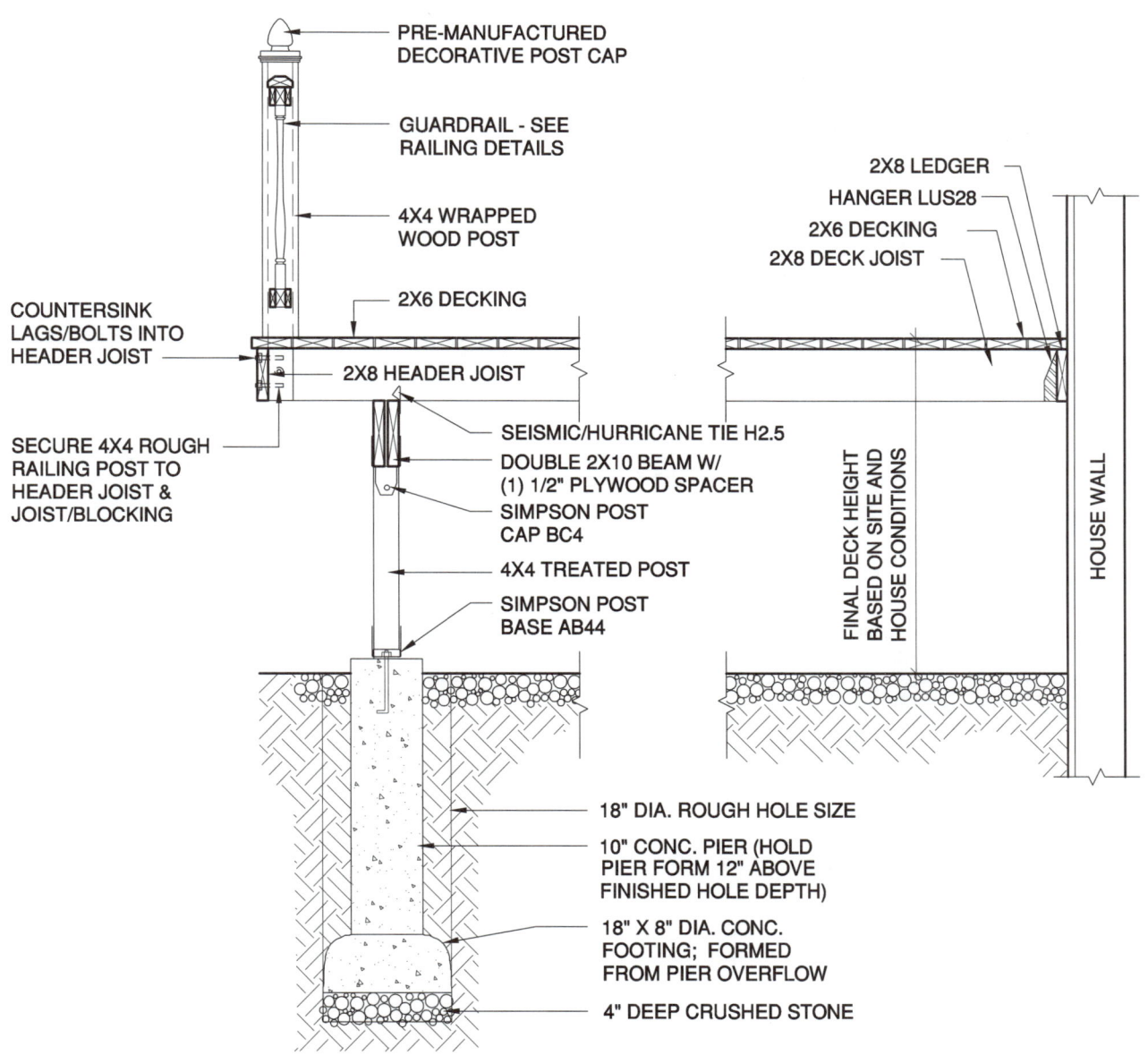

DETAIL C-C

GATSBY — Material List

FOUNDATION

Item	Location	Qty	UM
60# Concrete Mix	Pier	45	BG
10"x48" Fiber Tube	Pier	9	EA
2x4 - 10' Std. & Btr.	Batterboard	8	EA
1/2"x6" Anchor Bolt/Nut/Wash.	Pier	9	EA
Post Anchor (ABA44)	Pier	9	EA
Crushed Stone	Pier	18	BG
2x8 - 12' Treated	End Joist	1	EA
2x8 - 16' Treated	Ledger	1	EA
1x5 - 10' Zee Bar	Ledger/End Joist	3	EA
5# 16d Galv. Nails	General Framing	1	EA
3/8"x4" Lag Screws	Ledger/End Joist	42	EA
3/8"x1-1/2" Washer	Ledger/End Joist	42	EA
10 oz. - Paintable Caulk	Ledger/Bolt	3	TB

FRAMING

Item	Location	Qty	UM
2x10 - 8' Treated	Beam	2	EA
2x10 - 10' Treated	Beam	4	EA
2x10 - 12' Treated	Beam	4	EA
2x8 - 8' Treated	Joist	1	EA
2x8 - 10' Treated	Joist/Blocking	6	EA
2x8 - 12' Treated	Joist	18	EA
1/2" CDX - 5 Ply Plywd.	Beam	2	EA
4x4 - 10' Treated	Post	3	EA
Post Cap (PC44-16)	Post/Beam	9	EA
5# 16d Galv. Nails	General Framing	3	EA
2x8 Jst. Hngr. (LUS28)	Ledger/Beam	25	EA
2x8 Jst. Hngr. Angled	Beam	8	EA
Hurricane Tie (H2.5)	Joist/Beam	12	EA
Framing Anchor (A34)	Beam/End Joist	3	EA
1# 8d 1-1/2" Hanger Nails	Connector	3	EA
5# 8d Ctd. Box Nails	General Framing	1	EA

FINISH/RAILING/SKIRTING

Item	Location	Qty	UM
4x4 - 8' Treated	Post	10	EA
3/8"x4" Lag Screws	Post	8	EA
3/8"x1-1/2" Washer	Post	8	EA
Post Base (BC40)	Post	8	EA
2x6 - 12' Treated	Decking/Tread	31	EA
2x6 -16' Treated	Decking/Tread	23	EA
1# 2-1/2" Ctd. Screws	Decking/Railing	10	EA
2x12 - 6' Treated	Stringer	3	EA
3x5 Heavy Angle (HL35)	Stringer	4	EA
5/16"x1-1/2" Lag Screws	Heavy Angle	16	EA
Metal Stair Tread Angles	Tread	8	EA
2x6 - 4' Treated	Stair Nailer	1	EA
2x4 - 8' Treated	Cap Rail	3	EA
2x4 -10' Treated	Cap Rail	3	EA
1x3 - 8' Treated	Side Rail	12	EA
1x3 - 10' Treated	Side Rail	12	EA
2x3 - 8' Treated	Blstr. Blocking	6	EA
2x3 - 10' Treated	Blstr. Blocking	6	EA
1-3/8"x1-3/8" - 3' Trnd. Blstr.	Baluster	98	EA
1x4 - 8' Treated Post Wrap	Post	20	EA
1x6 - 8' Treated Post Wrap	Post	20	EA
Post Cap	Post	6	EA
2X8 - 8' Treated	Flush Beam	2	EA
2x8 - 12' Treated	Flush Beam	3	EA
2x10 - 8' Treated	Ridge Beam	1	EA
2x8 - 8' Treated	Rafter	14	EA
5# 16d Galv. Nails	General Framing	2	EA
5# 8d Ctd. Box Nails	General Framing	1	EA

THE NEWCASTLE

HPM-1115

Three levels triple the fun and function of this multi-level deck. Beyond the main deck, two octagonal deck levels offer extra space to lounge, dine and play. This stylish and eye-catching deck will complement any home.

Dimensions for this deck are 37' X 22'-6".

Newcastle — Plan View

Scale: 3/16" = 1'-0"

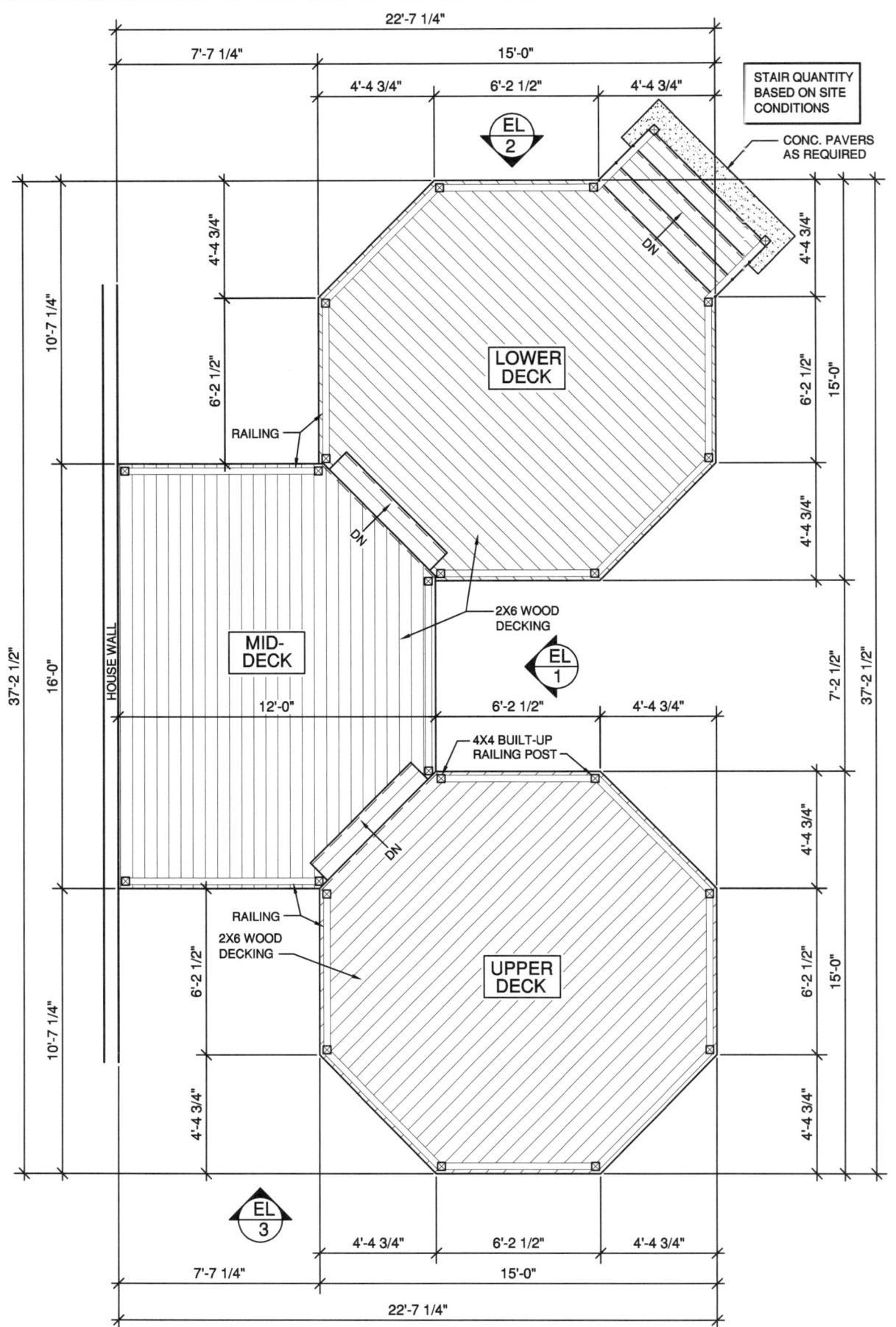

Newcastle — Pier Layout

Scale: 3/16" = 1'-0"

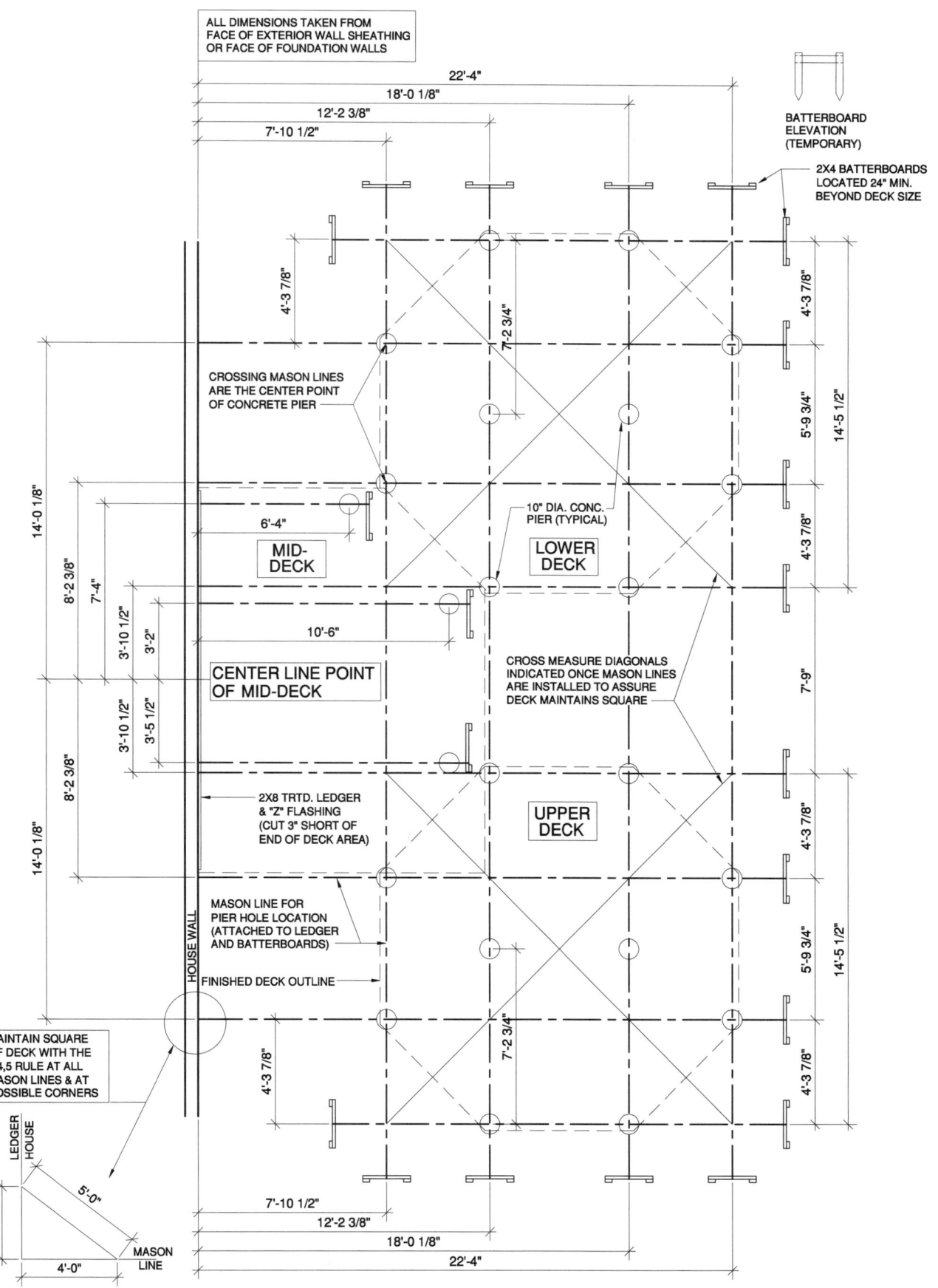

www.homedepot.com 167

Newcastle — Framing Plan

Scale: 1/4" = 1'-0"

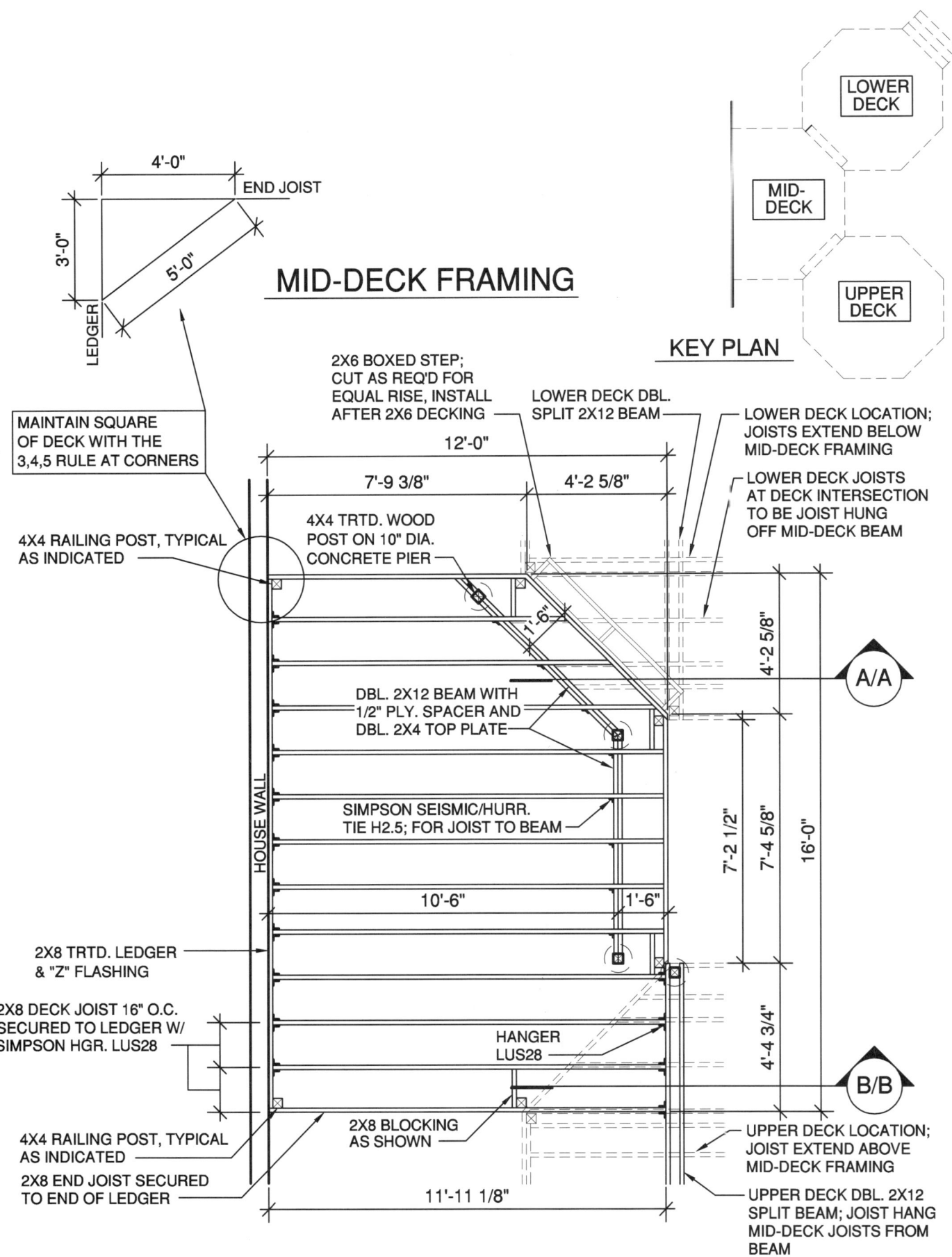

Newcastle | Framing Plan | Scale: 1/4" = 1'-0"

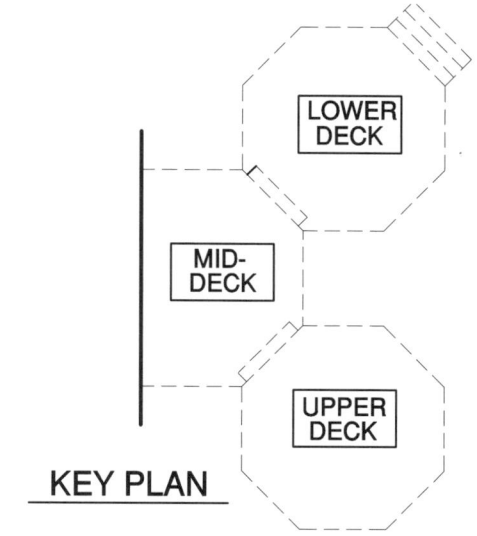

KEY PLAN

LOWER DECK FRAMING

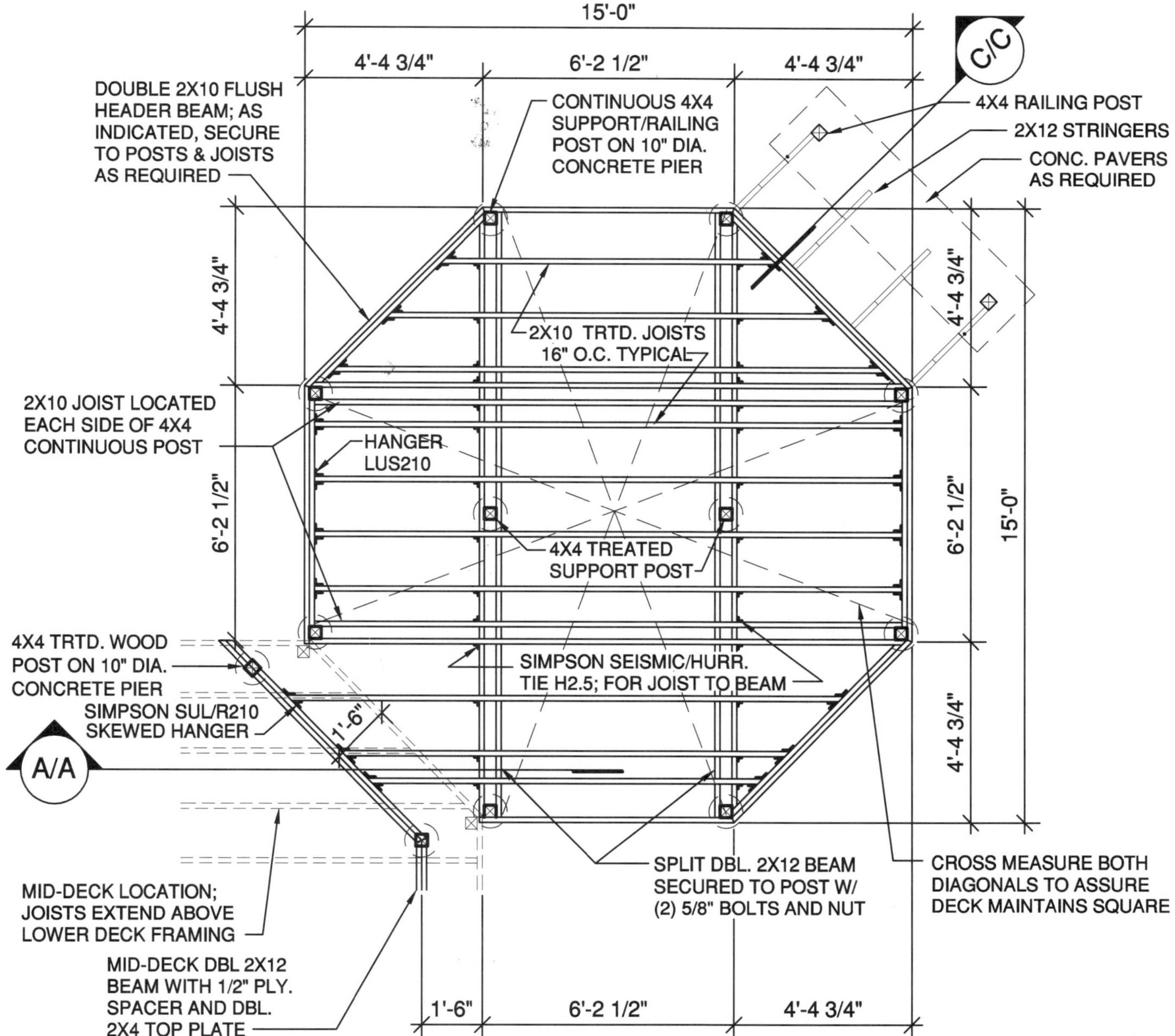

- DOUBLE 2X10 FLUSH HEADER BEAM; AS INDICATED, SECURE TO POSTS & JOISTS AS REQUIRED
- CONTINUOUS 4X4 SUPPORT/RAILING POST ON 10" DIA. CONCRETE PIER
- 4X4 RAILING POST
- 2X12 STRINGERS
- CONC. PAVERS AS REQUIRED
- 2X10 TRTD. JOISTS 16" O.C. TYPICAL
- 2X10 JOIST LOCATED EACH SIDE OF 4X4 CONTINUOUS POST
- HANGER LUS210
- 4X4 TREATED SUPPORT POST
- 4X4 TRTD. WOOD POST ON 10" DIA. CONCRETE PIER
- SIMPSON SEISMIC/HURR. TIE H2.5; FOR JOIST TO BEAM
- SIMPSON SUL/R210 SKEWED HANGER
- A/A
- MID-DECK LOCATION; JOISTS EXTEND ABOVE LOWER DECK FRAMING
- MID-DECK DBL 2X12 BEAM WITH 1/2" PLY. SPACER AND DBL. 2X4 TOP PLATE
- SPLIT DBL. 2X12 BEAM SECURED TO POST W/ (2) 5/8" BOLTS AND NUT
- CROSS MEASURE BOTH DIAGONALS TO ASSURE DECK MAINTAINS SQUARE

Dimensions: 15'-0" (4'-4 3/4" + 6'-2 1/2" + 4'-4 3/4"); 15'-0" (4'-4 3/4" + 6'-2 1/2" + 4'-4 3/4"); 1'-6"; 1'-6" + 6'-2 1/2" + 4'-4 3/4"

C/C

www.homedepot.com — 169

Newcastle — Framing Plan

Scale: 1/4" = 1'-0"

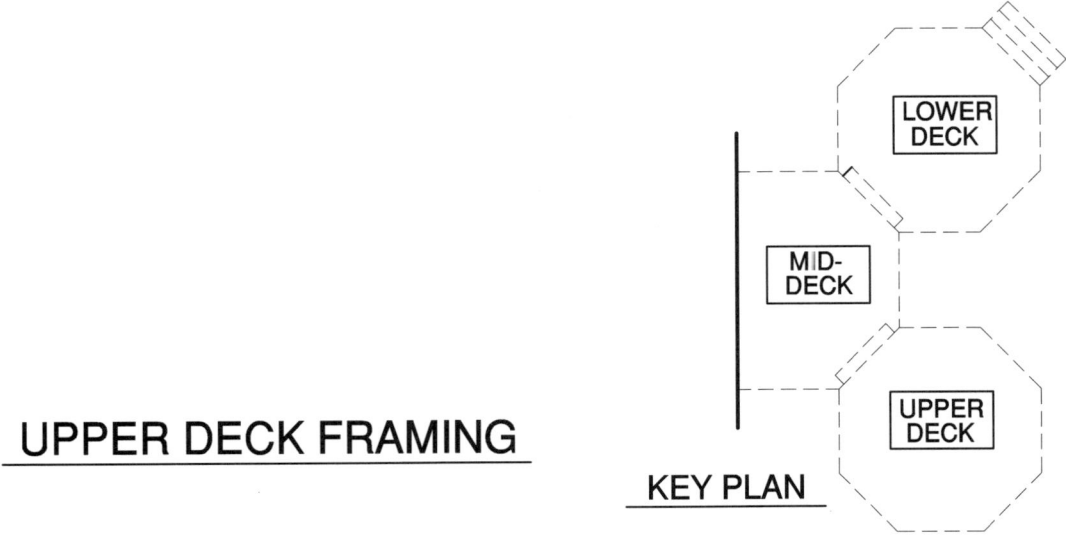

UPPER DECK FRAMING

KEY PLAN (LOWER DECK, MID-DECK, UPPER DECK)

- 2X6 BOXED STEP; CUT AS REQ'D FOR EQUAL RISE, INSTALL AFTER 2X6 DECKING
- MID-DECK LOCATION; JOISTS EXTEND BELOW UPPER DECK FRAMING & ARE JOIST HUNG FROM SPLIT 2X12 BEAM
- CONTINUOUS 4X4 SUPPORT/RAILING POST ON 10" DIA. CONCRETE PIER
- SPLIT DBL. 2X12 BEAM SECURED TO POST W/ (2) 5/8" BOLTS AND NUT
- SIMPSON SUL/R210 SKEWED HANGER
- 2X10 JOIST LOCATED EACH SIDE OF 4X4 CONTINUOUS POST
- 2X10 TRTD. JOISTS 16" O.C. TYPICAL
- DOUBLE 2X10 FLUSH HEADER BEAM; AS INDICATED, SECURE TO POSTS & JOISTS AS REQUIRED
- 4X4 TREATED SUPPORT POST
- CROSS MEASURE BOTH DIAGONALS TO ASSURE DECK MAINTAINS SQUARE
- SIMPSON SEISMIC/HURR. TIE H2.5; FOR JOIST TO BEAM

Dimensions: 4'-4 3/4" | 6'-2 1/2" | 4'-4 3/4" = 15'-0"

B/B

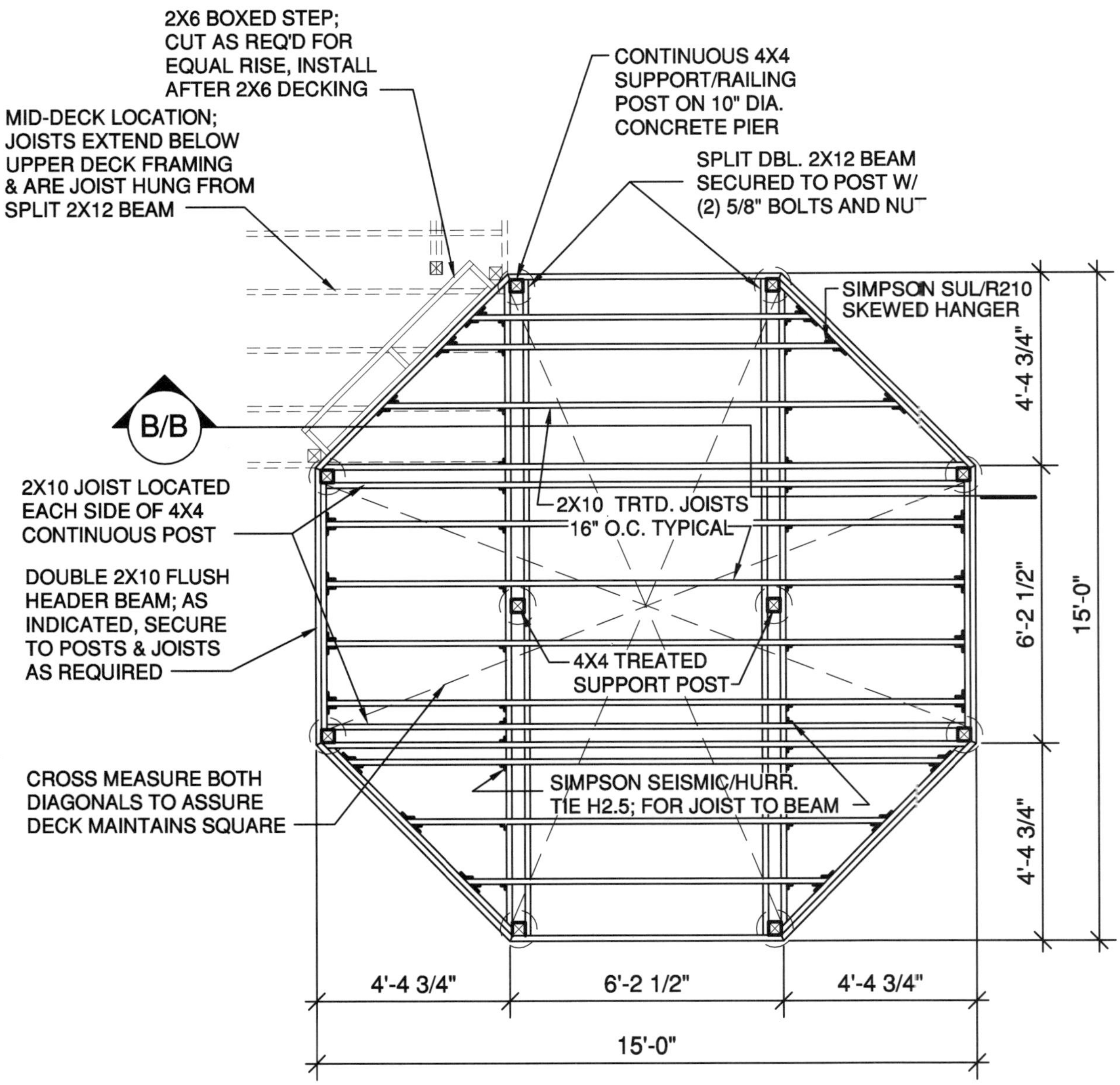

NEWCASTLE — Elevations

Scale: 3/16" = 1'-0"

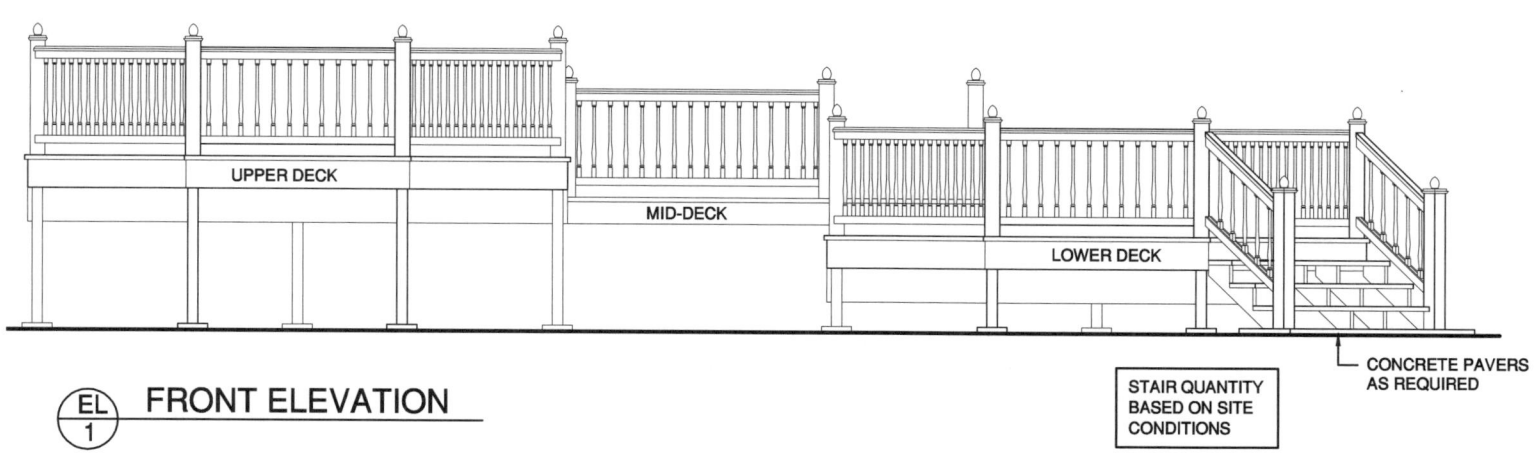

EL/1 **FRONT ELEVATION**

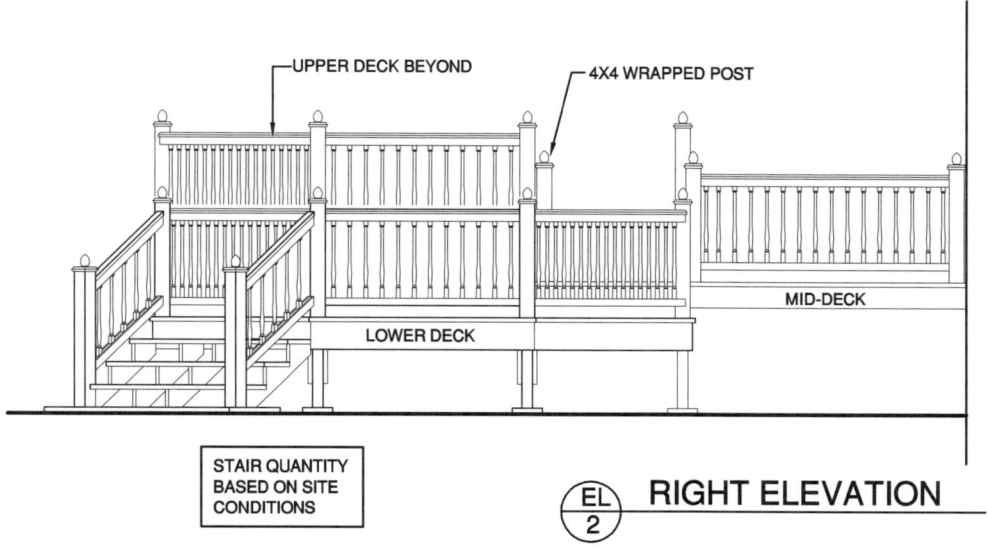

EL/2 **RIGHT ELEVATION**

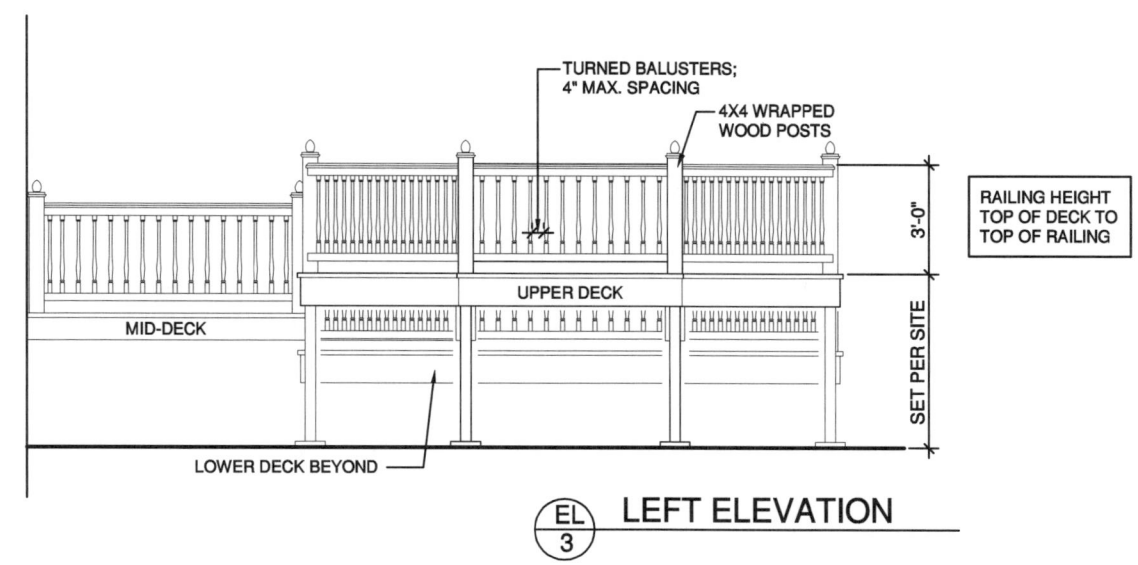

EL/3 **LEFT ELEVATION**

Newcastle — Detail

Scale: 1/2" = 1'-0"

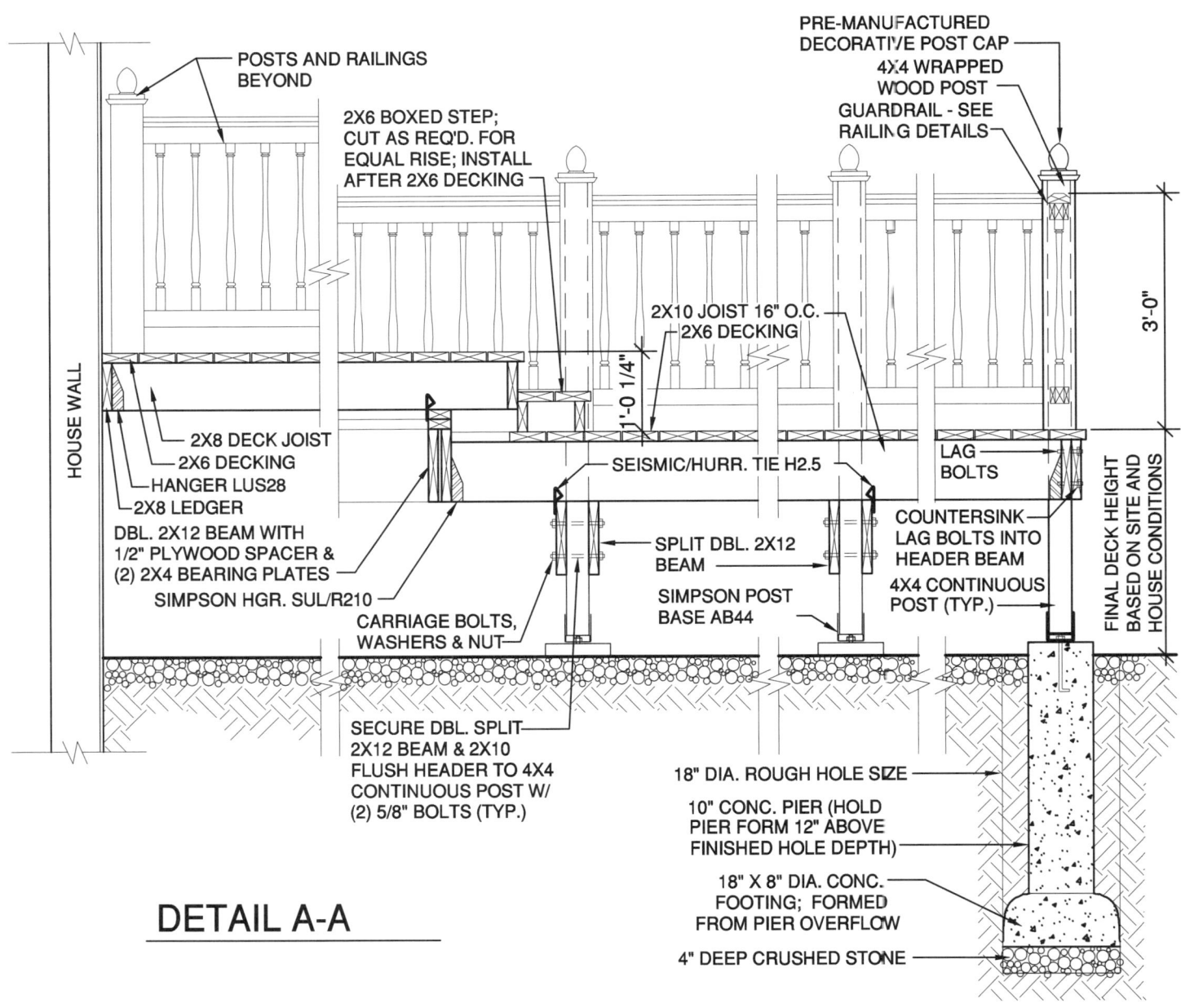

DETAIL A-A

Newcastle | Detail | Scale: 1/2" = 1'-0"

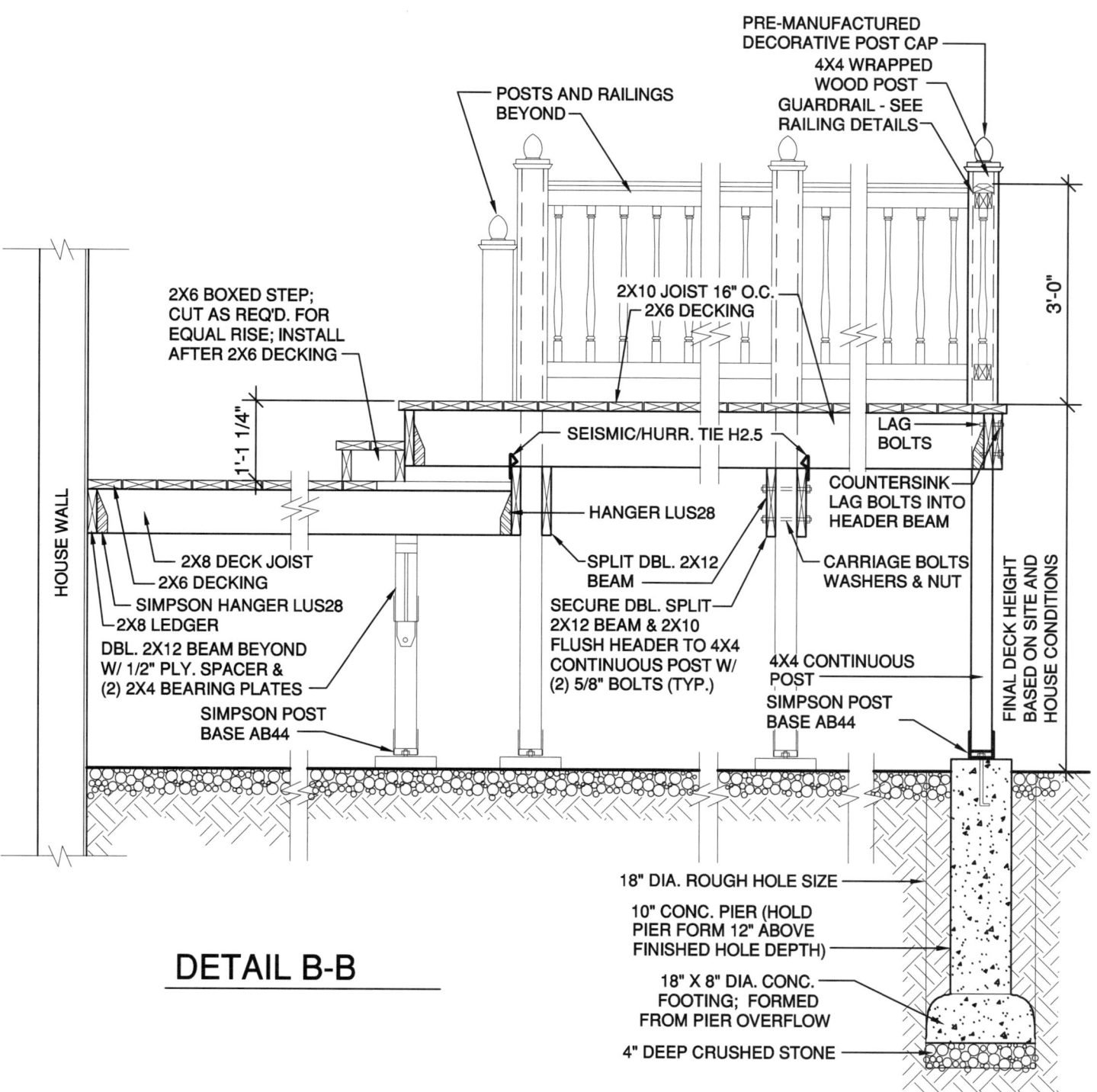

DETAIL B-B

NEWCASTLE Details

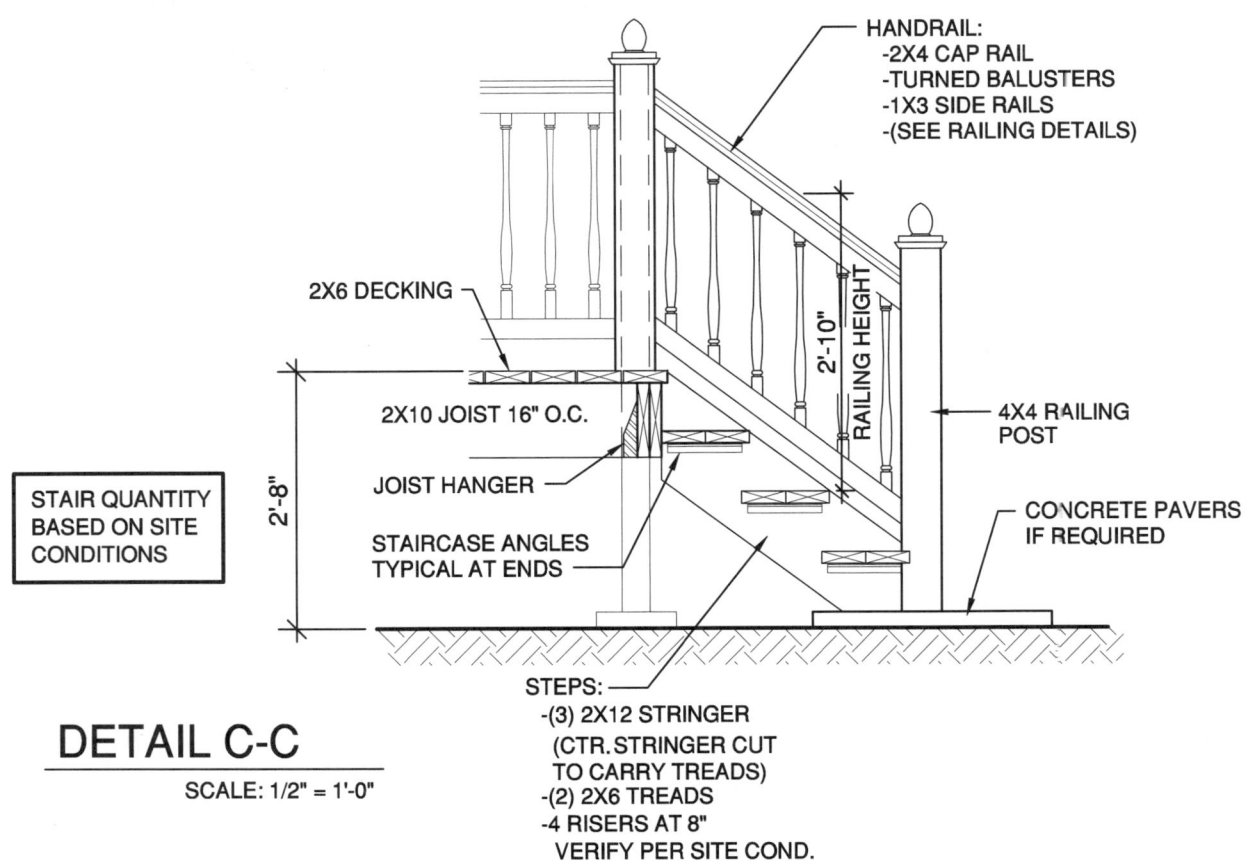

DETAIL C-C
SCALE: 1/2" = 1'-0"

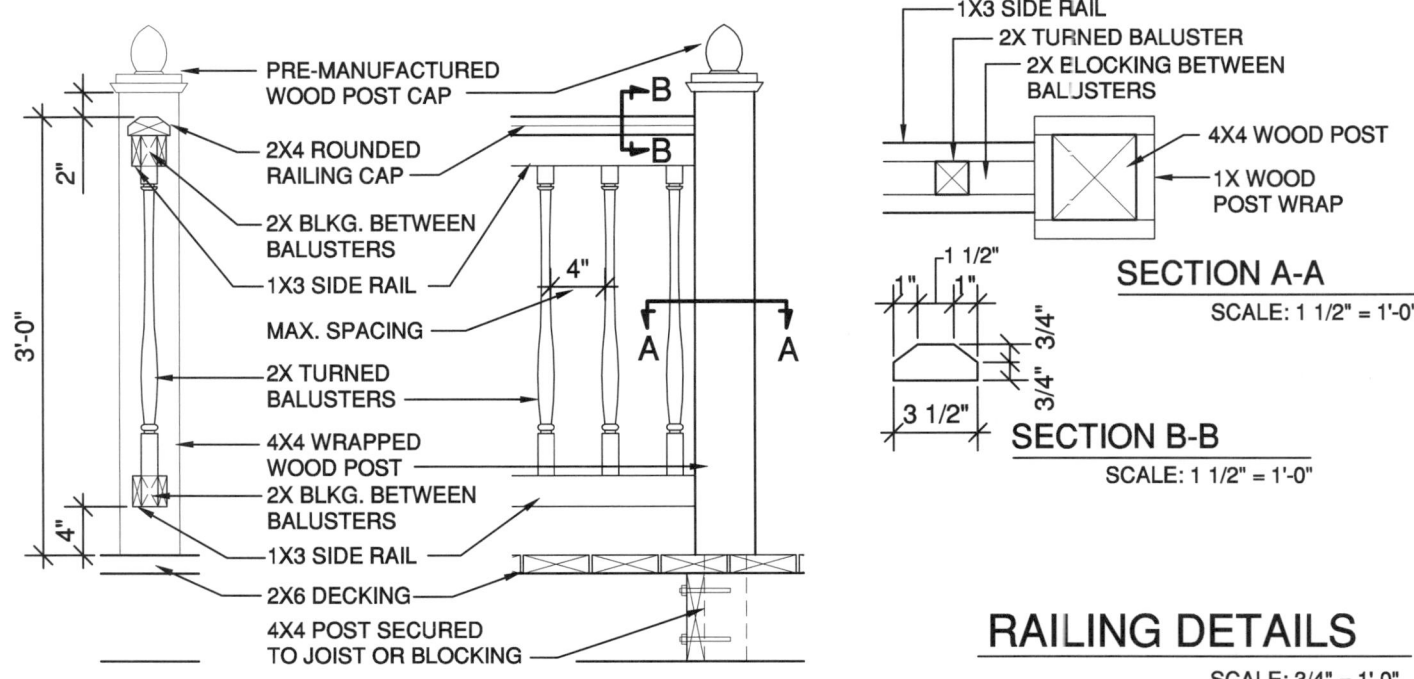

SECTION A-A
SCALE: 1 1/2" = 1'-0"

SECTION B-B
SCALE: 1 1/2" = 1'-0"

RAILING DETAILS
SCALE: 3/4" = 1'-0"

NEWCASTLE Material List

FOUNDATION

Item	Location	Qty	UM
60# Concrete Mix	Pier	115	BG
10"x48" Fiber Tube	Pier	23	EA
2x4 - 10' Std. & Btr.	Batterboard	13	EA
1/2"x6" Anchor Bolt/Nut/Wash.	Pier	23	EA
Post Base (ABA44)	Pier	23	EA
Crushed Stone	Pier	46	BG
2x8 - 16' Treated	Ledger	1	EA
1x5 - 10' Zee Bar	Ledger	2	EA
5# 6d Galv. Nails	General Framing	1	LB
3/8"x4" Lag Screws	Ledger	24	EA
3/8"x1-1/2" Washer	Ledger	24	EA
10 oz. - Paintable Caulk	Ledger/Bolt	3	TB

FRAMING

Item	Location	Qty	UM
2x10 - 14' Treated	Flush Header Bm.	10	EA
2x12 - 14' Treated	Beam	1	EA
2x12 - 16' Treated	Split Beam	8	EA
1/2" CDX - 5 Ply Plywd.	Beam	1	EA
2x4 - 16' Treated	Beam Plate	2	EA
2x8 - 8' Treated	Jst./Hdr./End Jst.	4	EA
2x8 - 12' Treated	Jsts./End Jst./Blkg.	14	EA
2x10 - 10' Treated	Joist/Beam	4	EA
2x10 - 12' Treated	Joist	4	EA
2x10 - 14' Treated	Joist	4	EA
2x10 - 16' Treated	Joist/Blocking	20	EA
4x4 - 8' Treated	Post	9	EA
4x4 - 10' Treated	Post	9	EA
5/8"x7" Lag Bolt/Nut/Wash.	Post/Beam	40	EA
4x4 Post Cap (PC44-16)	Post/Beam	3	EA
5# 16d Galv. Nails	General Framing	3	EA
2x8 Joist Hanger (LUS28)	Ledger Joist	15	EA
2x10 Jst. Hngrs. (LUS210)	Flush Header Bm.	16	EA
2x10 Jst. Hngr. (Angled)	Flush Header Bm.	24	EA
Hurricane Tie (H2.5)	Joist/Beam	64	EA
Framing Anchor (A34)	End Jst./Bm./Ldgr.	3	EA
1# 8d 1-1/2" Hanger Nails	Connector	3	EA
5# 8d Ctd. Box Nails	General Framing	1	EA

FINISH/RAILING/SKIRTING

Item	Location	Qty	UM
4x4 - 8' Treated	Post	4	EA
3/8"x4" Lag Screws	Post	16	EA
3/8"x1-1/2" Washer	Post	16	EA
2x6 - 12' Treated	Deck./Trd./Box Str.	64	EA
2x6 - 16' Treated	Deck./Trd./Box Str.	48	EA
1# 2-1/2" Ctd. Screws	Decking/Railing	10	EA
2x12 - 8' Treated	Stringer	2	EA
3x5 Heavy Angle (HL35)	Stringer	6	EA
5/16"x1-1/2" Lag Screws	Heavy Angle	24	EA
Tread Support Angle	Tread/Stringer	6	EA
2x4 - 8' Treated	Cap Rail	8	EA
2x4 - 12' Treated	Cap Rail	4	EA
1x3 - 8' Treated	Side Rail	32	EA
1x3 - 12' Treated	Side Rail	16	EA
2x3 - 8' Treated	Baluster Blocking	16	EA
2x3 - 10' Treated	Baluster Blocking	8	EA
1-3/8"x1-3/8" - 3' Trnd. Blstr.	Railing	242	EA
1x4 - 8' Treated	Post Wrap	24	EA
1x6 - 8' Treated	Post Wrap	24	EA
Post Cap	Post	24	EA
5# 16d Galv. Nails	General Framing	2	EA
5# 8d Ctd. Box Nails	General Framing	1	EA

Glossary

Anchor bolt
A J-shaped bolt used mainly to fasten posts to concrete piers. The curved end of the bolt is embedded in the center of the pier. The threaded section projecting upward attaches to the post anchor.

Baluster
Vertical member of deck railings, usually made from 2x2 lumber and fastened to rails spanning two or more posts.

Band board
A non-structural element installed around the edge of the deck to cover the end joists. Usually made from 2x6 stock.

Batterboard
A wooden assembly made up of two stakes and a third board spanning horizontally between them; used with mason's line to lay out deck foundation.

Blocking
Lengths of 2x4 fastened between joists to add support and structural rigidity on long spans.

Cantilever
To extend joists past the edge of the beams. Also refers to a deck jutting out over a steep incline.

Cap rail
The top section of a deck railing, usually laid flat and fastened to the tops of the railing posts.

Cleat
A small section of wood attached to the deck structure to support other members, such as on the inside of stringers to support stair treads.

Decay resistant
Refers to woods that are either naturally resistant to rot—such as cedar and redwood—or are treated with chemicals to be rot resistant.

Detail
Part of a deck plan showing a cutaway section of a particular view and revealing hidden structural elements.

Dimensional lumber
Graded for strength, this lumber is intended for the deck understructure; ranges in size from 2 to 4 inches wide and is at least 2 inches thick.

Elevation
Part of a deck plan that shows a side view. Included in the view are dimensions, materials, and in some cases, a detail of the view.

Face-nail
To drive a nail through the face of one board into another, with the nail perpendicular to the surface.

Footing
The wide concrete base under a concrete pier; serves to hold the pier firmly in place.

Framing connectors
Deck hardware that is used to connect structural members to form a stronger joint than is possible with conventional fasteners.

Frost line
The depth below grade to which the ground freezes in winter.

Galvanized
A process by which fasteners are coated with zinc to prevent oxidization due to contact with moisture. Hot-dipped galvanized fasteners are the highest quality.

Grade
The slope or incline of the ground; usually expressed in vertical inches per horizontal foot. A deck with a gentle grade will direct moisture away from the house.

Ground-fault circuit interrupter (GFCI)
An electrical device that shuts off power to a circuit when current leakage is detected. Usually required in outdoor wiring.

Header joist
A joist fastened to the ends of the other joists to enclose the structure and add extra support and rigidity.

Heartwood
The center or inactive section of a tree, usually where the highest grade of lumber is found. Heartwood redwood or cedar is resistant to rot and is very stable.

Lattice
Narrow strips of wood assembled in a woven panel and usually used for privacy screens, overheads or skirting.

Lath
A narrow strip of wood fastened to supports to provide shade or privacy on an overhead or arbor.

Ledger board
A large structural member, usually 2x10, fastened to the house wall to support deck joists.

Miter
An angled cut (other than 90 degrees), often used in diagonal or zigzag decking patterns.

On center
The span from the center of one supporting member to the center of another. Abbreviated on deck plans as "o.c."

Overhead
A structure built over a portion of the deck area for shade or privacy or to support climbing plants.

Pier
A cylindrical concrete foundation member set below ground level to support a deck post.

Plan view
A view of the deck structure with the decking in place seen from directly above, indicating mainly the dimensions of the deck perimeter.

Pressure-treated
A process by which chemical preservatives are forced into lumber under pressure, making it resistant to decay and insect damage.

Rise
The total height of a stairway from the ground to the deck surface.

Riser
One of the vertical sections of a set of stairs.

Site plan
A complete map of a lot indicating the position of all structures, including the proposed deck.

Span
The distance from the center of one supporting member to the center of another.

Stringer
The diagonal outer board of a stairway to which the treads and risers are fastened. Stringers can be notched or fitted with cleats to support the treads.

Toenail
To fasten two wood pieces together with a nail driven in at an angle.

Tread
A stair step.

Understructure
The supporting structure of a deck, made up of the posts, beams, ledger board and joists.